INDIA'S NEIGHBOURHOOD

THE ARMIES OF SOUTH ASIA

INDIA'S NEIGHBOURHOOD
THE ARMIES OF SOUTH ASIA

Editor

Vishal Chandra

idsa

INSTITUTE FOR DEFENCE STUDIES & ANALYSES
NEW DELHI

PENTAGON PRESS

India's Neighbourhood: The Armies of South Asia / **Vishal Chandra (Ed)**

First Published in 2013

ISBN 978-81-8274-706-7

Published by
PENTAGON PRESS
206, Peacock Lane, Shahpur Jat,
New Delhi-110049
Phones: 011-64706243, 26491568
Telefax: 011-26490600
email: rajan@pentagonpress.in
website: www.pentagonpress.in

In association with
Institute for Defence Studies and Analyses
No. 1, Development Enclave,
New Delhi-110010
Phone: +91-11-26717983

Printed at Syndicate Binders, A-20, Hosiery Complex, Phase II, Noida-201305

Contents

Foreword

Armies play a significant role in the maintenance of unity and integrity of states. However, their role, reputation, status and importance varies from state to state, depending upon the nature of political system, strength of the civil society and the institutions of state, intensity of popular participation in the affairs of the state, and above all, the attitude as well as ambitions of the leadership of the armed forces. In advanced democratic states, the armies usually function under civilian control and help consolidate the process of nation and state-building. In many post-colonial states—struggling with the process of democratisation—on the contrary, the civil-military relations have often been strained and the role of the army has been rather controversial. The armies, in some of these societies, have usurped power from civilian authorities and impaired the process of socio-political and economic growth and development.

In South Asia, the post-colonial record of the armies has been rather mixed. While the armies of India, Sri Lanka, Nepal and Bhutan have largely stayed under civilian control, in Pakistan, Bangladesh and to a certain extent in Afghanistan, the armies have staged coups, derailed democratic experiments and played their role as willing accomplices in propping up authoritarian systems of governance. The ideas, ideologies and aspirations guiding the functioning of such assertive armies have posed serious challenges to security at the regional level. In certain cases, the armies have perpetuated threat perceptions about their neighbours to legitimise their hold on power. This has had grave implications for inter-state relations and regional security.

In the South Asian context, therefore, it was felt necessary to study the armies of different countries in the immediate neighbourhood of India in detail, taking into account their origin, evolution, doctrinal orientation, organisational principles, relationship with civilian institutions, and their future trajectories. Given the tendency in the countries in the neighbourhood to define their security in relation to India's preponderance, and the temptation of the elites in these countries to project India as a hegemonic and interventionist power, such a study would be definitely useful for strategic analysts and policy makers in India.

Keeping this in mind, the scholars in the South Asia Centre at the IDSA have put together this volume under the IDSA neighbourhood studies programme. I commend their efforts and especially that of Vishal Chandra who has conceptualised and edited this volume with adequate care and attention.

I hope this study will be well-received in the wider strategic community in India and abroad.

October 2012
New Delhi

Arvind Gupta
Director General, IDSA

About the Contributors

Dr. Arvind Gupta is Director General, Institute for Defence Studies and Analyses (IDSA), New Delhi, India.

Mr. Vishal Chandra is Associate Fellow at IDSA.

Dr. Smruti S. Pattanaik is Research Fellow at IDSA.

Dr. Anand Kumar is Associate Fellow at IDSA.

Capt. (IN) Alok Bansal is currently Senior Fellow at the Centre for Land Warfare Studies (CLAWS), New Delhi. He was Member (Navy) at IDSA.

Dr. Nihar Nayak is Associate Fellow at IDSA.

Dr. Ashok K. Behuria is Research Fellow and Coordinator of the South Asia Centre at IDSA.

Ms. Sumita Kumar is Senior Research Associate at IDSA.

Dr. M. Mayilvaganan is Assistant Professor at the National Institute of Advanced Studies (NIAS), Bangalore, Karnataka, India. Formerly Associate Fellow at IDSA.

Acknowledgements

This study would not have been possible without the support, guidance and encouragement of Dr. Arvind Gupta, the Director General of the Institute for Defence Studies and Analyses (IDSA). Despite his many pressing engagements, he would always make himself available whenever his personal attention and advice was requested, especially as I was finalising the manuscript of this book. I am grateful to him for all his assistance, attention and encouragement.

I would also like to specially acknowledge the contribution of Dr. Ashok K. Behuria, Coordinator of the South Asia Centre at IDSA, in the successful completion of this book project. His vast scholarship on South Asian affairs proved to be an asset as I requested him to peruse through the final manuscript of this book. I would like to express my personal gratitude to him for his full cooperation and support.

I would be failing in my duty if I do not acknowledge the contribution of anonymous external reviewers who offered their valuable inputs on the draft of the chapters. All seven chapters were reviewed by two subject experts and their inputs have been taken into consideration by individual authors while finalising their respective chapters. I would also like to thank Mr. Vivek Kaushik, the Assistant Editor, who ensured timely refereeing and copy-editing of the draft chapters. I must also place my special thanks to the publisher of this book, Pentagon Press, for bringing out this edited volume in a relatively short time.

As editor, it is also my pleasant duty to personally thank my colleagues from the South Asia Centre who contributed chapters for this book, Dr. Ashok K. Behuria, Ms. Sumita Kumar, Dr. Smruti S. Pattanaik, Dr. Anand Kumar, Dr. Nihar Nayak, and our former colleagues, Capt. (IN) Alok Bansal and Dr. M. Mayilvaganan.

October 2012 **Vishal Chandra**

Abbreviations

AAF	Afghan Air Force
AG	Adjutant General
AFD	Armed Forces Division
AIA	Afghan Interim Administration
AIT	Advanced Individual Training
ALP	Afghan Local Police
ANA	Afghan National Army
ANAAC	Afghan National Army Air Corps
ANAP	Afghan National Auxiliary Police
ANATC	Afghan National Army Training Command
ANNISU-R	All Nepal National Independent Students Union-Revolutionary
ANP	Afghan National Police
ANSF	Afghan National Security Forces
APC	Armoured Personnel Carrier
APCSS	Asia Pacific Center for Strategic Studies
APEC	Army Physical Education Centre
APPF	Afghan Public Protection Force
ARSIC	Afghan Regional Security Integration Command
ARTD	Army Recruit Training Depot
ASFF	Afghan Security Forces Fund
ATA	Afghan Transitional Administration
ATC	Army Training Centre
ATS	Army Training School
AWACS	Airborne Warning and Control System
BAG	Budget Activity Group
BATT	British Army Training Team
BBC	British Broadcasting Corporation

BDGIE	Bangladesh Government-in-Exile
BDR	Bangladesh Rifles
BICS	Bangladesh Islami Chhatra Shibir
BIPSOT	Bangladesh Institute of Peace Support Operation Training
BMW	Band & Music Wing
BNP	Bangladesh Nationalist Party
BSF	Border Security Force
CA	Constituent Assembly
CARAT	Cooperation Afloat Readiness and Training
CARs	Central Asian Republics
CCMR	Center for Civil Military Relations
CDF	Ceylon Defence Force
CEITS	Communication, Electronics and Information Technology Service
CENTCOM	US Central Command
CENTO	Central Treaty Organisation (also often referred to as Central Eastern Treaty Organisation)
CFC-A	Combined Forces Command - Afghanistan
CGSC	Command and General Staff College
CHT	Chittagong Hill Tracts
CJTF	Combined Joint Task Force
CLS	Chief of Logistics Staff
CMC	Central Military Commission
COAS	Chief of Army Staff
COGS	Chief of General Staff
COS	Chief of Staff
CPC	Communist Party of China
CPN-Maoist	Communist Party of Nepal - Maoist
CRS	Congressional Research Service
CSF	Coalition Support Fund
CSTC-A	Combined Security Transition Command - Afghanistan
CT	Counter Terrorism
CTS	Combat Training School
CTT	Combat Trekker Team
CVF	Ceylon Volunteer Force

DDC	Directorate of Development & Construction
DDP	Directorate of Defence Production
DDR	Disarmament, Demobilisation and Reintegration
DIAG	Disbandment of Illegal Armed Groups
DITE	Defence Institute for Training and Education (Maldives)
DoD	US Department of Defense
DPR	Directorate of Public Relations
DPT	Druk Phuensum Tshogpa
DSCSC	Defence Services Command and Staff College
EME	Electrical and Mechanical Engineers
ETT	Embedded Training Team
EEZ	Exclusive Economic Zone
EU	European Union
EUPOL	European Union Police
FATA	Federally Administered Tribal Areas
FMF	Foreign Military Financing
FRS	Fire & Rescue Service
GAO	Government Accountability Office
GCE	General Certificate of Education
GPOI	Global Peace Operations Initiative
GWOT	Global War on Terrorism
HMI	Himalayan Mountaineering Institute
HuM	Harkat-ul Mujahideen
IBFH	Indo-Bhutan Friendship Hospital
IC	Interim Constitution
IG	Inspector General
IGT&E	Inspector General of Training and Evaluation
IJC	ISAF Joint Command
IMA	Indian Military Academy
IMET	International Military Education and Training
IMTRAT	Indian Military Training Team
IOJ	Islami Oikya Jote
IPCC	International Panel on Climate Change
IPKF	Indian Peace Keeping Force

IPSOT-SL	Institute of Peacekeeping Support Operations Training Sri Lanka
ISAF	International Security Assistance Force
ISI	Inter Services Intelligence
ITC	Infantry Training Centre
ITLOS	International Tribunal for the Law of the Sea
JCO	Junior Commissioned Officer
JeM	Jaish-e Mohammad
JIB	Jamaat-e Islami Bangladesh
JMB	Jamaat-ul Mujahideen Bangladesh
JMJB	Jagrata Muslim Janata Bangladesh
JRB	Jatiyo Rakkhi Bahini
JVP	Janatha Vimukthi Peramuna
KLO	Kamtapur Liberation Organisation
KMTC	Kabul Military Training Center
LeT	Lashkar-e-Taiba
LoC	Line of Control
LTS	Language Training School
LTTE	Liberation Tigers of Tamil Eelam
MAT	Military Advisory Team
MGO	Master General of Ordnance
MNDF	Maldives National Defence Force
MoU	Memorandum of Understanding
MS	Military Secretary/Medical Service
MSTS	Marksman Sniper Training School
NA	Nepal Army
NAB	National Accountability Bureau
NATO	North Atlantic Treaty Organisation
NCC	National Cadet Corps
NCO	Non Commissioned Officer
NCOTS	Non Commissioned Officer Training School
NDC	National Defence College
NDFB	National Democratic Front of Bodoland
NDU	National Defence University
NGO	Non Governmental Organisation

NMAA	National Military Academy of Afghanistan
NRB	National Reconstruction Bureau
NRP	Nepalese Rupee
NSS	National Security Service
NSSG	Naval Special Service Group
NTM-A	NATO Training Mission - Afghanistan
NWFP	North-West Frontier Province
OCC	Operation Coordination Centre
OMCA	Office of Military Cooperation Afghanistan
OMLT	Operational Mentoring and Liaison Team
OSCA	Office of Security Cooperation-Afghanistan
PAF	Pakistan Air Force
PAT	Police Advisory Team
PBAS	Programme Budget Accounting System
PBCP	Purba Banglar Communist Party
PBSP	Purba Banglar Sarabahara Party
PCJSS	Parbotiya Chattogram Jana Sanghati Samiti
PIA	Pakistan International Airlines
PLA	People's Liberation Army
PLOTE	People's Liberation Organisation of Tamil Eelam
PML-N	Pakistan Muslim League - Nawaz
PMS-Q	Pakistan Muslim League - Quaid-e-Azam
PN	Pakistan Navy
PoK	Pakistan occupied Kashmir
PPIMS	Project Planning, Implementation and Maintenance Service
PPP	Pakistan People's Party
PRC	People's Republic of China
PSO	Principal Staff Officer
QMG	Quartermaster General
QRF	Quick Reaction Force
RBA	Royal Bhutan Army
RBI	Reserve Bank of India
RBP	Royal Bhutan Police
RC	Regional Command
RCAC	Regional Corps Advisory Command

RDF	Rapid Deployment Force
RMB	Renminbi
RNA	Royal Nepal Army
RPP	Rastriya Prajatantra Party
Rs	Rupees
SAARC	South Asian Association for Regional Cooperation
SAC	State Affairs Committee
SEATO	South East Asia Treaty Organisation
SF	Special Forces
SLA	Sri Lankan Army
SLMA	Sri Lanka Military Academy
SOFA	Status of Forces Agreement
SPG	Special Protection Group
TAFII	Task Force Anti Illicit Immigration
Tk	Taka (Bangladeshi currency)
TS	Transport Service
UAE	United Arab Emirates
UAV	Unmanned Aerial Vehicle
UCPN-Maoist	Unified Communist Party of Nepal - Maoist
ULFA	United Liberation Front of Assam
UN	United Nations
UNCLOS	United Nations Convention on the Law of the Sea
UNCTAD	United Nations Conference on Trade and Development
UNDP	United Nations Development Programme
UNESCAP	United Nations Economic and Social Commission for Asia and the Pacific
UNMIN	United Nations Mission in Nepal
UPDF	United People's Democratic Front
US	United States (of America)
USPACOM	United States Pacific Command
VFTS	Volunteer Force Training School
WASA	Water and Sewerage Authority
WLDMS	Wangchuk Lo Dzong Military School
YCL	Young Communist League

List of Tables and Figures

Introduction

This book is a modest attempt to examine the role, relevance and status of the armies in the ever dynamic socio-political milieu of the countries in India's South Asian neighbourhood. It is part of an ongoing endeavour by the area/country specialists at the South Asia Centre of the Institute to further explore and understand the role of a key institution, the Army, in shaping the political destiny and defining the ideational evolution of the (nation-) states in India's South Asian neighbourhood. The book deals with the national armies of seven South Asian countries bordering India, namely Afghanistan, Bangladesh, Bhutan, Nepal, Maldives, Pakistan and Sri Lanka.

The countries in the region are in different stages of national evolution, and so are their key governing institutions and their role and influence in the national body politic and policy formulations—both foreign and domestic. The pace and the nature of state and identity formation varies from country to country, and is reflected in the diverse stages of political, economic, social and cultural development that one observes in the countries of the region.

Afghanistan, Pakistan and Nepal have had violent political transitions. Maldives too have had less than peaceful transitions. Bhutan presents an altogether different picture where a peaceful transition from an absolute to a constitutional monarchy is underway. Bangladesh and Sri Lanka are relatively stable democracies. In terms of periodic military rule and military's total dominance in state affairs, no country is comparable to Pakistan in the region. The Pakistan Army, historically, has had an overarching role and influence in the affairs of the state. The Pakistan Army's presence has been all-pervasive in the national life of Pakistan. It has had the last word right from defining the national identity of the Pakistan nation to determining the course of the country's domestic politics and foreign policy strategy. Though democracy in Bangladesh has had its tryst with long military interregnums, the strong role of political parties as well as enthusiastic participation of the people in the political process is a recognised fact in its national life.

The nature of threats (or perception of threats) also varies from country to country. If Pakistan and Afghanistan are threatened by radical Islamist ideologies and state-sponsored entities who freely take recourse to the most violent forms of terror tactics, Nepal and Sri Lanka until few years back were confronted with unrelenting Maoist and Tamil insurgency respectively. Apart from Pakistan, Afghanistan and Bangladesh, Maldives too has time and again faced serious threat from the rising influence of Islamist forces which are now well-embedded in the body politic of all of these countries.

Most of the countries in India's neighbourhood are thus in a state of social-political ferment and transition. They are up against great odds as they struggle to overcome and cope with a variety of often existential internal challenges, and even external challenges as in the case of Afghanistan.

The chapters in the book delve into the role and position of the armies in different states of South Asia in a contemporary setting. They are operating in a far more complex environment today compared to the Cold War period, as most of the countries in India's neighbourhood have either been on the verge of, or are in the state of remarkable political—and even social and economic—transition. The dominant negative perception of India in some of the neighbouring states, often for inexplicable reasons, poses a major challenge to India's foreign and military policy.

A newly independent sovereign, socialist, secular and democratic India had inherited a tough and an unfavourable neighbourhood. This has presented India with multiple challenges at different levels especially as India adjusts to the rapidly changing regional and global environment in the post-Cold War, or rather post-9/11 period. As the pivot of South Asia, it is necessary for India to constantly monitor the position and status of the armies given the centrality of their role and influence, overt or covert, in the national politics and policy- making of countries in its immediate neighbourhood.

Structuring of Chapters

Any pan-South Asian study is a complex multi-layered process. Perhaps, socially and culturally, South Asia is the most diverse and heterogeneous region of the world where countless languages, philosophies, ethnicities and belief systems have collided and merged into each other in due course of centuries of ceaseless cross-fertilisation processes. This has given rise to an inherently diverse yet geo-culturally distinct South Asian identity. The region is also amazingly diverse in terms of demography, geographical terrain, geological profile and natural resources. It comprises of countries completely landlocked, tucked away in the Himalayas; and countries with vast coastlines as well as Island states jutting into the Indian Ocean.

In order to present the study in a simple, lucid and reader-friendly way, an attempt has been made to structure the chapters in a uniform manner. However, at the same time, fully cognisant of the unique local context and socio-political settings in which the armies are operating, and the individual profile of the armies under study, necessary flexibility has been shown and modifications made in the structuring of certain chapters, especially chapters on Maldives, Bhutan and to an extent Nepal.

Centrality of the Army

What has come out very clearly from the discursive analysis offered in this book is the continuing and often increasing centrality of the Army, mostly as key guarantors of internal stability, in the national life of most of the countries in India's neighbourhood. None of these countries is actually faced with the prospect of an open and a full-scale inter-state war in a conventional sense.

However, the planned withdrawal of Western forces from Afghanistan by 2014, and continuing drone strikes inside Pakistan's tribal areas by the US, provides a different context to the situation in the Af-Pak region. The Afghan National Army (ANA), considered as critical to the security of the country post-2014, is the youngest Army in the region and would be needing long-term external assistance and support before it evolves into an effective national force.

The Pakistan Army, considered as the strongest and most organised of all institutions in the country, is faced with multiple challenges spanning from radicalisation within its ranks to the rapidly spreading influence of radical Islamist and terrorist groups in many parts of the country. The complex nature of long-standing nexus between the Army and Islamist militant groups of various hues now seems to be hitting directly at the social and political fabric of the country as suicide bombings and sectarian violence has become the order of the day. From the foreign policy point of view, managing an increasingly conflicting relationship with the US due to Army's complicity in protecting and nurturing a range of Islamist militant groups fighting against Western and Afghan government forces has been a major challenge before the civilian government in Pakistan.

Various factors have been attributed to a relatively more visible and tangible role of the national army in public affairs of some of the countries. Some of the key reasons identified may be summed up here as: (i) failure or weakening of civil institutions and state authority; (ii) loss of internal socio-political equilibrium leading to major structural changes in the political system; (iii) disorderly, inconclusive, uncertain and prolonged political transitions; and (iv) continuing threat from insurgencies. Perhaps, another key reason that can be attributed here is the failure of paramilitary forces and the local police systems to stand up to the challenges. In case of Pakistan and Bangladesh, the dominant role of Army has often been regarded as the key cause for lack of democracy and weak civilian institutions in the country.

Though there has been a spurt in democratic transitions in some of the countries bordering India—Afghanistan, Bangladesh, Nepal and Pakistan—this may not necessarily mean greater or full civilian control over the armed forces. Pandering to the Army is still considered critical to the survival of civilian regimes particularly in Pakistan and Bangladesh. The democratisation processes in these countries remain fragile and are confronted with great odds as prospects of civil war in Afghanistan and political instability in Nepal, Pakistan and even Maldives lurks in the background. Sri Lanka and Bhutan are exceptions here.

It is noteworthy that defence expenditure continues to register phenomenal growth in most of these countries as they seek access to latest technology and acquisition of advanced weaponry. Restructuring of forces and creation of new commands, as announced by Bangladesh recently, are manifestations of Army's growing relevance and its effort at self preservation by adapting to the changing national setting, and at times political leadership's security perception.

India's Challenge

The negative perception of India in most of the neighbouring countries, despite India's sustained confidence building measures and several unilateral economic and political initiatives, seems near constant. The change in regimes or even political systems in its neighbourhood would at best lead to a brief interregnum in otherwise unabated anti-India tirade. Apart from political leadership, often militaries in these countries have used anti-India national constructs, based on imagined or perceived threat from a hegemonic India, to consolidate and strengthen their own position within the national politics and in cases even to bargain for assured external assistance.

This certainly has not been a desirable situation for India, especially in view of the growing thrust on promoting regional connectivity and trade in its policy towards neighbouring countries and regions to meet its own rising energy demands and commercial interests. The old stereotypes and imagined constructs about India, that have been institutionalised and perpetuated, often in a systematic manner, over many decades, have shaped the perception of the people in India's neighbourhood. Sometimes it is re-engineered and recalled to define nationalism and patriotism (basically nationalistic jingoism), or as a time-tested political ploy of diverting nation's attention from lingering domestic issues of concern. Be it a faltering political regime or a discredited military coup seeking self-justification, invoking anti-India constructs and maintaining the façade of an existential threat from India would often help in altering and setting a new national discourse.

So, what are the available options or viable approaches from the military point of view for India? Is there enough space and scope for a robust military diplomacy with certain countries, and would it make a valuable addition to India's ongoing effort to engage its immediate neighbourhood? Perhaps, the answer could be both yes and no.

The military diplomacy in South Asia region, in fact, has not been quite appreciable as has been brought out in various chapters. However, at the same time, despite a pervasive sense of negative mutual perceptions and rhetoric, the political realism or *realpolitik* dictated by convergence of interests in tackling common threats necessitates better communication and engagement among the armies of the region. Pakistan Army remains a strong exception here. India has been conducting joint exercises with the armies and navies of most of the South Asian countries, now including even Bangladesh.

India has had an institutionalised training programme for some of the South Asian armies. The first Indian Military Training Team (IMTRAT) was deployed in Bhutan in 1960. Indian forces were despatched to save President Gayoom's regime in Maldives when it was threatened by a local dissident group backed by a Sri Lankan Tamil rebel group in 1988. A large number of Gurkhas from Nepal, around 40,000 as stated in the chapter on Nepal Army, are serving with the Indian Army. Indian military assistance to Bangladesh and Sri Lanka going back to decades too has been brought out in the chapters dealing with the armies of the two countries. India has also been offering training courses to Army officers from foreign militaries at its own military academies, including officers from Sri Lanka, Nepal and Afghanistan.

But all this has not translated into or provided India with any strong leverage either within the military or the political establishments of the neighbouring countries who remain distrustful of India. They are instead diversifying their sources of weaponry and bilateral relationships while continuing their engagement with India at the same time. This is simply unavoidable as India's stature grows and certain extra-regional countries raise their stakes in the region for geo-political and often for economic reasons as well.

It is a given that India needs to constantly monitor the developments and the changing nuances of politics in its dynamic neighbourhood, and to further examine the perceptions of the military, and that of the various political groups, and how people in general perceive both, within those countries. This book is a step in that direction. It is also understood that a differentiated approach is required to engage and deal with different armies in the neighbourhood. Whether engaging the Army within a bilateral framework would in some cases undermine the civilian or democratic institutions, or would it help in thawing the relationship long marred by negative perceptions and boxed up thinking, is worth enquiring.

Meanwhile, the continuing centrality of the Army in India's neighbourhood as societies aspire for change and struggle to define and redefine a just political order is part of the inevitable power politics and quest for state preservation. While this is an ongoing process, there are certain factors that are simply undeniable and remain constant, such as, shared geography and fundamentals of geo-economics, irrespective of how national interests are defined or on what terms states or their key institutions interact within a region. Getting the fundamentals right and engaging with one another in a constructive spirit is the way forward for both India and its neighbours.

Chapter One

Afghanistan's National Army: Expectations and Scepticism*

Vishal Chandra

We can help train an army, we can help equip an army, we can help build facilities for the army, but only the Afghan people can breathe a soul into that army.

—Gen. Karl Eikenberry, former Commanding General, CFC-Afghanistan, January 2007

It cannot be predicted what the security situation will be like in 2014. But considering the current security situation...Afghanistan will need a security force numbering more than 400,000 to transition power in 2014.

—Afghan Defence Ministry Spokesman Gen. Zaher Azimi, January 2011

Introduction—The Security Environment of the Country

The Afghan situation is extremely uncertain and its future predictably less than hopeful. Afghanistan is awaiting another major transition in 2014-15 as the US and North Atlantic Treaty Organisation (NATO)-led troops are in the process of ending their combat mission by 2014. This coincides with the presidential and parliamentary elections due around the same time in Afghanistan. The West has been busy revising its objectives and intensifying its exit strategy on an annual basis. The Taliban and their allies, with full support from the Pakistani establishment, have over the years expanded their area of guerrilla operations beyond their traditional strongholds, making the Afghan war unsustainable and unviable for the Western coalition.

At the larger geo-political level, more than the Taliban and its affiliates,

*Few sections of this chapter have been drawn from the author's earlier publication. Vishal Chandra, "Making of the New Afghan National Army: Challenges and Prospects", *Strategic Analysis* (Routledge), 33 (1), January 2009, pp. 55-70.

it is the Pakistani establishment which has been positioning for a grand bargain in anticipation of a post-withdrawal situation in Afghanistan. One is inevitably reminded of the Pakistani role in the aftermath of the Geneva Accord of 1988 as the then Afghan President Mohammad Najibullah unsuccessfully struggled for support for his national unity initiatives, prior to stepping down in April 1992.

The ongoing confusion and divisions within the Western alliance as well as between the US and its regional allies continue to complicate the already complex Afghan situation. The US Administration had deployed nearly 33,000 additional troops as part of the military 'surge' announced in 2009, which had taken the over-all Western troop levels in Afghanistan to well above the 100,000 mark. The idea was to degrade the Al-Qaeda and reverse the Taliban momentum before any substantive reduction in Western troop level takes place. As the Afghan war peaks, so does the uncertainty over the future of Afghanistan.

The phased transition of security responsibilities from the NATO-led International Security Assistance Force (ISAF) to the Afghan National Security Forces (ANSF), and simultaneous withdrawal of the US and NATO-led troops, as agreed upon during the NATO's Lisbon Summit in November 2010, has been underway since July 2011. The security transition process is stated to be 'irreversible', even as the Haqqani-Taliban network with support from Pakistan's military establishment continues to push deeper into the Afghan heartland. Nearly 33,000 US troops are stated to have withdrawn so far—10,000 in 2011 and another 23,000 in September 2012. This means that the current US troop levels have come down to the pre-2009 level, i.e., about 68,000 American troops are still deployed.

Nothing has thus far been stated about the likely pace of withdrawal in the next two years (2013-14). Perhaps, it would be decided after the US presidential elections in November 2012, based on terms and conditions of the Bilateral Security Arrangement being negotiated between the US and Afghanistan. Meanwhile, in May 2012, President Karzai announced the beginning of the third phase of security transition. Afghanistan is expected to enter into the last phase of security transition by mid-2013, which means the ANSF is expected to take the lead in security responsibilities across the country by the end of 2013.

According to the declaration of the NATO Summit at Chicago in May 2012:

> The pace and the size of a gradual managed force reduction from the ANSF surge peak to a sustainable level will be conditions-based and

> decided by the Government of the Islamic Republic of Afghanistan in consultation with the International Community. The preliminary model for a future total ANSF size, defined by the International Community and the Government of Islamic Republic of Afghanistan, envisages a force of 228,500 with an estimated annual budget of US$4.1 billion, and will be reviewed regularly against the developing security environment.[1]

This means that the size of the ANSF would be pruned 2015 onwards from 352,000 to nearly 228,500 as stated above. Interestingly, nothing was said or plans were put forth for nearly 120,000 trained ANSF personnel who would have to be retrenched after 2014. The declaration further stated that:

> As the Afghan economy and the revenues of the Afghan government grow, Afghanistan's yearly share will increase progressively from at least US$500 m in 2015, with the aim that it can assume, no later than 2024, full financial responsibility for its own security forces.

On the eve of the Chicago Summit, it was reported that as per a US-backed plan, the Afghan Government is expected to contribute $500 million, the NATO countries $1.3 billion, and the remaining shortfall in the total amount required will be taken care of by the US and other countries. More than $1.1 billion was pledged at the summit's end, including contributions from Canada, Australia, Denmark, Italy, Germany and others.[2] According to another report, the "Afghan funding commitments so far include $100 million annually from Britain, $120 million from Italy, $110 million from Canada, $100 million from Australia and $20 million from Turkey."[3]

Though the prospect of a complete US and NATO withdrawal from the region is ruled out, the nature and level of their engagement post-2014 is far from clear. The US Administration has already signed an *Enduring Strategic Partnership Agreement* with Kabul in May 2012, wherein it has committed to remain engaged in Afghanistan until 2024. The Bilateral Security Agreement is to be concluded by May 2013, within a year of the signing of the Partnership Agreement.[4] Until it comes through, the ambiguity over the nature and level of US engagement after 2014 would remain. However, as of now, it is sufficiently clear that the US would be maintaining some military presence and would continue to assist Afghanistan for at least a decade after 2014. Interestingly, within two days of the NATO Summit, Gen. John R. Allen, commander of ISAF and the US forces in Afghanistan, during an interview made it clear that his troops will be requiring "significant firepower" in 2013-14 and that he owes the US president "some real analysis on this."[5]

In recent years, the West has explicitly staked its exit strategy on two processes: development of the ANSF, comprising both the Afghan National Army (ANA)[6] and the Afghan National Police (ANP); and reconciliation with key Pakistan-backed Afghan insurgent groups, particularly the Taliban leadership. It is a foregone conclusion now that both the processes will not be delivering the desired results by 2014-15. Despite several attempts, no tangible progress has been made or is likely to be made on the reconciliation front in the near-term. A strong sense of pessimism is reported to have set in within the US establishment over the idea of direct talks and reconciliation with the Taliban leadership. The focus is said to be shifting from the current policy of finding ways to directly engage the Pakistan-based Taliban leadership to working towards an intra-Afghan dialogue after 2014.[7] However, it is still too early to conclude that the US would be completely backing off from the idea of negotiating deals with the Taliban leadership. Perhaps, the US, after November 2012 presidential elections, might rework its strategy towards the Haqqani-Taliban network and even towards Pakistan, as 2014 approaches and Western forces drawdown from Afghanistan. As of now, there is no reason to believe that the Haqqani-Taliban network would agree to a negotiated political settlement, or the ANSF would be able to manage the combined Haqqani-Taliban onslaught without massive long-term external aid and assistance.

However, a strong ANA is still regarded as critical to the transition of security responsibilities and withdrawal of the bulk of Western forces by 2014. Given the rising cost of the Afghan war, both in terms of funding and casualties, building up a capable Afghan Army and Police is seen as a more economical option. In the above context, it is worth pondering if ANA at all has the potential to emerge as an effective unifying and a sustainable national force after 2014.

It is pertinent here to factor in the geo-strategic position of Afghanistan, and identify key internal and external threats to the country, and take a holistic view of the challenges that lie ahead in rebuilding Afghan state, particularly such key institutions as the national army.

(i) Geo-political/strategic Significance of the Country

Afghanistan's geo-strategic location has significantly contributed to the shaping of its social and political matrix, both in historical and present times. A quick glance through history reveals that Afghanistan, as we know today, has both immensely benefited and suffered on account of its geographic location. Being at the crossroads of South, West and Central Asia, Afghanistan was the melting pot of cultures and philosophies that flourished around it and those from distant lands that criss-crossed the region.[8]

Afghanistan's landlocked status and its nearly 5, 529 km long land borders with seven countries—Pakistan 2,430 km, including Pakistan occupied Kashmir (PoK) which is an integral part of the Indian Union; Tajikistan 1,206 km; Iran 936 km; Turkmenistan 744 km; Uzbekistan 137 km; and China 76 km—places the country in a unique geo-strategic context. Coupled with this is the amazing multitude of tribes, clans, ethnicities and languages that comprise the Afghan mosaic. Afghan communities often have remarkably overlapping or multiple identities, and it is not always easy to neatly differentiate or categorise them into separate ethnic or linguistic groupings.

It is notable that the major ethnicities comprising Afghanistan have their co-ethnics residing right across the borders of the country. There are more Pashtuns, known as Pakhtuns across the Durand Line, in Pakistan than in Afghanistan; similarly, the Afghan Tajiks, Uzbeks, Turkmen and Kyrgyz have their co-ethnics across the Amu Darya in the Central Asian Republics (CARs). Though no proper census has ever been conducted in the country, it is generally believed that minority ethnic groups taken in together outnumber the Pashtuns. The dominance of Persian culture among the heterogeneous Afghan *Farsiwan* or Dari-speakers that include a wide array of Afghan populace—the Shia minorities, such as, the Hazaras, Ismailis and Qizilbash; the predominantly Sunni Tajiks and Turkic Uzbeks and Turkmen, and even Sunni Pashtuns settled in parts of northern and western Afghanistan, is notable.

The Pashtuns, divided into intensely hierarchical social structures and tribal sub-cultures, are spread over a wide expanse extending from south-western Afghanistan to north-western Pakistan. Such a complex social diversity with cross-border cultural affinities has provided the Afghan groups as well as the neighbouring countries with certain socio-political leverages and continuing interface. This somewhat explains the much talked about 'proxy politics', arguably a two-way affair, in the context of Afghan civil war. If the neighbouring countries sought to engineer and exploit the Afghan situation to their advantage, the Afghan groups too have been known for masterfully taking advantage of their supposed allies and foes alike.

At the geo-economic level, if Afghanistan lay at the heart of the Old Silk Route in ancient and medieval times, today it is considered a vital transit corridor from the resource-laden but landlocked Caspian region to the energy-hungry countries in South Asia. Afghanistan is being increasingly projected as the connector of the region, a gateway to Eurasia and regions beyond. The notable geo-strategic significance of Afghanistan has thus remained undiminished, politically and economically, since centuries unknown.

Often caught in imperial rivalries, be it between the Iranian Safavids and the Indian Mughals in medieval times or British India and Czarist Russia in colonial times, and more recently as the last battle ground of the highly-contested Cold War, Afghanistan has nevertheless been able to carve out its own unique identity as a political entity though with varying degrees of independence and internal consolidation. The evolution as well as the destruction of Afghanistan as a state thus has been influenced by both external and internal dynamics.

The impact of adversarial bi-polar Cold War politics and competing regional geo-politics on Afghanistan's dynamic internal power play has been remarkable since the 1970s. It led to the withering of key Afghan institutions and the traditional balance of power both at the state-province and societal levels. This partly explains the north-south divide and the challenges faced in the building of national institutions of governance and enforcement in Afghanistan since 2001. The making of the new Afghan Army as a viable institution is no exception here. How 'national' is the new Afghan Army in terms of social representation and regional balance is often a subject of debate and scepticism.

(ii) Geographical Terrain

Afghanistan has a diverse and challenging geographical terrain and its impact on the social, economic and political diversity and history of the country is apparent. Two-thirds of the country has a mountainous terrain. The sprawling Hindu Kush Mountains divide the country into north and south-west. Afghanistan has three broad geographic regions: (i) The Central Highlands (ii) the Northern Plains, and (iii) the South-Western Plateau. Each of these regions varies in terms of soil composition, vegetation, agricultural productivity, altitude, and climate.

The Central Highlands are mountainous and dry with extreme temperatures in summer and winter. The soil varies from desert-steppe to meadow-steppe type. Much of the southern and western parts have high plateaus and deserts. The soil is infertile, except along river valleys, and sand storms are not unusual. This area is the epicentre of poppy cultivation in the country since poppy is said to be drought-resistant and does not need much irrigation. The Northern Plains are extremely fertile and agriculturally highly productive. This region is relatively rich in mineral resources and has deposits of natural gas as well.

The guerrilla style warfare comes naturally to the Afghans given the rough mountainous terrain of the country. For centuries, Afghan fighters have used the uneven terrain to their advantage, inflicting heavy casualties on the vastly superior foreign armies. Over the centuries, it has helped numerically weak

Afghan forces to present the challenge of asymmetric warfare to their enemies. Here in lies the importance of developing capabilities for high-altitude mountain warfare and counter-guerrilla operations, without which the ANA cannot be an effective force against the Taliban and its allies.

(iii) Threat Perceptions—Key Domestic and External Challenges

The prevalent ethno-political divide and the factionalised Afghan power politics remain a major internal challenge. The Afghan Government's position today is far more precarious and uncertain. The post-2001 political process has largely failed in stabilising the country as violence reaches record levels with every passing year. Kabul's authority remains limited as the Taliban and allies have expanded their reach beyond their traditional strongholds. Though the US has deployed thousands of additional troops since 2009, the security situation so far remains dismal and continues to deteriorate.

The US decision in December 2009 to simultaneously declare a military surge as well as plans for force withdrawal has only added to the confusion over the Western intent and strategy. It has emboldened the Pakistani establishment and a range of Islamist militants operating from their safe havens within Pakistan to continue with their *jihad*, especially when, in their perception, the Western coalition is on the verge of defeat. No wonder, the supposedly Kabul-led reconciliation initiatives aimed at the Taliban leadership are yet to elicit any positive response. After 2014, both insurgency and terrorism would thus continue to pose a major challenge to Afghanistan. Pakistan too is not likely to de-Talibanise its Afghan policy, especially as the West is bent on withdrawing its forces. It is notable that despite the Barack Obama Administration prioritising the process of re-building the Afghan Army and Police, the preparedness and capability of both so far remains questionable. Efforts are on to evolve a framework whereby the Western countries could remain engaged in Afghan theatre for at least a decade after 2014. Series of conferences have been organised in this regard, beginning with Bonn II on December 5, 2011 where it was decided that the West would remain engaged for a decade after 2014, which is referred to as the "Decade of Transformation (2015-24)."[9]

Origin/Evolution of the New National Army

On December 2, 2002, during a meeting with representatives from the UN and the donor countries at Petersberg in Bonn, Germany, Hamid Karzai, then chairman of the Afghan Transitional Administration (ATA), had issued a decree for the establishment of the ANA. The "Petersberg Decree" declared that the US would be 'the designated lead nation for ANA restructuring' under the overall command of the 'legitimate Afghan civilian authorities.' It also designated the UN with Japan as the lead donor nation for preparing a comprehensive programme for the Disarmament, Demobilisation, and Reintegration (DDR) of various militia groups to augment the process of establishing the ANA. The decree initially envisaged a multi-ethnic and an all-volunteer national army of 70,000.[10] However, the US Green Berets had already started training the first batch of Afghan soldiers in May 2002. The US soon partnered with the UK, France, Canada, Germany, New Zealand, Romania, Bulgaria and Mongolia to build a functional national army for Afghanistan.

Interestingly, according to the official website of the ANA, which has not been made available since 2008, the ANA has been 'active' from the 1880s to the present. However, according to analysts like Ali Ahmed Jalali, former colonel in the old Afghan Army and later interior minister (2003-05) in Karzai's cabinet, this was the fourth time in the last 150 years that the Afghan military is being rebuilt.[11] Jalali identifies at least three occasions since the late 19th century in the military history of Afghanistan when the Afghan monarchs had to recreate the Army—(i) in the 1870s by Amir Sher Ali Khan during the second Anglo-Afghan War (1878–1880); (ii) in the 1880s by Amir Abdur Rahman; and (iii) after the third Anglo-Afghan War of 1919 when the Army was remodelled by King Amanullah Khan. The newly remodelled Army, however, suffered a lot during the civil war of 1929. As a result of this, King Nader Shah had to recreate the Army after his accession in 1929 which continued to grow under successive regimes until 1992. With the collapse of the Najibullah regime, the Afghan Army simply withered away.

Training and Mentoring

Following the decree, various camps and coalition/combined task forces were established by the Western countries and the partners in and around Kabul to train the new Afghan Army and to provide necessary logistics with regard to it. Camp Phoenix, established in early 2003 on the outskirts of Kabul and led by the Combined Joint Task Force (CJTF) Phoenix of the US coalition, soon began conducting broad-based training, mentoring, and assistance programmes for the ANA. The CJTF Phoenix has since undergone various rotations and has played a key role in establishing the ANA's five corps. The CJTF Phoenix VI later took up the additional responsibility of assisting in the training of the Afghan police.[12] Similarly, Camp Black Horse, located on the outskirts of Kabul, which hosts the Canadian Afghan National Training Centre Detachment, too has been providing training and mentorship to the ANA.[13] The US Special Forces are said to be training the ANA commando battalions at Camp Morehead in the south of Kabul.

The Combined Joint Task Force 82 (CJTF-82), headquartered at Bagram Airfield, has also played an important role in the training of the ANA, even though its main mission was "to conduct operations to destroy remaining Al-Qaeda/hostile Taliban command and control and other hostile anti-Islamic elements."[14] It operates directly under the US Central Command (CENTCOM), and functions as Regional Command (RC)-East of the NATO-led ISAF in Afghanistan.[15]

All programmes relating to training and mentoring of the ANA since 2002 were initially coordinated by the Office of Military Cooperation Afghanistan (OMCA) under overall US command. Later OMCA came under the command of Combined Forces Command-Afghanistan (CFC-A), which was established in November 2003. Satisfied with the progress made on the development of the ANA, the US expanded the OMCA's role to include the entire Afghan security sector. On July 12, 2005, the OMCA was re-designated as the Office of Security Cooperation-Afghanistan (OSCA). On April 4, 2006, the OSCA was in turn re-designated as Combined Security Transition Command-Afghanistan (CSTC-A) under the US CENTCOM.

However, in April 2009, the US and NATO agreed to establish NATO Training Mission-Afghanistan (NTM-A) to oversee institutional training for the ANSF. This shifted the responsibility for ANA's development from the US to the ISAF. NTM-A/CSTC-A's headquarter elements were fully operational by February 2010 and it now operates as an integrated NATO and US command with the mission of developing the ANSF.[16] While NTM-A/CSTC-A focuses on training recruits and building institutional training capacity, the ISAF Joint Command (IJC) now takes responsibility for training Afghan soldiers in the field as well as for conducting combat operations. Having achieved full operational capacity in November 2009, the IJC provides training to ANA units in the field through training teams and partner units. Both NTM-A/CSTC-A and IJC report to the commander of the ISAF and the US forces in Afghanistan.[17]

On the ANA side, all training and education is managed and implemented by the newly formed ANA Training Command (ANATC). The Kabul Military Training Centre (KMTC) also comes under ANATC-HQ. Formal education and professional development courses for the senior ANA officers are conducted by US and Turkish military instructors at the newly established National Military Academy of Afghanistan (NMAA). The Command and General Staff College (CGSC), built by France in early 2004, prepares mid-level ANA officers to serve on brigade and corps staffs. A team of French Army instructors oversees operations at the school. The basic infantry training course for ANA troops was initially for ten weeks, which later varied from eight to 14 weeks.

Headquartered at Camp Eggers, the CSTC-A, established in April 2006 and operating directly under US CENTCOM, coordinates all programmes relating to training and mentoring of the ANA. It is "a joint service, coalition organisation with military personnel from the US, UK, Canada, Poland, Albania, Germany, France and Romania, as well as contracted civilian advisors, mentors and trainers."[18]

To boost the ANA's regional commands, an Afghan Regional Security Integration Command (ARSIC) has been attached to it. The objective is to carry forward the mission of the CSTC-A at the regional command level. Each ARSIC comprises a Regional Corps Advisory Command (RCAC) responsible for planning, training, and mentoring at the level of regional corps and below. Within each RCAC are a number of US-led Embedded Training Teams (ETTs) whose functions range from "daily mission planning and preparation to safety, unit training and moral and ethical training" for the ANA.[19] Then there are ISAF-led Operational Mentoring Liaison Teams (OMLTs) attached to regional commands in support of ARSIC.

In due course of time, the British forces were tasked with the training of Non-Commissioned Officers (NCOs) of the ANA; the Canadians began conducting a two-week training programme in squad and platoon level tactics; the French forces assisted in training the ANA officers; the German forces provided trainers and mentors for the ANA armour (tanks); the Romanian forces were responsible for the ANA Advanced Individual Training (AIT); Mongolia provided instructors for the ANA field artillery; and Croatian, Italian, Dutch, Norwegian, Slovenian, Swedish, and Polish forces provided OMLTs. The US forces, however, remain responsible for the overall mentoring and training of the ANA from the Afghan Ministry of Defence (MoD) to the company level.[20]

At first, the ANA soldiers were given a brisk two-month course and then sent out to battle the Taliban insurgents. But now, the training at KMTC is for 15 weeks, including six weeks of basic training, and nine weeks of Advanced Infantry Training, during which soldiers are given specialised training, from rifleman to artillery to more elite commando duties. The NTM-A/CSTC-A reportedly follows a three-step approach: training Afghan recruits, training Afghans to be trainers, and training Afghans to assume control of their systems and institutions. It is said to be currently in the process of moving from the first step to the second and third steps.

Military Doctrine/Strategic Thought of the National Army

The Afghan National Army is said to be acquiring strength and confidence despite all uncertainty, but it is difficult to assess its doctrinal focus. The slogan of *Khuda, Watan and Wazifa* is still to characterise the new Army. The senior officers are said to be a mix of veterans of the old pro-Soviet Afghan Army of the 1970s and 80s including the deserters and defectors from the old national army, elements from the anti-Soviet resistance, and more recently veterans of the anti-Taliban resistance. The diversity of the multi-national entities involved in the training and mentoring process has, to an extent, led to a complex mix of doctrines and approaches within the ANA. There are US/NATO/Soviet trained officers and instructors working with the ANA and their over all impact on the orientation of the new Afghan Army as well as at operational and coordination levels is yet to be assessed. The expansion of the ISAF and its role in training the ANSF further diversified the military doctrines and policy approaches to the development of the ANA.

Equally important is the training of officers and NCOs. The only veteran NCOs available are ones who had served in the old Soviet-trained Afghan Army. NATO has different standards for NCOs, with sergeants expected to lead, supervise and take responsibility. The training of the officer corps also presents similar challenges. The Soviet style varied from the NATO style of officer training, position and orientation Since many of the mid-level and senior officers have been recruited from among old factional commanders and officers trained by the Russians, they are often at variance with the younger officers being trained on West Point or Sandhurst model.

Structure/Formation of the National Army, including Ethnic Composition; and Budgeting

Structure/Formation of ANA[21]

The ANA is said to comprise six ground manoeuvre corps and one air corps. The ANA is suppose to comprise '76 battalions or *Kandaks*[22] organised into 13 light infantry brigades, a mechanised brigade, a commando brigade, enabling units and the initial operation of an air corps by the end of fiscal year 2009.'[23] The ANA is said to be 'primarily a light infantry based army equipped with towed artillery and mortars.'[24] The ANA, as of now, has a Capital Division and six regional corps commands:

- 111th Capital Division (Kabul)
- 201st *Selab* or Flood Corps based in Kabul (Central Command);
- 203rd *Tandar* or Thunder in Gardez (Eastern Command);
- 205th *Atal* or Hero in Kandahar (Southern Command);
- 207th *Zafar* or Victory in Herat (Western Command); and

- 209th *Shaheen* or Falcon in Mazar-e-Sharif (Northern Command); and
- 215th *Maiwand* in Lashkar Gah, Helmand.

The first regional corps command headquarters outside Kabul was established in Kandahar on September 19, 2004. The other three regional commands were soon established in late 2004 and early 2005. The 215th sixth corps command was formally established in April 2010. A new division, the 111th Capital Division, was created from the 201st Kabul Corps and it became operational in April 2009.

According to the US Government Accountability Office (GAO):

> The ANA personnel are counted toward the force size after they have successfully passed vetting procedures. In order to pass vetting procedures, recruits must validate that they are Afghan citizens between 18 and 35 years old; present two vouchers of recommendation (often written by village elders); and pass a physical and mental examination and a drug test. Recruits also undergo biometric testing to verify that they are not assigned to any other armed forces unit and have not been involved in previous attacks against US, NATO, or Afghan forces.[25]

Afghan National Army Air Corps (ANAAC)

The ANAAC was re-established in January 2005 and at that time comprised of few ageing Russian helicopters and transport planes. The Russians had helped in overhauling 11 of them in 2004. It was also reported that the Afghan defence ministry had sought the return of 26 aircrafts including nine helicopters, five bombers, eight fighters, two trainer jets and two transporters—19 of which are in Pakistan and seven in Uzbekistan.[26] In October 2005, there were reports suggesting that Russia will be supplying four helicopters and military equipments worth $30 million to the ANA.[27] The Czech Republic had also committed to supply six helicopters to the Air Corps.[28] Since then, efforts have been on to re-equip the ANAAC.

According to *The Long War Journal*, as of April 2010, the ANAAC had an estimated 3,000 personnel and a total of 46 aircrafts. The total cost of building the ANAAC, from its start in May 2007 to the completed organisation of 130-140 aircrafts, and nearly 8,000 personnel by the end of FY2015 is expected to be approximately $5 billion (for details, see Annexure).

The ANAAC is organised into three air wings and four regional support detachments (for further details, see Annexure I):

- Kabul Air Wing—Houses ANAAC headquarter, Supports National Commando Brigade, Fixed wing transport, VIP transport, attack, ISR.
- Kandahar Air Wing—Supports Regional Command (RC)—South/ 205th Corps, Fixed wing transport, attack, ISR.

- Shindand Air Wing—Supports RC—West / 207th Corps. Center for pilot training.
- Jalalabad Regional Support Detachment—Support RC-Central/201st Corps.
- Mazar-e-Sharif Regional Support Detachment—Supports RC-North/ 209th Corps.
- Gardez Regional Support Detachment—Supports RC-East / 203rd Corps.
- Herat Regional Support Detachment—Supports RC-West / 207th Corps.

Ethnic Representation

The ethnic composition of the ANA remains a tricky issue. Striking the right ethnic balance at various levels in the Army remains a continuing challenge. It is a key factor in determining people's perception and trust in the ANA as a national institution. Though the ANA is said to be multi-ethnic in nature, imbalance at certain levels, especially the officer corps which is often stated to be dominated by the Tajiks, seems unavoidable for the time being given the prevalent socio-political equations within the country. Moreover, in the absence of proper census figures, the demographic composition of the country itself has been a controversial issue. In order to address the above issue and to lend a national character to the ANA, the Afghan defence ministry is reported to have set targets for the ethnic composition of the ANA. Ethnic quotas have been introduced especially at the level of officers—about 40-45 per cent for Pashtuns, 30-35 per cent Tajiks, 10-12 per cent Hazaras, and 8-10 per cent for Uzbek and other groups.[29]

The implementation of ethnic quota in the Army may have invariably ended the dilemma over what is more urgent to its survival—ethnic balancing or professionalism. The Afghan view seems to be divided on this issue. Some are of the view that the priority should be given to first developing a highly professional national army. The issue of ethnic balance though important can be taken care of later. The other viewpoint is more in favour of first ensuring proportionate ethnic representation without which it would not be possible to build a legitimate national army.[30]

Despite efforts made from time to time to augment Pashtun representation, getting recruits from the south and east has been a major challenge. According to an estimate, only about three per cent of recruits are actually Pashtuns from southern provinces.[31] However, some success has been achieved at the officer level in recent years. Apart from the ethnic imbalance, the regional imbalance too has the potential to trigger centrifugal tendencies within the Army in times to come. Much would, however, depend on the political configuration post-2014.

Funding

The US Central Command (CENTCOM) has the primary responsibility for managing the Afghan Security Forces Fund (ASFF). CSTC-A, under CENTCOM uses the ASFF to fund its mission. The ASFF provides for the equipment, supplies, services, training, facility, and infrastructure repair, renovation and construction.

The ASFF is divided into Budget Activity Groups (BAG), both for the ANA, ANP, and for related activities, including detainee operations. The ANA Budget Activity Group is further divided into Sub-Budget Activity Groups (SAG). Both the BAG and SAG are monitored through the Army's Programme Budget Accounting System (PBAS) and a separate Afghan-run database. The international donor support for the ANA includes over 40 donor nations and international organisations, contributing approximately $470 million (as of October 2010) worth of equipment to the ANA. In addition, as of October 2010, the other donor countries had reportedly provided about $210 million in funding in support of ANA development, with nearly another $200 million pledged. The donor nations have provided funding for the army through the NATO-ANA Trust Fund which was established in 2007 'to support activities such as ANA training, equipment purchases, and transportation of donated equipment'.[32] As of May 2012, contributions and pledges made to the Trust Fund totalled • 489,088,425.[33]

Between 2003 and 2009, the US is said to have spent $20 billion to finance the Afghan Army and Police. During 2010-11, the amount spent was $9 billion. Of the approximately $20 billion provided by the US, about $17.9 billion, or nearly 90 per cent, came from the DOD-managed ASFF. Of the $17.9 billion, the largest amount—about $7.0 billion, or 39 per cent—has been directed toward equipment purchases.[34]

In January 2011, Gen. William B. Caldwell, commander of NATO's training mission in Afghanistan, had announced that the US and its NATO allies plan to spend $11.6 billion during 2011-12 on building Afghanistan's security forces. This is said to be the largest yearly sum to date as the Western forces begin transferring security responsibilities to the ANA in certain parts of the country. The new funding pushes the total for 2010-11 to nearly $20 billion, as much as in the seven previous years combined. It was also reported that, among other things, 24,000 Ford Rangers, 108,000 9-mm pistols, 74,000 handheld radios, 44 helicopters and four bomb-sniffing robots have already been purchased from the funds available for the year.[35]

Interestingly, a large chunk of the ANA funding goes towards salaries. In 2002, recruits were offered $50 per month after they completed their basic training, while NCOs and officers were paid $50-70 and $150, respectively. The following year witnessed high levels of desertion and attrition, understandably linked with soldiers' dissatisfaction with poor pay. In 2003, a recruit's salary was increased to $70 per month while a battalion commander's salary was increased to $300 per month. As an added bonus, soldiers received two dollars for each day spent on field operations.[36]

The idea has also been to discourage defections in the ANSF as the Taliban part-time fighters were said to be better paid. In the summer of 2006, the Taliban were reportedly offering three times the daily pay of the ANA, approximately $300 a month for the equivalent of a first-year ANA soldier. Additionally, the Taliban reportedly offered "$10 to $20 per day for joining attacks on Western forces, $15 to launch a single mortar round into nearby coalition military bases, and US $1,000 for the head of a government worker or a foreigner."[37] Since then, pay for the Afghan Army and Police have been revised from time to time with the objective of checking the high desertion rate. As of 2010, Afghan police officers and soldiers make on an average $165 a month; forces serving in the Helmand province and other such places get an additional $75 as hostile environment pay.[38]

Strength of the National Army—Logistics (Sources and Nature of Weaponry) and Weaknesses/Limitations of the National Army

Interestingly, there are no definitive figures on the current as well as future potential strength of the ANA. Initially the strength of the ANA was projected at 70,000, but the targeted strength has since been revised several times. Later, as the US began shifting its focus back from Iraq to Afghanistan in 2008-09, the targeted strength of the ANA was revised from 70,000 to 134,000. In January 2010, it was decided during the London Conference on Afghanistan to further augment its strength to 171,000 by October 2011. As per the new US plan, about 10,000 troops were supposed to be trained each year for four years beginning in 2010. In August 2010, it was said that the West has increased the capacity to train about 75,600 recruits from 27,000 annually, a nearly three-fold increase since January 2008. A further revision in the targeted strength of the ANA from 171,000 to 240,000 is already said to be under consideration. The current strength of the ANA (as of October 2012) is said to be around 195, 000. However, according to ISAF, the current strength of ANA stands at 184,676 or almost 99 per cent of the 187,000 to be inducted by December 2012 and fielded by December 2013.[39] For increase in the size of the ANSF since 2003, see Table 1.

The sustainability of the projected strength of the ANA has been the subject of debate in recent years. Though senior Afghan Army officials have been of the view that an army of at least 150,000-200,000 and a maximum of 300,000-400,000 would be needed to stabilise the country, the West had its reservations, fearing that it might undermine the authority of the nascent civilian government in Kabul. Arranging and sustaining necessary levels of external funding and direct assistance for a large Afghan Army and Police for at least a decade after 2014 is also considered as a huge challenge. It was stated in the NATO Summit in Chicago that the over all size of the ANSF would have to be reduced after 2014 depending on the ground situation and, more importantly, availability of funds.

Table 1: Size of Afghan National Security Forces on Duty, 2003-12

Month	*Ministry of Defence Forces (ANA)*	*Ministry of Interior Forces (ANP)*	*Total ANSF*
End 2003	6,000	—	6,000
End 2004	24,000	33,000	57,000
End 2005	26,000	40,000	66,000
End 2006	36,000	49,700	86,000
End 2007	50,000	75,000	125,000
October 2008	68,000	79,910	147,910
December 2009	100,131	94,958	195,089
December 2010	149,533	116,856	266,389
December 2011	179,610	143,800	323,410
March 2012	194,466	149,642	344,108

Both ANA and ANP met manning goals set for October 2011. The goal for ANA by November 2012 is 195,000 soldiers and the goal for ANP is 157,000 security forces by the same time.

Source: Above figures have been drawn from the *Afghanistan Index* published by Brookings. See Ian S. Livingston and Michael O'Hanlon, Size of Afghan Security Forces on Duty, 2003-12, Figure 1.4, *Afghanistan Index*, Brookings, September 18, 2012, p. 6, at http://www.brookings.edu/~/media/Programs/foreign%20policy/afghanistan%20index/index20120918.pdf

Sources and Nature of Weaponry

The nature of weaponry with the ANA has been predominantly of Soviet origin. However, attempts to make the ANA adapt to Western/American weaponry have met with several hurdles. It has been a contentious issue as most of the veteran commanders and militia fighters integrated into the new Army prefer Soviet weaponry. The US has in recent years acquiesced to the idea of buying Russian-made weapons and helicopters for the ANA. Equipping the rapidly expanding Army and the need to ramp up maintenance services has raised several issues critical to the sustainability and orientation of the new Afghan Army.

In 2006, the NATO Equipment Donation Programme was introduced. The Programme "provides a mechanism through which Allies donate essential equipment, from uniforms and medical equipment to ammunition and helicopters." Similarly, the NATO-Russia Council (NRC) Helicopter Maintenance Trust Fund was launched in March 2011. The NRC Trust Fund "provides vitally-needed maintenance and repair capacity, including the provision of spare parts and technician training, to the Afghan Air Force helicopter fleet."[40] However, there have been serious differences between the NATO and the Afghan Army officials on what constitutes the right weaponry for the Afghan Army. The ANA officials have often complained about poor equipments as well as inadequate and incompatible weaponry.

Limitations/Weaknesses

A number of limitations are inhibiting the development and growth of an effective national army in Afghanistan. These can be broadly categorised as: (i) logistical in terms of training and mentoring, weaponry and support structures; (ii) lack of internal cohesion and often motivation in terms of ethnic factionalism and under-representation; (iii) high attrition rate, desertions, absenteeism and low enlistment; (iv) rampant drug abuse and illiteracy; (v) occasional friction between the recruits and their foreign trainers and mentors; and (vi) Taliban infiltration.

The last of the two has emerged as a major challenge in recent times. There has been a phenomenal spurt in what is generally referred to as 'green-on-blue' or 'insider' attacks, which as of now seems to be making a devastating impact on the very core of the post-2014 Western strategy. The idea of Western troops moving into a supportive role and focussing on training and mentoring of the ANSF long after Western forces have ended their combat mission in 2014 could be jeopardised if such attacks do not abate. It is already weakening the coordination between the Afghan recruits and the Western military trainers and instructors.

According to the data provided by *The Long War Journal*, the 'green-on-blue' attacks account for nearly 15 per cent Coalition casualties this year (as of October 16, 2012). In previous years, they accounted for six per cent casualties among Coalition troops in 2011, two per cent in 2010, two percent in 2009, and less than a per cent in 2008. Since January 2008, a total of 65 such attacks (38 in 2012, 15 in 2011, five in 2010, five in 2009 and two in 2008) have taken place, with maximum number of incidents reported from Helmand and Kandahar, both known Taliban strongholds. They have resulted in total 118 Coalition casualties (55 in 2012, 33 in 2011, 16 in 2010, 12 in 2009 and two in 2008), with 121 wounded (as of October 16, 2012).[41]

Various reasons have been cited for the sudden spurt in what is now being more commonly referred to as 'insider' attacks during 2011-12. Initially, it was believed to be due to cultural differences and personal grievances within the ANA, but now given the emerging patterns and rising frequency of attacks, the Haqqani-Taliban network is understood to be behind most of these attacks. According to a recent report by the *Associated Press*, based on internal US military analyses, "a number of shooters were recruited into the Afghan army or police forces from Pashtun areas in eastern Afghanistan—including the provinces of Paktika, Paktia and Khost—where the Haqqanis wield great influence." The report added, "In some cases these Afghans—most of whom had served in uniform for six months or less—returned to those areas on leave from their army or police duties, or briefly crossed into Pakistan, shortly before turning their guns on American or allied soldiers."[42]

Another notable aspect is the near absence of credible and detailed information on casualties among the ANSF and its impact on the morale of both Army and Police. The ISAF recently indicated that in 2012 the casualty among the ANA personnel averaged 243 killed and wounded *per month*, and among the ANP averaged 292 killed and wounded *per month*.[43] Yet another missing aspect is the 'green-on-green' attacks that too have increased within the Army and Police. According to a recent report by the *Associated Press*, quoting US military statistics, about 135 Afghan policemen and soldiers have been killed in insider attacks since 2007, which is much more than the number of Western troops killed in such attacks. At least, 53 Afghan soldiers and policemen are said to have been killed until August this year.[44] Such 'insider' attacks where Afghan security personnel attack their compatriots would add to the general distrust and weaken the ANSF from within.

There are also several reports suggesting that the Afghan Army is incapable of fighting insurgency on its own. Rampant ethnic factionalism, illiteracy, drug addiction and desertion are highlighted as key limiting factors. In the words of a senior ANA official from the national recruiting centre, "There are drug traffickers who want to use our units for their business, enemy infiltrators who want to raise problems, jailbirds who can't find any other job." He also candidly observed that, "The news of the American withdrawal has weakened our morale and boosted the morale of the enemy" and "if the international community abandons us again, we won't be able to last."[45]

Lack of motivation and disoriented sense of loyalty has also impacted the performance levels. It has been aptly observed that, "the rank and file soldiers are confused about what kind of culture they should follow. The US and NATO (too) are learning. The training has improved in recent months. But they have not created a message or an idea that the soldiers can believe in. What is it that they must be loyal to? What do they defend?"[46]

Attrition and absenteeism has been a particularly worrying feature. For instance, from November 2009 to October 2010, the ANA is reported to have lost over 30,000 soldiers due to attrition. In September 2010, it was reported that only 69 per cent of soldiers were present for duty. An analysis of data provided by IJC indicates that, from January to September 2010, on an average, over a quarter of the ANA was absent during any given month.[47] Recently, in October 2012, it has been reported that, "a third of the Afghan Army perpetually consists of first-year recruits fresh off a 10- to 12-week training course. And in the meantime, tens of thousands of men with military training are put at loose ends each year, albeit without their army weapons, in a country rife with militants who are always looking for help." In fact, a four-year programme has been proposed to order the recall of nearly 22,000 deserters.[48]

Illiteracy too is widely prevalent in the ANA. General Rahmatullah Raufi, the former corps commander in Kandahar, was on record having stated that 80 per cent of the soldiers in his corps are illiterate, 50 per cent of the officers are illiterate, and only 20 per cent of his soldiers have a professional knowledge of how to serve in an army; the rest are former militia fighters or young recruits.[49] At the more critical field level, there is a tremendous shortage of NCOs. As of October 2010, about one-quarter of NCO positions in ANA combat units were said to be lying vacant.

Civil-Military Relations

The training and mentoring of the ANA has been a Western-led and sponsored process since 2002, right from creating infrastructure to providing necessary funds; and from preparing the training modules to providing trainers and instructors and weaponry for the ANA. Kabul so far hardly has had any say in the above process. The only way whereby Kabul gets to exert its influence over the ANA is when it comes to the appointment and promotion of senior officers in the Army through the defence ministry. Its involvement at the technical level has been largely symbolic. Though views have been expressed by the relevant Afghan ministries from time to time about the supposed numerical strength of the ANA, the over-all process of rebuilding the Army largely remains a Western prerogative.

It is still too early to be looking at the emergence of the ANA in terms of civil-military relations and its likely role in the context of an increasingly fragile and reversible state-building process in Afghanistan. The future of ANA in terms of internal cohesion and loyalty to the government in Kabul will thus be greatly determined by the reversibility and the irreversibility of the West-sponsored political process and the West's future engagement in Afghanistan as well as Pakistan.

National Army in People's Perception

The ANA is believed to enjoy a positive reputation. It is generally regarded as relatively less corrupt and an institution that often evokes cautious optimism and pride among the Afghan people. However, despite greater focus on developing the ANSF, the growing confusion over the Western commitment and Kabul's renewed efforts for reconciliation with the Taliban is invariably giving way to growing scepticism over the future prospects of the ANA.

The idea of creating Afghan Public Protection Force (APPF) or Afghan Local Police (ALP) to address the shortfall in the ANSF or the gap in local security by way of arming the tribes, especially in south-eastern parts of the country, to protect themselves against the Taliban, has wide implications for the development and future prospects of the ANSF. Both are supposed to have been formed on the basis of lessons learnt from the earlier experience with the Afghan National Auxiliary Police (ANAP). The ANAP was created in 2006 and had to be disbanded within two years of it as it largely comprised of local militia, criminals and men involved in drugs trade. Though APPF and ALP too are supposed to be temporary in nature as members of these forces are to later merge into the ANA or ANP, but such parallel informal structures may in the long run strengthen the culture of private militias and undermine the credibility of both ANA and ANP in people's perception.

Future Prospects

Though the Obama Administration has prioritised and accelerated the process of building up the ANSF, the Army is decades away from being an effective and a professional national institution. It is clear that the ANA will not be in a position to either fully take on the security responsibilities from the Western forces or carry out counter-insurgency/terrorism operations on its own by 2014 or even later. In fact, the present ANA cannot survive without sustained external assistance and will require generous financial and logistical support for long years to come.

It is said that the Afghan Government currently spends almost $450 million of its approximately $1 billion annual revenue on security, which is a small fraction of the total cost.50 According to a projection by the International Monetary Fund (IMF) released in January 2010, it will not be possible for Afghanistan— before 2023— to be able to cover all expenses relating to the Army.[51] As the Army grows, so is the need for infrastructure to sustain such a huge army across the country. In January 2011, it was pointed out by the US inspector general overseeing American contracts in the country that hundreds of new Afghan outposts, barracks and garrisons are "seriously behind schedule, making it doubtful that the construction efforts would keep pace with recruitment and training." He stated that "of 884 projects for completion over the next two years, only 133 are finished. Another 78 are under way, but 673 have not begun."[52]

Much would also depend on how the politics of Afghanistan shapes up; and the nature of US and NATO's involvement beyond 2014. It is still to be seen how successful and irreversible the security transition would be in years to come. The internal cohesion of the ANA is likely to remain fragile on account of competing agendas of various domestic and external actors involved in the Afghan war. Despite greater Western focus and investment, the ANA is still logistically speaking a chronically deficient force. The NATO training mission have for long been short of hundreds of trainers and mentors. The Western effort has notably failed in creating and developing indigenous Afghan instructors and mentors critical to the continued growth of the ANA. Some of the neighbouring countries who could have immensely contributed towards the rebuilding of the ANA were deliberately kept out of the whole process.

The challenges before ANA are thus immense in proportion and diverse in nature. A range of internal and external factors are arrayed against it. Pakistan, a critical element in the West's Afghan policy, has been strongly averse to the idea of a huge and a powerful Afghan Army on its western frontiers. The process of building institutions of governance in Afghanistan is today far more constrained than in the early years of the war on terror. The failure of the UN-led and externally-sponsored disarmament and demobilisation programmes, such as, the DDR and Disbandment of Illegal Armed Groups (DIAG) aimed at various private militias across the country; the prevalent socio-ethnic divide in the Afghan polity; fragmented Western efforts and its failing Af-Pak strategy, are factors impacting the development of the ANA.

At the domestic level, the future prospects of the ANA will to an extent also depend on the perceptions of the war-weary population, and the capacity of the national police to effectively respond to local security needs and sensitivities of the Afghan people across the country. The development of an efficient and well-resourced national police too is thus critical to the emergence of the ANA.

The rush to increase the numerical strength of the Army within a short span of time and without any emphasis on quality soldiering or developing a strong professional core too does not bode well for the future of the ANA. The centrifugal tendencies within the ANA have the potential to wreck the Army from within if the Afghan conflict expands and the West fails to neutralise the Taliban and their numerous allies operating from across the

Durand Line with support from the Pakistani establishment. The continuing short-termism in the Western approach towards 'stabilising' the Af-Pak region could lead to the undoing of the ANA as the 'stakeholders' of all shades and hue could be preparing for the next round of civil war in Afghanistan.

NOTES

1. "Chicago Summit Declaration on Afghanistan", Issued by the Heads of State and Government of Afghanistan and Nations contributing to the NATO-led International Security Assistance Force (ISAF), May 21, 2012, at http://www.nato.int/cps/en/SID-C2334E22-719429FC/natolive/official_texts_87595.htm
2. Carol E. Lee, Adam Entous and Stephen Fidler, "NATO Leaders Seal Afghan Exit Plan", *The Wall Street Journal*, May 21, 2012, at http://online.wsj.com/article/SB10001424052702304791704577418271228255322.html?mod=world_newsreel
3. Matt Spetalnick and Missy Ryan, "NATO sets "irreversible" but risky course to end Afghan war", *Reuters*, May 21, 2012, at http://www.reuters.com/article/2012/05/21/us-nato-summit-idUSBRE84J02C20120521
4. "Enduring Strategic Partnership Agreement between the United States of America and the Islamic Republic of Afghanistan", *The White House*, May 2, 2012, at http://www.whitehouse.gov/sites/default/files/2012.06.01u.s.-afghanistanspasignedtext.pdf
5. "General says Afghanistan will need 'combat power'", *Reuters*, May 23, 2012, at http://www.reuters.com/article/2012/05/23/us-usa-afghanistan-idUSBRE84M1DH20120523
6. The national army is known as *Ordou-e Melli* in the local Dari language.
7. Matthew Rosenberg and Rod Nordland, "U.S. Abandoning Hopes for Taliban Peace Deal", *The New York Times*, October 1, 2012, at http://www.nytimes.com/2012/10/02/world/asia/us-scales-back-plans-for-afghan-peace.html?_r=1&pagewanted=all
8. The influence of pre-historic cultures; the Sindhu (or Indus) Civilisation and the Harappan culture; the early Aryan cultures (Vedic and non-Vedic); the Zoroastrian Persia, the Hellenistic/Ionian Greek and subsequent Gandhara tradition; the Indic Brahmanical and Mahayan Buddhistic religious traditions; the Turkic; the Mongoloid; the Sinic; the Islamic (Perso-Arabic) with conspicuous Sufi tradition; the European thought; the Soviet Communism; and later 19th and 20th century strands of revivalist and anti-colonial political Islamism, are a well-noted fact of Afghan history.
9. Vishal Chandra, "The Bonn II Conference on Afghanistan: A Step Forward Amidst Uncertainty", *IDSA Comment*, December 19, 2011, at http://www.idsa.in/idsacomments/TheBonnIIConferenceonAfghanistan_vchandra_191211
10. "Rebuilding Afghanistan: Peace and Stability", Petersberg (Bonn, Germany), December 2, 2002, at http://www.unama-afg.org/docs/_nonUN%20Docs/_Internation-Conferences&Forums/Bonn-Talks/decree%20on%20army.pdf.
11. See Ali A. Jalali, "Rebuilding Afghanistan's National Army", *Parameters*, 32 (3), Autumn 2002, pp. 72–86.
12. See the official Website of the Combined Joint Task Force Phoenix VI, at http://www.taskforcephoenix.com/.
13. For details, see http://www.globalsecurity.org/military/world/afghanistan/kabul.htm.
14. See "Combined Joint Task Force-82", September 7, 2007, at http://cjtf-a.com/index.php/About/About.html.
15. Ibid.
16. NTM-A was established on November 21, 2009, bringing together NATO and national training efforts under one umbrella. It works in close partnership with the Afghan Ministry

of Defence and Ministry of Interior, as well as in collaboration with the European Union Police Mission in Afghanistan (EUPOL) and the European Gendarmerie Force. There are currently 38 nations contributing to NTM-A. Training and mentoring of ANSF is carried out by NATO's Military Advisory Teams (MATs) and Police Advisory Teams (PATs). Additional ISAF advisor teams are provided to the Afghan Operation Coordination Centres (OCCs), which support the ANSF commanders in coordinating the employment of forces in their areas. As of May 11, 2012, nations contributing full MATs are—Albania 1, Australia 6, Belgium: 1, Bulgaria 3, Croatia 3, Czech Republic 1, Denmark 1, France 7, Germany 8, Greece 1, Hungary1, Italy 9, Latvia 1, Lithuania 1, Norway 1, Poland 3, Portugal 1, Romania 3, Slovakia 1, Slovenia 1, Spain 4, Sweden 1, Turkey 6, United Kingdom 7, United States 75, and Multinational 5. See "Afghan National Security Forces (ANSF): Training and Development", at http://www.nato.int/nato_static/assets/pdf/pdf_topics/20120516_media_backgrounder_ANSF_en.pdf

17. "Afghanistan Security: Afghan Army Growing, but Additional Trainers Needed; Long-term Costs Not Determined", *Report to Congressional Addressees*, United States Government Accountability Office, January 2011, p. 5.
18. "CSTC-A Fact Sheet", December 1, 2007, at http://www.cstc-a.com/mission/CSTCAFactSheet.Html.
19. "Fact Sheet on Afghan Regional Security Integration Command", September 2007, at http://www.cstc-a.com/mission/ARSIC.html.
20. "Coalition Forces Information", March 4, 2008, at http://www.taskforcephoenix.com/cofor.htm.
21. For detailed information on ANA structures, logistics & equipment, see C.J. Radin, "Afghan National Army", Afghan National Security Forces Order of Battle, *The Long War Journal*, at http://www.longwarjournal.org/multimedia/ANSF%20OOBpage4-ANA.pdf
22. The *Kandak* or battalion comprising 600 troops is the basic unit of the ANA. Most of the present Kandaks are infantry units.
23. The strength and composition of some of the ANA units/sub units have been revised and accurate figures are not available in this regard.
24. "Fact Sheet Afghan National Army", September 2007, at http://www.cstc-a.com/mission/AfghanistanArmyFacts.htm
25. Government Accountability Office, no. 17, p. 3.
26. "Afghan military seeks return of fugitive planes", *Associated Press*, January 11, 2005, at http://msnbc.msn.com/id/6814109/.
27. "Russia to Supply Afghan Army", *Washington Post*, October 10, 2005, at http://www.washingtonpost.com/wp-dyn/content/article/2005/10/09/AR2005100900985.html
28. "Afghan National Army gets three attack helicopters", *Pajhwok Afghan News*, December 2, 2008, at http://www.pajhwok.com/viewstory.asp?lng=eng&id=66215
29. "Afghan army struggles with ethnic divisions", July 27, 2010, at http://www.cbsnews.com/2100-202_162-6717786.html
30. Based on author's personal observations during his research trips to Afghanistan.
31. Government Accountability Office, no. 17, p. 1
32. Ibid, pp. 9-10.
33. "Afghan National Security Forces (ANSF): Training and Development", at http://www.nato.int/nato_static/assets/pdf/pdf_topics/20120516_media_backgrounder_ANSF_en.pdf
34. Government Accountability Office, no. 17, p. 7.
35. Joshua Partlow, "U.S. and NATO allies plan to spend $11.6 billion this year for Afghan security", *Washington Post*, January 5, 2011, at http://www.washingtonpost.com/wp-dyn/content/article/2011/01/05/AR2011010503337.html

36. Antonio Giustozzi, "Auxiliary Force or National Army? Afghanistan's 'ANA' and the Counter-Insurgency Effort, 2002-06", *Small Wars and Insurgencies*, 18 (1), March 2007, pp. 45-67.
37. Samuel Chan, "Sentinels of Afghan Democracy: The Afghan National Army", *Military Review*, January-February 2009, at http://usacac.army.mil/CAC2/MilitaryReview/Archives/English/MilitaryReview_20090228_art006.pdf.
38. Ray Rivera, "Support Expected for Plan to Beef Up Afghan Forces", *The New York Times*, January 16, 2011, at http://www.nytimes.com/2011/01/17/world/asia/17afghanistan. html
39. "ISAF Factsheet on Current ANSF Status", October 2012, at http://www.isaf.nato.int/article/isaf-releases/isaf-factsheet-on-current-ansf-status.html
40. "Afghan National Security Forces (ANSF): Training and Development", at http://www.nato.int/nato_static/assets/pdf/pdf_topics/20120516_media_backgrounder_ANSF_en.pdf
41. Bill Roggio and Lisa Lundquist, "Green-on-blue attacks in Afghanistan: the data", *The Long War Journal*, at http://www.longwarjournal.org/archives/2012/08/green-on-blue_attack.php
42. Robert Burns, "US: Haqqani tie to Afghan insider attacks possible", *Stars and Stripes*, October 6, 2012, at http://ap.stripes.com/dynamic/stories/A/AS_AFGHANISTAN_INSIDER_ATTACKS?SITE= DCSAS&SECTION=HOME&TEMPLATE=DEFAULT&CTIME=2012-10-05-14-58-51
43. "Over 500 Afghan security forces killed or injured per month", *Khaama Press*, October 16, 2012, at http://www.khaama.com/over-500-afghan-security-forces-killed-or-injured-per-month-349/?utm_source=feedburner&utm_medium=email&utm_campaign=Feed%3A+khaama+%28 KHAAMA+PRESS+%7C+Afghan+Online+Newspaper+%26+Magazine%29
44. Deb Riechmann, "Afghan forces also suffer from insider attacks", September 30, 2012, at http://news.yahoo.com/afghan-forces-suffer-insider-attacks-185712158.html
45. Rod Nordland, "Afghan Army's Turnover Threatens U.S. Strategy", *The New York Times*, October 15, 2012, at http://www.nytimes.com/2012/10/16/world/asia/afghan-armys-high-turnover-clouds-us-exit-plan.html?_r=1&nl=todaysheadlines&emc=edit_th_20121016&pagewanted=all
46. Simon Tisdall, "Behind the politics, Afghan army has a mountain to climb", *The Guardian*, December 3, 2009, at http://www.guardian.co.uk/world/2009/dec/03/training-afghan-army-kabul
47. Government Accountability Office, no. 17, p. 19.
48. Rod Nordland, no. 45.
49. Scott Baldauf, "A 'half full' Afghan army", *Christian Science Monitor*, February 10, 2006, at http://www.csmonitor.com/2006/0210/p06s02-wosc.html?s=hns.
50. "Costly coalition plan to recruit thousands more Afghan forces draws concerns", *Washington Post*, January 17, 2011, at http://www.washingtonpost.com/wp-dyn/content/article/2011/01/17/AR2011011702058.html?sub=AR.
51. "Islamic Republic of Afghanistan: Sixth Review Under the Arrangement Under the Poverty Reduction and Growth Facility, Request for Waiver of Non Observance of a Performance Criterion, Modification and Performance Criteria, and Rephasing and Extension of the Arrangement", *International Monetary Fund*, Country Report No. 10/22, January 2010.
52. Ben Farmer, "Plans for Nato withdrawal could be hit by base construction delays", *The Telegraph*, London, January 25, 2011, at http://www.telegraph.co.uk/news/worldnews/asia/afghanistan/8281330/Plans-for-Nato-withdrawal-could-be-hit-by-base-construction-delays.html.

ANNEXURE

Current Status of ANAAC (April 2010)

Personnel: 3000

Total aircraft: 46

Rotary wing aircraft:

- 22 × MI-17v5 transport
- 3 × MI-17DV VIP transport
- 9 × MI-35 attack
- 3 × C-27
- 5 × AN-32
- 1 × AN-26
- 3 × L-39

Operations for 2008: 6,754 sorties; 469,706 kilograms of cargo; 80,653 passengers.

End State Goal (by end 2015)

Capabilities: VIP transport, CASEVAC, MEDEVAC, operational airlift, tactical battlefield mobility, training, intel/surveillance/reconnaissance, light ground attack, air superiority

Personnel: 8000

Total aircraft: 130-140

Rotary wing:

58 MI-17v5 (battlefield mobility)
3 Mi-17 (VIP transport),
6 training helicopters
Mi-35 will be replaced by armed Mi-17 by FY14

Fixed wing:

20 C-27 (18 operational airlift, 2 VIP transport configurable)
4 propeller cargo aircraft based ISR
14 propeller light attack/ISR
20 light multi role attack/air superiority jets
8 propeller basic training aircraft,
6 propeller advanced training aircraft
AN32/AN-26 will be replaced by C-27 by FY12

Total cost ~$5billion

FY2009 to FY2011 goal: 100 aircraft, 4900 airmen.

- Build English skills, focus on air-mobility, develop logistics and sustainment, build initial infrastructure, and build training capability.
- Initiate training 48 pilots per year. Sent to US for 2 years.
- Acquire 20 × C27 cargo aircraft. First four arriving end 2009 and two per quarter thereafter.
- Acquire 58 Mi-17v5

FY2012 goal:

- ANAAC takes full control of all airfields, except Bagram Air Base.
- Add more training capability. Add trainer aircraft

FY2013 to FY2015 goal: 130-140 aircraft, 8000 airmen.

- Add light attack capability (single-engine turboprop with precision attack capability)
- Add intelligence, surveillance, and reconnaissance capability.
- Add attack/air sovereignty

Source: C.J. Radin, "Afghan National Army Air Corps (ANAAC)", Afghan National Security Forces Order of Battle, *The Long War Journal*, at http://www.longwarjournal.org/multimedia/ANSF%20OOBpage5-ANAC.pdf

Chapter Two

Bangladesh Army: Evolution, Structure, Threat Perception, and its Role

Smruti S. Pattanaik

Introduction

The process of state formation in Bangladesh, the experience of Pakistani rule, and military dictatorship—pre- and post-liberation—greatly shaped the discourse on the role and the organisational ethos of the Bangladesh Army. It also influenced the outlook of the political leaders who directed the liberation war towards the armed forces in which the military played an important role. Moreover, their sufferings under the military rule in the erstwhile Pakistan strongly influenced their decision regarding the organisation and strength of the Bangladesh military. The political leaders were initially convinced that Bangladesh did not need a powerful Army as it did not perceive any threat to its sovereignty and territorial integrity—not at least from India given its support in the liberation war.

To give shape and direction to Indo-Bangladesh relationship, Sheikh Mujibur Rahman signed the *Treaty of Peace and Friendship* as Bangladesh shared the longest land border of 4,053 kilometres with India. Its border with its eastern neighbour, Myanmar, is only 193 kilometres long. Initially, it was thought—given the Pakistani experience– that the Army may emerge as a force challenging the civilian authority. The leadership of the armed movement against Pakistan forces did play an important role in the liberation war, and the declaration of independence by Major Ziaur Rahman, first in his name and later in the name of Mujibur Rahman, was indicative of the initial tension between the civilian leadership and the armed forces.[1]

The armed forces' opinion of the civilian leadership and the manner in which they conducted the liberation war did not escape the eyes of the politicians. Therefore, the civil-military relations were problematic from the beginning and the factionalism within Army accentuated this further. In the initial years, the Army struggled to establish a chain of command that had been broken due to the politicisation of armed forces and the percolation of extreme leftist ideology that did not recognise hierarchy. Several factors heightened the Army's suspicions regarding the politicians, apart from the high expectations relating to governance issues. Bangladesh's relations with India and the creation of *Jatiyo Rakkhi Bahini* (JRB),[2] which was trained by India, also fostered distrust within an Army that had largely inherited the perceptions of the Pakistan Army *vis-à-vis* India.

The fragility of the state was the result of weak institutions rather than the societal structure as Bangladesh is one of the most homogeneous states of South Asia with hardly any ethno-nationalistic assertions that would threaten the state. Bangladesh, post-Mujib, dissolved the *Jatiyo Rakkhi Bahini* and re-established the command structure disrupted by coups and counter-coups in the Army between August 1975 and April 1977 when General Ziaur Rahman took over as the President and Chief Martial Law Administrator from Justice Abusadat Mohammad Sayem. General Zia concentrated on building a strong Army, redefined its security perceptions, and took steps to prevent any group from posing a challenge to the state. For example, the state's consolidation over territory was achieved by resettlement of the Bengali Muslim population in the Buddhist-majority Chittagong hill region to thwart any threat to its integrity.

The nationality discourse in the state moved from Bengali nationalism to Bangladeshi nationalism, having unique religious diacritics that defined Bangladeshi state and the identity of its citizen *vis-à-vis* the state. To deal with the internal dissent that threatened the command structure, General Zia removed many officers who participated in the liberation war and relied more on repatriated officers (repatriated from Pakistan) to strengthen his hold on to power. However, the emergence of an authoritarian state structure with democratic trappings could not give Army the legitimacy to rule. Politicisation of the bureaucracy that had started during Mujib's regime got further accentuated as the military captured power. Emergence of vested interests—Islamists, petty bourgeoisie, and military's institutional interest—eroded the culture of democracy that required accommodation and toleration of contrarian political views. Weakening of institutional structures led to further erosion in state's authority and gave rise to multiple centres of power led by political parties, NGOs, civil society, Islamists and mafias. While the political forces remained divided, the Army emerged as an important player. However, given the factionalism within the Army and other external factors, the Army's ability to hold on to power directly has eroded over the time.

The Security Environment of the Country

The security environment of the country is conditioned by external and internal factors. It is also influenced by its geo-strategic location that impinges on the thinking of the Army and colours its perceptions.

(i) Geo-Political and Strategic Significance of the Country

The geo-political location of Bangladesh, as that of any other country, has largely shaped its threat perceptions. It is surrounded by India from all the three sides. Added to this is the political relationship with India which has been fairly rocky, and has created the perception that their interests could clash. Interestingly, China has overtaken India as the largest bilateral trading partner of Bangladesh in recent years. It also remains a major source of weapons procurement for Bangladesh. Many in Bangladesh, especially those close to the Bangladesh Nationalist Party (BNP), have been arguing for strong defence ties with China to balance India.

The Chinese presence in the neighbourhood is of great concern to India which has had difficult relations with Bangladesh, especially during the years when the BNP was in power. India shares a porous border with Bangladesh and in the past the BNP regime had offered shelter to insurgents from India's north-east as a strategic asset to be used against India. Its geo-political location makes it indispensable for the economic development of India's north-eastern region as well. Similarly, the terrain of the region is such that it often works to the advantage of smugglers and insurgent groups.

Due to the Chinese presence in Myanmar, and given Bangladesh's geo-political location close to the Bay of Bengal, the United States (US) in 1998 had contemplated and proposed a Status of Forces Agreement (SOFA) with Bangladesh. The US also held the view that such an agreement would be a graduation from a relationship based on MoU that basically dealt with training and joint exercises between the two militaries. The US later clarified that it was not a military pact and was aimed at helping Bangladesh in conducting relief operations during natural calamities.[3] However, this proposal was rejected by the Awami League Government which did not want to annoy India.[4] The navies of the two countries conducted their first joint exercise on September 18, 2011 which was referred to as Cooperation Afloat Readiness and Training (CARAT) on maritime safety and preparedness. The US counter terrorism force is present in Bangladesh as part of capacity-building in counter-terrorism efforts. Politically too, Bangladesh's status as the second largest Muslim country in the world is important.

The significant shift in the international security environment especially after 9/11 has made many analysts portray Bangladesh as a hub of terrorism in view of some media reports suggesting that some Bangladeshi Taliban had reached Chittagong Port after the US attacked Afghanistan.[5] Though such reports were dismissed by the Bangladesh Government, later the country-wide bomb blasts, attack on judiciary and suicide attacks proved that radicalism had in fact emerged as a major challenge. Western NGOs are playing a major role in providing social and developmental aid to ensure the economic and political empowerment of the people that would help Bangladesh emerge as a modern Muslim country. However, the role of the NGOs funded by the West Asian countries remains controversial.

Bangladesh's geographical location also makes it a land-bridge between South Asia and South-East Asia. The Chittagong Port has the potential to emerge as a major hub for international trade for many countries of South Asia. Its immense geo-strategic and economic potential is yet to be harnessed due to the divisive internal politics that colours its relations with India, which is an important neighbour. The Bangladesh Government has already invited China to help build the Chittagong Port whereas India has extended a $1 billion credit line for building infrastructure that would revolutionise communication out of which $200 million has been converted into a grant. After Sheikh Hasina assumed power, Bangladesh offered services of its ports—Chittagong and Mongla—to Bhutan, Nepal and India for trade. Talks have already been held between the officials of these countries to work out tariffs and other modalities to operationalise this offer. Nepal has already started using the Chittagong Port to import fertilizer from Morocco.

(ii) Geographical Terrain

Bangladesh is a deltaic country criss-crossed by several rivers that flow into the country. Floods and cyclones have devastated it periodically, affecting large areas of the country as well as the livelihood of the people. Bangladesh faces threat from the rising sea levels and other consequences of climate change. It also has high population density of 1263.16 people per square kilometre. The northern part of Bangladesh is affected by drought called *Monga* every year. Given its deltaic character, agriculture is the main livelihood of the people. Around 84 per cent of the total population depend directly or indirectly on it.

Its geographical terrain is suitable for guerrilla warfare which is an advantage in country's defence planning. This had worked against the Pakistan army's ability to defend East Pakistan during the 1971 war. The Chittagong Hill Tracts (CHT) are hilly and mountainous with thick vegetation that at one point of time had allowed the *Shanti Bahini* to operate and engage the Bangladesh Army. The porous border with India allows local insurgents to cross over into India which frustrates any unilateral operation by the Bangladesh Army. Thus, without India's cooperation it is difficult for Bangladesh to achieve success in counter insurgency operations. Same holds true for India. Moreover, given the conflict in Myanmar, many ethnic Rohingyas who are staying in Bangladesh as refugees awaiting repatriation are exploited by religious fundamentalists. In the past, they were trained and sent to Afghanistan to fight against the Soviet occupation.

Bangladesh's location at the mouth of the Bay of Bengal further adds to its vulnerability. It has emerged as a major transit point for illegal arms, most of it carried through the seas. It has also had long-standing maritime disputes with both India and Myanmar. Discovery of oil has further complicated the dispute. In the past, conflict over the ownership of oil blocks in the Bay had led to the mobilisation of the navies of Bangladesh and Myanmar. Bangladesh and India have now gone for international arbitration to settle their maritime boundaries that would allow them to jointly explore their exclusive economic zones (EEZs). So far, the International Maritime Boundary Dispute Settlement Tribunal set up by the International Tribunal for the Law of the Sea (ITLOS) in Hamburg, Germany, has settled the maritime boundary between Bangladesh and Myanmar in its verdict passed in March 2012. It is expected that the dispute between India and Bangladesh too will be settled by the world body by 2014.

(iii) Threat Perception: Key Domestic and External Challenges

(A) Domestic Challenges

Ideological Polarisation and Political Contestation

Political contestation based on zero sum game has been endemic to Bangladesh since its emergence as an independent state. Fifteen years of democracy has sharpened ideological divisions within the country, greatly affecting the emergence of consensual politics. This contested politics, characterised by a zero sum game, has led to *hartals* and *bandhs* that have paralysed Bangladesh from time to time. Streets rather than parliament have emerged as a ground to show political strength and put pressure on the government.

The electoral calculations and politics of alliance that have divided the broad centre-left and centre-right parties have led to political degeneration in Bangladesh. This has in turn led to political uncertainty and has affected investment climate leading to lack of faith among international investors. The BNP's alliance with religious right has strengthened the Islamist forces in Bangladesh. In the past five years that they were in power, they have succeeded in penetrating the state institutions as well as socio-cultural, economic and educational institutions to attain their objective of bringing in an Islamic revolution. Similarly, the approach of Awami League towards the opposition political parties, mainly the BNP, has not helped the matter either.

The institutionalisation of democracy in Bangladesh has been hampered by years of military rule. A politicised bureaucracy and armed forces have posed a serious challenge to civilian oversight. Though both the political parties have tried to manage and satisfy the military and their institutional needs, there have also been attempts from time to time to involve military politically often on the plea to 'protect democracy.'[6] The January 11, 2007 incident when the military-backed caretaker government took over power to establish the writ of the state due to wide-scale political violence is a case in point of military's dominance and relevance in establishing political order. To keep the armed forces on the right side, both the political parties in the past have appointed ideologically closer army officers as army chief disregarding seniority.

A contested national identity, the stance of the two political parties on liberation war, discourse on collaborators and debate on the direction of Bangladesh's foreign policy, have all contributed to a horizontal polarisation of Bangladesh politics. Issues have often been contested from ideological point of view for short-term political benefits, at times compromising the larger interest of the country.[7] There is a lack of consensus on almost every issue creating mistrust and suspicion between the political parties. The political parties, by exercising brute majority, have often marginalised the view of the opposition resulting in the opposition boycotting the parliament and taking the issue to the street and paralyzing the state for days together.[8] As a result, political instability remains a major internal threat.

Islamic Radicalism

Islamic radicalism has emerged as a serious challenge to the largely secular social fabric of Bangladesh. During the rule of the BNP-led four-party alliance, the religious political parties like the *Jamaat-e Islami Bangladesh* (JIB) and *Islami Oikya Jote* (IOJ) were important coalition partners. The government turned a blind eye to the growing Islamic militancy and denied its existence for a very long time. During the alliance government period, many Islamic NGOs funded by countries from the Middle East registered themselves under the social welfare ministry and started operations in Bangladesh.[9] They funded various Bangladeshi madrassas to spread orthodox Wahabi Islam and as a result there was a significant increase of madrassas in Bangladesh. The approach of the BNP Government towards Islamic militancy further added to the problem.[10] It used groups like the *Jagrata Muslim Janata Bangladesh* (JMJB) to get rid of radical left which had got criminalised over the years. Moreover, by encouraging Islamic groups, the BNP thought it would be able to ideologically deal with the alliance between the Awami League (AL) and the left parties.

Both the BNP-led alliance government and later the caretaker government considered militancy as a law and order issue and refused to treat it as the rise of fundamentalist forces which in the long-run could affect the stability of the country. This approach limited the government's efforts aimed at arresting the militants and there were no investigations to find their patrons and sources of their financial sustenance. According to the present Law Minister Shafique Ahmad, around 122 organisations were involved in terror activities in Bangladesh.[11] A London-based NGO in Bhola District was reported to have provided arms training to militants in a madrassa that was ostensibly meant for the orphan.[12]

The mystery surrounding several bomb blasts in Dhaka in the late nineties is yet to be resolved.[13] These attacks were directed against cultural organisations, street plays (*jatras*), cinema halls and Bengali New Year celebrations. An analysis of the events targeted by extremist forces reveals that these were either Awami League meetings or cultural organisations; both considered as 'enemies' by the Islamic parties. The campaign launched by the BNP and Islamic parties at that time was to divert the attention from the internal malaise. Some Bangladeshis felt that extremism was fuelled by external powers to tarnish Bangladesh's image as a 'moderate' Muslim country.[14] The Awami League after assuming power in December 2008 election conducted a probe into these incidents. It has arrested several leaders of the *Jamaat-e-Islami* and has made them face some of the arrested militant leaders who have admitted to the party's role in encouraging the *Jamaat-ul Mujahideen Bangladesh* (JMB).

During the alliance government period, many Islamic NGOs registered themselves under the social welfare ministry and started their operations in Bangladesh.[15] It is reported that 15 out of 34 foreign funded NGOs, registered with the NGO bureau of the Government of Bangladesh during the BNP rule, were actively promoting Islamic values and culture. There are also several hundred local Islamic NGOs registered with the Social Welfare Ministry which was then headed by the JIB Secretary General Ali Ahsan Mujaheedi, who is well-known for his opposition to Bangladesh's liberation in 1971 and collaboration with the Pakistan Army. These local NGOs act as affiliate organisations of the foreign funded large NGOs and promote their agenda in the country.[16] The funds at their disposal are estimated to be to the tune of Taka 1,200 crores, which they had earned from business investments in the country.[17] It is also believed that some of the Islamic scholars, leaders of religious political parties and heads of madrassas regularly visit the Middle Eastern countries and collect *zakat* and *fitra* which is generally meant for the charitable organisations and orphanages. No account was maintained for this money which is generally channelled through *hundis.*[18] In the name of spreading Islam of the Wahabi variety, these organisations strengthen the hand of radicals who perceive the Islam practiced in Bangladesh as being less authentic. Money is spent on building mosques and madrassas and other charitable activities in the name of promoting Islamic culture. It is important to note that the Bangladesh expatriates, especially those working in the Middle East, often contribute liberally for religious purposes which remain largely unaccounted. Militant Islam will remain a bigger challenge to country's stability given their international linkages.

Insurgency and Conflict in the CHT

The CHT tribes feel marginalised in the state structures. Soon after independence, call for Bengali nationalism was resisted by Manabendra Larma, a Chakma leader who said they are Chakmas and not Bengalis. This was followed by General Zia's decision in 1979 to settle Bengali population in the CHT to counter tribal dominance in this strategically located region which had raised the Indian flag in 1947 to oppose Chittagong becoming part of Pakistan. The process of resettling population, however, had begun before the liberation. The 1962 constitution of Pakistan converted the CHT from being an excluded area into a tribal area. However, soon afterwards, the ban on entry and settlement was lifted in 1964 by an act of parliament and the CHT ceased to be an exclusive tribal area and the administration of the area was slowly transferred to the Bengalis. In 1979, the resettlement policy introduced by General Zia changed the definition of non-Hillman resident. This policy has reduced the indigenous population from 97.5 per cent in 1947 to 50 per cent at present.[19] Earlier, the establishment of Kaptai Hydroelectric Project in 1960 had dispossessed the tribes of 40 per cent of the cultivable land in this region. Given the subsequent insurgency, the genesis of which can be traced back to East Pakistan days, the Army has established permanent camps since the Chakma issue threatens peace in Bangladesh. Many a time violence was allegedly instigated by the Bengali settlers supported by the Army to continue with the military presence.[20]

A peace accord was signed in 1997 between the Awami League Government and *Parbotiya Chattogram Jana Sanghati Samiti* (PCJSS, Chittagong Hill Tracts Regional Council).[21] However, peace continues to elude the CHT as there was no time frame for the implementation of this accord. Most of the refugees who returned after the conclusion of peace accord are yet to get their land back which continues to be occupied by the Bengali Muslim settlers. The BNP that came to power in 2001 was opposed to the accord and thus refused to implement it in its true letter and spirit. The land commission was dysfunctional and the Regional Council was paralysed due to political interference. The United People's Democratic Front (UPDF), a faction that has been opposed to the accord is supported by the BNP.

Assumption of power by the Awami League Government raised expectations regarding implementation of the CHT Accord. Unfortunately, violence in the hill tracts has become a recurring feature between Bengali settlers and the tribes in Rangamati. In August 2009, the AL Government announced the single biggest withdrawal of the troops (which involved withdrawal of as many as 35 army camps) so far but without giving any time frame. Rehabilitation of the refugees displaced during conflict continues to pose a challenge. The three Hill Development Councils are yet to become functional and the CHT Land Dispute Resolution Commission Act established in 2001 needs to be amended to implement the accord in true spirit. There are frequent clashes between the indigenous people and the Bengali settlers as well as between various other groups which have impacted the security situation in the CHT. Moreover, the controversy generated by the Bangladesh Foreign Minister Dipu Moni who questioned the indigenousness of the Chakmas in response to the report of the United Nations special rapporteur on the status of implementation of 1997 Accord to the Permanent Forum on Indigenous Issues, has created misgivings among the people of the CHT regarding the seriousness of AL to resolve their problem.[22] However, the withdrawal of the Army and the return of land to the original owners remain a major issue with the tribes. Any contradictory action is regarded as a move to dispossess them of their property. Some people feel that the anti-Buddhist violence in the CHT in February 2010 was instigated by the opposition political parties to divert attention from the main issues and to delay the military withdrawal.

The CHT remains a festering problem and is a challenge to the integrity and unity of the country. Land rights remain the most controversial issue. In July 2001, the Awami League Government, before handing over power to the caretaker government, hurriedly passed the CHT Land (Disputes Settlement) Commission Act 2001. The provisions of this Act contradict the original CHT Accord of 1997. In a meeting held in January 2012, the government decided to bring amendment to the 2001 Act as per recommendations of the CHT Regional Council and the CHT Affairs Ministry in the winter session of the Parliament. This is likely to have an impact on the land rights of the tribals which is a highly contested issue and has led to frequent clashes.

Small Arms Proliferation and Drug Trafficking

The Chittagong arms haul in April 2004 demonstrated how Bangladesh has emerged as a major transit point for the illegal transfer of arms. It also indicated close relations between the state machinery, the arms proliferators, and the Indian insurgent groups that were patronised by the state. The cache included 690 (7.62 mm T-56-I sub-machine guns or SMGs), 600 (7.62 mm T-56-2 SMGs), 150 (40 mm T-69 rocket launchers), 840 (40 mm rockets), 400 (9 mm semi-automatic spot rifles), 100 Tommy Guns; 150 rocket launchers, 2,000 grenade launchers, 25,020 hand grenades, 6,392 magazines of SMG and other arms, 700,000 rounds of SMG cartridges, 739,680 rounds of 7.62 mm calibre, and 400,000 cartridges of other weapons. Most of the arms and ammunition were reportedly of Korean, Italian, Chinese and American make.[23] Recent investigations have indicated complicity of the official intelligence agency in the transfer of arms which were meant for the United National Liberation Front of Assam. The ex-national security intelligence director and deputy director were arrested after the Awami League came to power in 2008. Similarly, the government has questioned Salauddin Qadeer Chawdhury in whose jetty these arms were unloaded as well as the present *Amir* of *Jamaat-e Islami*, who was then the industry minister, about their possible roles. The alleged role of Bangladeshi intelligence agencies in transferring these arms to the Indian militants operating in Assam is now being probed.

Political Violence

Political violence has been a major challenge to socio-political stability of the country. Clashes between various groups affiliated to the major political parties are a permanent feature of student politics in Bangladesh. This creates law and order problem with the potential to transform into bigger political problems and leading to clashes between the students and law enforcers.[24] Factors like political instability, intolerance and patronage to *mastans*,[25] have created a violent political atmosphere in the country.[26] Between 2001 and 2006, 2,389 people were killed and 64,954 people were injured.[27]

Factional fights within the parties' local units and between the political parties have led to regular incidents of violence affecting the law and order situation in the country from time to time. According to the annual report of *Odhikar*, between January and December 2011, "135 persons were reported killed and 11,532 injured in political violence". A number of incidents of intra-party violence were also recorded during this period (340 for Awami League with 22 dead and 3770 injured, and 104 for BNP with 3 dead and 1234 injured).[28]

Outlawed left wing extremism is another major cause of concern. The *Purba Banglar Communist Party* (PBCP; its two factions are *Lal Pataka* and *Jonojodha*) and the *Purba Banglar Sarbahara Party* (PBSP) are active. It needs to be mentioned that the BNP Government had used Islamic radicals like the *Jagrata Muslim Janata Bangladesh* (JMJB) to deal with these groups noted for extortion.[29]

Environmental Degradation

Rising sea levels, shrinking coast line, increase in the salinity of ground water and encroachment on the river banks are some of the problems related to environmental change that Bangladesh is facing today. Pollution leading to the loss of natural habitats primarily due to deforestation and encroachment of wetlands would have negative consequences on environment and impact on Bangladesh's growth.[30] Retarded growth will have implications for political stability as it would lead to the displacement of population.

According to the Inter-governmental Panel on Climate Change findings, a 45 cm sea-level rise will inundate almost 10.9 per cent of Bangladesh's territory and will displace 5.5 million people in the coastal regions.[31] A rise in the sea level would result in the submerging of *char* lands in Bangladesh. This may lead to communal tension given the scarcity of land as well as propel migration to India giving rise to tension between the two countries.[32]

External Challenges

External challenges to Bangladesh are not many. However, given the fact that it is surrounded by India on three sides, its military strategy is formulated with India in mind. The India threat has been nurtured by a psyche that looks at India through the prism of the two-nation theory—an inheritance of the Pakistan Army mind-set that came into dominance with the military takeover in 1977. Bangladesh's maritime imperatives are confined to securing maritime resources, the exclusive economic zone and patrolling the Bay of Bengal. However, the threats to Bangladesh's security are mostly internal.

The threat of small arms, criminal groups who challenge law and order very frequently, and environmental security are the core concerns of the nation. Apart from these internal threats, the frequent exchange of fire on the border with India has been a major concern.[33] The CHT problems and the likelihood of renewed insurgency is another area of concern for the Bangladesh Army. The rise of religious fundamentalism and the 459 bomb blasts orchestrated in the 63 districts out of total 64 districts of Bangladesh on August 17, 2005 were also perceived as threats to stability.[34] A donor dependent economy, it is concerned about the international attention the terrorist activities may attract. Growing radicalisation would impinge on the work of various international donors whose focus remains women, education and gender equality.

Distrust of India

Bangladesh's threat perception is characterised by a deep distrust of India. Its geographical location of being surrounded by India on the three sides has not helped the matter. Not only does it carry the historical baggage of an inherited strategic culture of Pakistan that has been traditionally anti-India, but also the perception of repatriated soldiers and officers who later formed the bulk of the Bangladesh Army. Moreover, some of the nationalist freedom fighters from the Army viewed India's participation in the liberation war from a different perspective. In the words of a Bangladeshi scholar: "...Bangladesh's gratitude to India for the latter's role in 1971 may be reasonably tempered by the realisation that India had certain well-conceived and cogent calculations of its own in extending assistance to Bangladesh."[35] Another scholar also echoes similar sentiments: "...India's intention was to "transform this natural pre-eminence into an imposed pre-dominance."[36] While such perception may have been in vogue at one point, in the era of globalisation the dynamics of relationship is changing.

There is a view that India's military capacity and Bangladesh's reluctance to be part of India's security architecture may lead to future military confrontation. In fact, Bangladesh is reluctant to be part of any common security architecture. The 1972 *Treaty of Peace and Friendship* could not take off due to the resistance of Bangladesh Army which took over power in 1977 and perceived this Treaty as an imposition of India's natural pre-eminence. Though India's contribution to the liberation war is now being recognised, the Army continues to make its contingency plans with India in mind. The underlying parameter of defence preparedness is to have a defensive posture and hold on to its territory till the international community intervenes. Relation between the two armies was strengthened during the military caretaker regime. In fact, General Moeen Ahmad's visit to India in 2008 took place after several years. Subsequently, various army chiefs visited India in 2010 and 2011 to bolster military ties. India and Bangladesh conducted the first ever joint anti-terror exercise in February 2009 in West Bengal's Jalpaiguri District,[37] despite mutiny in the Bangladesh Rifles (BDR). Later, the two countries carried out joint exercises in counter-terrorism and counter-insurgency operations, known as *Sampriti I* and *II*, in Jorhat in India's north-eastern state of Assam in November 2010 and in Sylhet in Bangladesh in

October 2011. The Indian soldiers who participated in the liberation war of 1971 were for the first time invited to participate in Bangladesh's Victory Day celebration in 2008. It is argued that the "maintenance of enhanced military to military contacts with Bangladesh by Indian Army is mutually beneficial to the strategic interests of both the neighbours."[38]

The two countries are increasingly realising that without cooperation they will not be able to meet the common challenge of terrorism, drug smuggling, and arms proliferation network that have used the porous border with impunity. The Article 9 of the framework agreement for cooperation and development signed in September 2011 during Prime Minister Manmohan Singh's visit states: "To cooperate on security issues of concern to each other while fully respecting each other's sovereignty. Neither party shall allow the use of its territory for activities harmful to the other."[39] The two countries have agreed on a mechanism for joint and simultaneous patrol of the border to prevent illegal activities in the border region. The Border Security Force (BSF) of India has agreed to use rubber bullet to prevent people from violating border. Firing on the border has now reduced.

However, increased incidents of smuggling has been noted by the BSF which feels that such an agreement that expects them not to fire without cooperation from the Bangladesh Border Guards allows the smugglers to operate with impunity as some time they do not hesitate to use fire arms against the BSF.[40] Illegal migration has been a major issue from the perspective of India as Bangladesh refugees to accept the problem which prevents any initiative to address the issue. Exchange of enclaves and land in adverse possession along with border demarcation that the two countries agreed upon during Prime Minister Singh's visit would go a long way in addressing some of the border related incidents.[41]

Issues with Myanmar

In the recent past, Bangladesh's relations with Myanmar have been marked by tension.[42] Earlier, the two countries had a problem relating to the Rohingya refugees who had taken shelter in Bangladesh. Their repatriation remains a major issue after several rounds of talks between the two countries. According to media reports, the Jamaat's student organisation, the *Bangladesh Islami Chhatra Shibir* (BICS), has made inroads and some Rohingyas have participated in pan-jihadi movements.

The treatment meted out to the Rohingya Muslims in Myanmar has frequently marred Bangladesh-Myanmar bilateral relations. Violence against the Rohingyas in July 2012 which led many of them to flee Myanmar and seek refuge in Bangladesh created bilateral tension. Bangladesh has refused to accept these people as refugees in spite of international pressure. It has also asked international charities to stop providing care to the refugees as it feared, such generosity could encourage further influx from Myanmar.

In November 2009, the navies of the two countries were in confrontational mode when Myanmar tried to prospect for oil near a disputed area which is claimed by both the countries to be falling under their respective maritime zone. The situation was de-escalated by reported Chinese intervention. Maritime boundaries between the two countries have been demarcated by the ITLOS on March 14, 2012. Bangladesh has agreed to build a road connecting to Myanmar and then to the proposed Asian Highway. The proposed road transport project and rail network[43] would link Bangladesh through Myanmar to China (Kunming) and South-East Asia. Sheikh Hasina had visited Myanmar in December 2011 to strengthen the bilateral relations.

US and the European Union

Though Bangladesh shares a good relationship with the US and countries of the European Union (EU), there is a certain scepticism regarding the US among the centre right parties. The US action in Iraq and Afghanistan has raised popular sentiments against the US in Bangladesh. However, the Islamic political parties have good relations with the US Embassy in Dhaka. The US in fact accepts the *Jamaat-e-Islami* as a moderate Islamic party. The US plays a visible role in Bangladesh's politics by advising the political parties publicly.

The US foreign assistance in the FY 2010 was $168.5 million.[44] The US foreign military financing (FMF) to Bangladesh in 2009 was $590 thousand and $787 thousand was given for international military education and training and $3,600 thousand was given for non-proliferation, anti terrorism and de-mining.[45] Though there is cooperation between the two countries on counter-terrorism, US is extremely critical of the treatment meted out to former Grameen Bank founder and Nobel Prize winner Mohammad Yonus.

The EU countries are mostly involved in social sector development providing developmental funding. They are, per se, not considered a threat. However, their role in women's empowerment, gender equality and their criticism of governance, inequality, human rights and minority rights issues are considered as intrusive.

(B) Origin and Evolution of the National Army

After liberation, the Bangladesh armed forces mainly comprised of the East Bengal Regiment, East Bengal Rifles, and some members of the *Mukti Bahini.*

Later some Army officers and soldiers who were repatriated from Pakistan joined the Bangladesh Army. In 1975, the Bangladeshi armed forces consisted of 36,000 men. The air force and navy had 5,500 and 500 men, respectively. The Bangladesh Rifles numbered 30,000[46] and the *Jatiya Rakkhi Bahini or JRB*, a force raised from the *Mujib Bahini* and the *Mukti Bahini*, around 25,000.[47] There were 1200 officers in 1975 and senior officers above the rank of Major were 250.[48] About 28,000 men including 1000 officers were repatriated from Pakistan.

The repatriation of officers from West Pakistan led to a sharp division within the Army affecting the Army as an organisation and also its command structure. The division within the Army that comprised of nationalists, the radical left and the repatriates created several fault lines. General Zia increased the police force from 40,000 to 70,000 and raised the allocation for defence from Taka 750 million (13 per cent of total revenue budget in 1975) to Taka 2,062 million (32 per cent of the total revenue budget in 1977).[49]

The nationalist forces felt that the contribution of the armed forces in the liberation war was not recognised and that the military had been made ineffective. As discussed earlier, the signing of the 1972 *Treaty of Peace and Friendship* with India and raising of the JRB was perceived to have been against the interest of the Army. However, Sheikh Mujibur Rahman was very clear regarding the future strength of the armed forces. His experience under the Pakistani military regime had taught him not to have a strong military that would threaten the democratic regimes. He had said, "I do not want to create a monster like the one we had in Pakistan."[50] The JRB was trained and armed by India and had a budget which was equivalent to the Army. After Mujib's death, members of the JRB willing to join the Army were absorbed in the military and the force was disbanded.[51]

After Ziaur Rahman took over, he reorganised the Army and restored the command structure, purged the Army of leftist elements and elevated the repatriated officers to senior position. This was done to strengthen his hand and address the grievances of the repatriated officers—several of whom were junior to their contemporaries in Army who had got out of turn promotion for participating in the liberation war.

(C) Structure/Formation of the National Army

(i) **Structure:** Bangladesh's population is 98 per cent Bengali and 88 per cent practice Islam as their religion. Bangladesh is one of the most homogeneous countries of South Asia. The Bangladesh Army is homogenous in its structure and most of its soldiers are Muslims, given the numerical strength of the community in the country. There are few minorities but numbers are not known. Minorities like the Hindus have alleged that they have not been given proper representation in the Army. The Chapter IV, Part 4 of the Bangladesh Constitution deals with the defence services of the country. At present, the Bangladesh armed forces consist of 126,153 personnel in the Army, 16,900 in Navy and 14,000 personnel in the Air Force. Apart from this, it includes 20,000 paramilitary, 5000 armed police, 38,000 border guarding force, and 900 coast guards.[52] Women began to be recruited in 2000. The Bangladesh Infantry Regiment was added in January 2001.

The Army has seven divisions; headed by the army chief who till recently was a three-star general. In January 1972, there were 11 infantry units (excluding the 5th, 6th and 7th), and later 8 more units were raised. Most of the soldiers recruited were able-bodied Bengalis from the *Mukti Bahini*. After independence, a need for five infantry brigades in the five cantonments of the country was felt. Three infantry brigades, which were already operational during the liberation war, were asked to move to the newly designated cantonments. The Z force (consisting of the 1st, 3rd and 8th Bengal Regiment) commanded by General Ziaur Rahman operating in the Sylhet area during the liberation war moved to the Comilla Cantonment, the S force (2nd and 11th Bengal Regiment) under Colonel Saifullah formed the infantry brigade in Dhaka, the K force (4th, 9th and 10th EBR) commanded by Lt. Col. Khaled Musharraf moved from Chittagong to Jessore Cantonment and two infantry brigades were raised at Chittagong and Rangpur.

In April 1972, separate headquarters for the three services were established. The Bangladesh Armoured Corps was started in 1974 with Egyptian T-54 tanks and was known as the 1st Bengal Lancers. The Bengal Lancers who were involved in the killing of Sheikh Mujib was dismantled when it organised a coup against General Zia with the help of former coup leaders. The Armoured Corps now has six regiments. Armoured brigades and units are controlled by the Armour Directorate. There is also an artillery regiment.

The government has approved *Reconstitution of Bangladesh Army and the Forces Goal 2030* for short, medium and long-term plan to strengthen and modernise the armed forces. Accordingly, the government has approved the creation two Commands—the Eastern and the Western Command—in the Bangladesh Army headed by an officer of the rank of Lieutenant General. Reference to the creation of three commands was stipulated in the 1974 Defence Policy though the Army chose to create only two commands.[53] The creation of commands may entail a new force restructuring, rearranging the existing command and control into two zones. However, the creation of new command structures coming during the Awami League rule suggests that it has a political connotation. Like in the past, the AL has always addressed the Army's demand pertaining to procurement to maintain cordial relations with the force with which the AL has had historical mistrust.[54]

While opening the Army HQ Selection Board, Prime Minister Hasina stated, "A well-disciplined and strong army could play a supplementary role in establishing democracy in a country."[55] This reference to Army while speaking of its role in democracy has been frequently emphasised by the two political parties. Strategic affairs analyst Brig. Anam feels that the creation of command has nothing to do with this regime rather the "timing is purely coincidental."[56] The new command structure would lead to the expansion of the Army and involve fresh recruitment. The government also plans to create 29 headquarters/units in the medium-term and another 25 headquarters/units in the long-term.[57] The aforesaid plans for the expansion of the Bangladesh Army has mostly been considered as an appeasement of the Army by the AL regime especially as it had to earlier face the BDR mutiny and was later threatened by an Islamist coup.[58]

(ii) Recruitment/Selection Procedure

The age for entry into the Bangladesh Army is 17-20 years both for combatants and non combatants. It is 17-40 years for commissioned ranks, 17-21 years for commissions in the navy and 17-20 years for sailors. A cadet has to undergo training for two years and a sailor for 18 months. For the air force, the age for entry is 16.1/2 years to 21 years for a flight cadet, and 16-21 years for airmen. The Bangladesh Army advertises in the national newspapers that lay down academic qualification, age and physical requirements. It holds written and physical, psychological and medical fitness tests of the candidates.

Training for commissioned ranks in the army, navy and flight cadet in the air force is a minimum of two years.[59] Recruitment to the Bangladesh Navy takes place at two levels—permanent commission and short service commission. Candidates from the science stream of the HSC examination undergo a selection procedure and later take an Inter-Services Selection Board Test. A Master's degree is essential for the non-commissioned category.[60]

The Bangladesh Military Academy at Bhatiary was established in 1974. The School of Infantry and Tactics established in 1973 is based at Sylhet in the Jalalabad Cantonment. The Defence Service Command Staff College at Mirpur established in 1977 is a training institution with separate wings for the three services. There is a National Defence College and Military Institute of Science and Technology which provides technical training to the technology branches of the services.[61]

(iii) Budgeting

The ministry of defence is responsible for the defence services of Bangladesh and armed forces attached to or operating with any of the armed forces of Bangladesh excluding planning, co-ordination and arrangement of mobilisation of the defence services on declaration of national emergency/ war and co-ordination and control of the activities of the defence services when deployed in aid of civil administration.[62]

During General Zia and General H.M. Ershad's time, the ministry of defence functioned under the direct control of the president's office and some of its function like preparing the budget, etc., was transferred to the Supreme Commander Headquarter that is now known as Armed Forces Division (AFD). After the establishment of democracy in 1991, the defence ministry has traditionally been under the direct control of the prime minister who also looks after the portfolio of defence minister.

Bangladesh, which was initially reluctant to have a large army after the liberation war increased its defence budget after 1977, when military took over power. For the financial year 1988, defence spending amounted to 17.2 per cent of the budget; and if expenditures for paramilitary forces and the police are added to the defence budget, the figure rises to nearly 23.8 per cent of the budget.[63] In the current year, the budget for 2011-12 proposes an 11 per cent increase over the previous year which is 1.5 per cent of the GDP and 7.5 per cent of the total national expenditure to modernise the Army.[64] There has been over spending on defence over the past years and as a result it has been given additional funds that generally get reflected in the revised estimates.

As regards the budget for 2012-13, the finance minister said, "We are pledge-bound to build up a strong and modern defence force capable of addressing the challenges of the 21st century." The budget for 2012-13 is Tk 120.985 billion which is an increase of 8.5 per cent over the previous year and 6.77 per cent of the total budget.[65] The defence budget of Bangladesh is not discussed in the parliament and the finance minister in his budget speech would mention the procurements for the armed forces and requirements for modernisation while presenting the defence budget.[66]

(D) Strength of the National Army

Internally, the Bangladesh Army performs three important functions: counter insurgency operation, managing essential services and disaster management. The Army has aided the government in times of national calamity. It also helps the civil administration in identifying and providing assistance to the affected people under the flood relief programmes. The Army has also been

Fig. 1: Trends in Budget Allocation: 2002-09

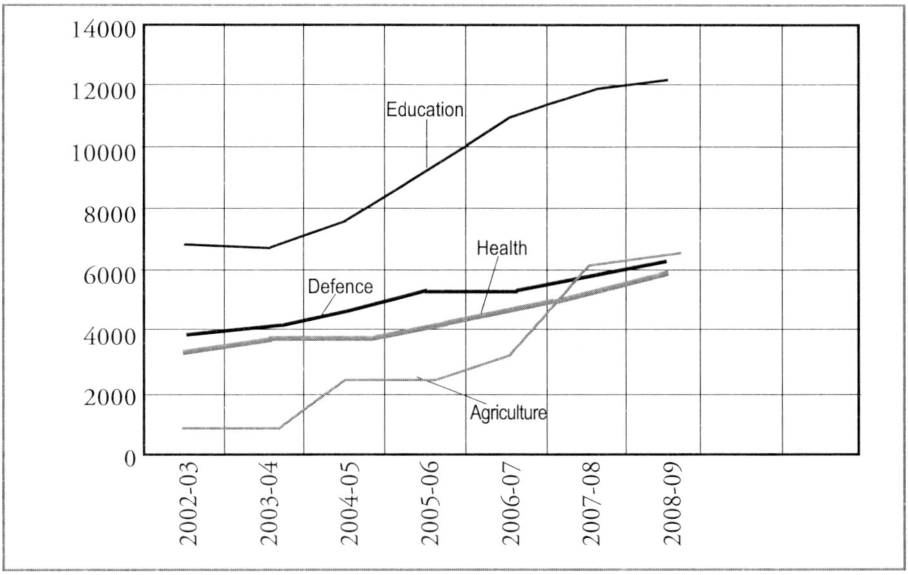

Source: Air Cdre. Ishfaq Ilahi, "Bangladesh Defence Budget 2008-09: An Analysis", *The Daily Star*, July 5, 2008, at http://www.thedailystar.net/story.php?nid=44241

deployed during the national elections held in 1991, 1996, 2001 and 2008. It aids the civil administration by patrolling the area of responsibility, standing by to meet any emergency, coordinating with civil administration, and assisting the police and civil administration and returning officers to maintain law and order and to ensure security during the counting of votes. In 2003, it was deployed in *Operation Clean Heart* undertaken against criminals. Under the military-backed caretaker government, it assisted the Election Commission in making national photo-cum-voter identity cards. It secures the key installations and helps in the distribution of drinking water when the Water and Sewerage Authority (WASA) fails to supply adequate drinking water during summer months. The Army has been involved in the construction of Hazrat Shah Jalal International Airport, in building embankments, and constructing roads in Chittagong.

Logistics and Source of Weaponry

China, Pakistan and Eastern Europe are the major defence suppliers to Bangladesh.[67] Between 2005 and 2008, the US provided $2.2 million in grant and aid funding (Foreign Military Financing) for the purchase of Defender Class small boats for the coast guard of Bangladesh, and allocated

$934,000 for IMET (International Military Education and Training) for 2007.[68]

Bangladesh has an ordnance factory in Ghazipur set up under an agreement between Bangladesh and China which would produce 10,000 BD-08 model sophisticated rifle per annum. It was reported that Bangladesh "successfully test-fired land attack anti-ship cruise missile C-802A with a strike range of 120 km from the frigate BNS Osman near Kutubdia Island in the Bay of Bengal" in May 2008.[69] For the Army, the government is planning to acquire "44 modern MBT-2000 tanks, three armoured recovery vehicles, two weapons locating radars, 18 self-propelled guns, one electronic mate station, two pieces of sound raising equipment, 200 surface-to-surface missiles, 130 short-range anti-tank guided weapons, 10 automatic grenade launchers, seven light mortars, one ground surveillance radar, and 25 machine guns."[70]

The Bangladesh Army advocates jointmanship for efficient management of war effort taking into consideration budget constraints. Lt. Col. ABM Azizul Islam argues:

> In context of strategic encirclement of Bangladesh by the potential adversary, synergy of resources and asymmetric imbalance in military might and economy in favour of our potential adversary, the defence services need to fight as an integrated team. The geographical realities of our country, perception of threat to our national security along with the pattern of our relations with the neighbours demand a force larger than the present size with predominant land force. But influences of many related factors do not prescribe large land force for Bangladesh. As such, the logical option open to the nation is to emphasize on qualitative uplift of forces and formulation of suitable strategy and concept of operation instead of following numerical superiority.[71]

China has had extensive relationship with the Bangladesh military. China and Bangladesh signed a Defence Cooperation Agreement in 2002 though the terms of the Agreement are not available in the public domain. There have been several interactions between the top officials of the People's Liberation Army (PLA) and the Bangladesh Army from time to time.

The Bangladesh Navy will be acquiring two more frigates from China taking its number to seven. Strengthening the navy has become a priority especially after the Bangladesh-Myanmar conflict over exploration of gas that had led to tension in 2008. The India factor in the defence cooperation is extremely significant. According to the former Army Chief of Bangladesh Mahbubur Rahman, "To achieve a military deterrence in land, air and sea, Bangladesh should also look for friends. China could help Bangladesh to strengthen its defence capability."[72] The two countries have already signed an agreement on peaceful usage of nuclear energy in 2005. The Defence Cooperation Agreement of 2002, signed during Begum Zia's visit to China, according to an analyst was kept "unarticulated, flexible and ambiguous, so as to allow Bangladesh to reap the benefits of a strategic partnership with a nuclear power without involving itself in any defence arrangement."[73] China is an important factor in Bangladesh's balance India policy especially for its military and the BNP. In the recent past, many Bangladeshi officers have been trained in the People's Republic of China (PRC) and in Pakistan.

The Chinese are the largest suppliers of weapons to Bangladesh. The Army equipment includes Chinese W-531 Type 85 armoured personnel carriers, T-62 light tanks and T-59 main battle tanks. According to its declaration to the United Nations in 2007, China sold 65 large-calibre artillery systems, including 18 122mm howitzers and 16 rocket launchers to Bangladesh in 2006.[74] There are plans to acquire 155mm PLZ-45/Type-88 (including transfer of technology) and 122mm Type-96 as well as MBRLS from China by 2011.[75] The Bangladesh Army's armoured vehicles include 1,080 Russian-built BTR-80 and BTR-70 wheeled armoured vehicles, as well as 60 Egyptian-made Fahd 28s and several Turkish and Romanian 6x6 RN-94 armoured personnel carriers (APCs).[76]

The Bangladesh Navy's inventory includes the Jianghu-class 1,500-ton F-18 Osman frigate, four 175-ton Huangfeng-class guided-missile patrol boats (PTG), five 68-ton Houku-class PTGs, a torpedo boat, patrol boat, submarine hunter, minesweeper, landing craft, tugs and survey craft.[77] Bangladesh had also placed an order for anti-ship and air defence missiles and is reported to have already test-fired one of them from its frigate *BNS Osman* on May 12, 2008.[78] The government is planning to purchase two off the shelf [readymade] frigates, two large patrol crafts, two maritime patrol aircraft, and five patrol crafts.[79]

The Bangladesh Air Force is equipped with two squadrons of Chengdu F-7Ms and Guizhou FT-7s, one squadron of Nanchang A-5Cs and Shenyang FT-6s, and one trainer squadron of Nanchang PT-6s.[80] In 2000, the Air Force bought 9 MIG 29s from Russia. According to a report, it plans to "set up facilities to upgrade its Chengdu F-7 fighters and various Russian-made helicopters. By 2021, it hopes to begin replacing the older aircraft, says the report. It also hopes to introduce airborne early warning capability into the air force."[81] The government now plans to purchase 16 fighter planes, three MI-17 SH helicopters, and two air defence radars which will be bought in 2011-12.[82]

Bangladesh has been the second largest contributor to the UN peacekeeping missions in various parts of world since 1988. This has been one of the major sources of foreign exchange for the country. In fact, since many in the Army considered serving in the UN peacekeeping as a lucrative option, the UN used it as a pressure tactic during the January 10, 2007 takeover by the military-backed caretaker government.[83] This is also one of the reasons that restrained the Army from contemplating a military takeover. It has currently about 10,900 peacekeeping military and police personnel in 12 UN peacekeeping missions in 11 countries. It ranks first in terms of police contingents.[84]

Dhaka has established the Bangladesh Institute of Peace Support Operation Training (BIPSOT) at Rajendrapur to provide training to its soldiers involved in peacekeeping operations. France gives linguistic training to Bangladeshi officers as some of them are sent to French-speaking African countries for peacekeeping. It trains around 50 military officers each year for this.[85] The Bangladesh Army earns around $200 million from its peacekeeping operations.[86] Bangladesh has signed an agreement in 2004 with Kuwait to train the Kuwait Army. Around 3,741 armed forces personnel were sent for three years on deputation to Kuwait under this agreement.[87] They have an international liaison headquarter in Kuwait.

(E) Civil-Military Relations

The armed liberation groups played an important role in the liberation war. Their expectation from the new state, to a very large extent, was based on their role in the liberation war. The uprising in Chittagong by a section of East Bengal Rifles was the first organised attempt to challenge the Pakistan regime. The Bengali armed force officers kept a close watch on the political developments and on the negotiations between General Yahya Khan and Sheikh Mujib. One of the former military officers narrating the feelings that prevailed in the cantonment at that point of time wrote that many expected that Mujib's March 7 speech will be a declaration for independence.[88] However, the speech fell short of calling for independence. The March 25, 1971 crackdown brought the Bengali officers and politicians together.

During the liberation war, the Bangladesh Government-in-Exile (BDGIE) tried to keep both the military and political direction of the movement strictly under its control though in the operational matters it closely coordinated with the Eastern Command of the India Army. To maintain political control over the Bengali armed groups, which included politicians and Bengali officers and soldiers, it appointed M.A.G. Osmany, a member of National Assembly belonging to the Awami League, as commanding officer. The 177 members elected to the National Assembly and 270 members elected to the then provincial assembly of East Pakistan in the 1970 elections were given the ranks of major general and brigadier respectively to establish political control over the armed forces and other groups fighting in the liberation war.[89] The Army's opinion of politicians and politics was influenced by the fact that these officers had long been a part of the Pakistan Army. Some officers like General Zia resented the role of Indian Army officers who were in the overall command of the liberation war. Apart from this, some officers like Colonel Abu Taher and Colonel Ziauddin were influenced by the Maoist idea of a people's army and resented the civilian leadership who took over power after the liberation war arguing that the Bangladesh revolution was an unfinished revolution as it was conducted by bourgeoisie elements to retain their control over the state.

From the beginning, the civilian leadership and the Army were greatly suspicious of each other. Some of the policies adopted by Mujib after the liberation war further aggravated the tension between the two. The signing of the Indo-Bangladesh *Treaty of Peace and Friendship* was not liked by many as it was felt that Bangladesh would not be able to pursue an independent foreign policy as its security was tied to India. Clause 10 of the Treaty which reads: "Each of the parties solemnly declare that it shall not undertake any commitment, secret or open, towards one or more states which may be incompatible with the present treaty" was considered as restrictive.

The raising of the *Jatiyo Rakkhi Bahini* (JRB) was seen by the armed forces as inimical to their institutional interests. In fact the JRB was raised to help the government under the 'aid to civil' provision of the government. As Sheikh Mujib himself had seen how the deployment of armed forces in aid to civil administration had exposed them to local politics and politicised them, he did not want to replicate the Pakistani experience. He also did not perceive any military threat to Bangladesh and preferred to have a small army which would not threaten the nascent civilian government. It can be said that during the period 1972-75, the government and some of the senior officers in the armed force did not share a comfortable relationship.

The armed forces were also divided and ridden with factionalism, each of them pursuing a different political agenda disregarding its chain of command and political authority. While the freedom fighters were asserting their superiority—at times at the cost of repatriated officers—some other officers were planning to replace Mujib to restore the glory of the nation and the armed forces. Around 35,000 officers who were repatriated from Pakistan in 1973 were absorbed into the Army without promotion, seniority and regularisation of their service which undermined the morale of these officers.[90]

Civilian control over the armed forces is exercised through the Armed

Forces Division (AFD) attached to the prime minister's office. The Commander in Chief Secretariat established in 1978 later came to be known as Supreme Commander Headquarter under General Ershad in 1986 and in 1989 it was given the status of a Division known as Supreme Commander Head Quarter Division. He shifted matters relating to appointment, promotion, training procurement and other organisational issues from the ministry of defence to the president's office. After Bangladesh became a parliamentary democracy in 1991, it came to be known as the Armed Forces Division and functions like a ministry. The defence ministry was expected to confine its work to finance and other procedural matters not involving hardcore military issues like defence acquisitions. The ministry has regulatory power over the three services, defence production and procurement board, department of military lands and cantonments, inter-service intelligence and co-ordination board, defence science organisation, the ordnance factory in Gazipur, and the Fauji Foundation

The AFD decides matter of defence policy, monitors pacts and agreements, and formulates purchase policy, co-ordinates inter-service posts and foreign training of the military personnel. It has the authority, direction and control over services on operational and administrative matters and functions under the direct supervision of the Prime Minister.[91] The AFD has overarching authority which includes operation and plan directorate, civil military relations directorate, training directorate, administration and logistic directorate. This often creates dissention within the Army when politically motivated transfers and promotions are done. An Army officer spoke in exasperation when Sheikh Hasina visited Senakunj on March 2, 2009 after the BDR mutiny, "Don't destroy the Army, don't destroy the unity...there is conspiracy to destroy the Army." The officers accused the political parties of doing politics in the name of transfer, not giving security clearance for promotion to officers who do not believe in their political ideology. These officers further said "don't drag Army into politics. Why should the Army get divided between the AL and the BNP, why should we get promotion with the direction of the politicians where one can get promoted from Lt Col. to Brigadier within two years due to his political affiliation."[92]

Though some of these officers who had raised their voice against the prime minister were quietly removed or forcefully retired, however the allegation of politicisation of the Army remains a crucial determiner of civil-military relations.[93] The issues of 15th Amendment to Bangladesh Constitution that restored secularism as one of the foundational principle also ruffled the feather of Islamic-minded officers leading to the failed attempted coup in Bangladesh Army last December. According to

International Crisis Group (ICG) report, the attempt of Parliament Standing Committee on Defence to make the Army's allegiance of constitution compulsory also became a source of irritation as many felt that owing to their allegiance to the religion, a soldier would be far more willing to die for his faith rather than something as abstract as constitution.[94] The handing over of the Indian insurgents, considered as strategic assets by some in the Bangladesh Army, and agreeing to provide transit to India too has its impact on the civil-military relations in the country. According to a retired senior military officer, this "concedes Bangladesh's sovereignty to the arch enemy."[95] However, it needs to be mentioned that the change in India-Bangladesh relations was brought about by the former Army Chief Moeen U. Ahmed who for the first time invited Indian soldiers who had participated in the liberation war and felicitated them.

The civil-military relations would continue to remain a matter of concern with both the political parties vying to please the Army by allowing procurement of arms and strengthening the Army. The Army will remain a last resort to deal with political instability and will have the support of the masses to restore order. This would make the Army relevant to politics and will continue to impinge on civil military relations in Bangladesh.

(F) Bilateral/Multilateral Defence/Security Cooperation

China

China which recognised Bangladesh in 1975 after Mujib's assassination and twice blocked its entry to the UN is considered to be a friend of Bangladesh. The two countries have since not looked back and share close relations. China is an important supplier of weapons to the Bangladesh Army and its personnel do not require a visa to visit China. The two countries signed a defence cooperation agreement in 2002. Both the Awami League and the BNP have bipartisan approach to their relations with China.

Many security analysts in Bangladesh believe that the country needs to cultivate close relations with China to balance India. Sheikh Hasina visited China in 2010 and in a ten-point comprehensive *joint communiqué* agreed to enhance trade, investment and building of infrastructure in Bangladesh. Dhaka has requested China to build the Chittagong Port which will connect Kunming province with Chittagong through Myanmar. It is also building a deep sea port at Sonadia and Bangladesh cabinet has already approved Sonadia Deep Seaport Act and China's Harbour Engineering Company is going to build it. China has also offered RMB 150 million for the socio-economic development of Bangladesh.[96] Chinese Vice President Xi Jinping visited Dhaka in June 2010 to celebrate 35 years of diplomatic relations between the two countries.

Bangladesh is reportedly planning to buy 44 new tanks and three armoured recovery vehicles from China as part of the modernisation of its Army. These would be delivered within the next 27 months.[97] The Chinese are also involved in various power projects in Bangladesh. It has now offered to build Padma bridge which got mired in corruption scandal leading the World Bank to stop funding the project. China has multifaceted relations with Bangladesh and has engaged political parties, parliamentarian, civil society and the army.[98]

Bangladesh has close defence ties with the People's Republic of China and the US. During a visit to Bangladesh on April 26, 2008, the Chinese Foreign Minister Yang Jichie showed an interest in helping Bangladesh set up a nuclear power plant in Rooppur in Pabna.

(G) National Army in People's Perception

The Bangladesh Army played a valiant role in the liberation war. They are perceived by the people as freedom fighters, defenders of country's independence and territorial sovereignty. However, people have not been supportive of the political role played by the Army as demonstrated during the caretaker government period.

However, the size of the Army, defence budget and their role has often been discussed by intellectuals and retired armed force officers. This is based on two important criteria: Firstly, what kind of defence is required for the security of a small state like Bangladesh which is surrounded by India? Secondly, depending on its defence doctrine, how much of defence expenditure is affordable.

Many believe that Bangladesh needs a strong armed force to back its defensive military doctrine. There is a feeling that a defensive doctrine would help them to hold on to their territory in case of an aggression and while diplomatic efforts are made to deal with such a threat. At the same time, many people often fear that a large defence budget is simply not affordable for a country like Bangladesh. There is also an apprehension that a too strong army is not conducive to individual liberty and democracy as Bangladesh in the past has been under military rule.[99] To deal with these issues Colonel Abu Taher and later General Ershad had proposed a People's Army.[100] However, both had different reasons for doing so. Taher's suggestion was based on affordability and liability of maintaining a large defence force. In an interview to *The Guardian* newspaper in London, Ershad had said, "...if the army participates in the administration of the country, then they will probably have a feeling they are also involved, and they will not be frustrated."[101] However, Bangladesh's troop contributions to UN peacekeeping missions act as a safety valve for the Army and prevent their direct intervention in civilian affairs. This was evident when the UN warned the Army not to support partisan election scheduled for January 22, 2007 saying its peace keeping role otherwise will have to be reconsidered.[102]

While the concept of a strong army finds acceptability in Bangladesh, many people are averse to them playing a political role. The Army has been trying to push for a role in decision-making on security affairs that have remained unfulfilled. From time to time, there have been demands for establishing a national security council which will give the Army a larger say in the security affairs of the country. Some reports suggest that the Army has also slowly developed business interests over a period of time. Though the UN peacekeeping remains a lucrative option, the Bangladesh Army's business interest includes several hotels, the Trust Bank, universities, schools and colleges. It is also involved in the business of bakery and even has a cement factory. The *Sena Kalyan Sangstha* which looks at some of these interests was established in 1998 during the Awami League regime.[103]

The people of Bangladesh look at the Army as a stabilising force given the contested politics that Bangladesh is witnessing now. Unwillingness of the two political parties to compromise or work out an agreed solution to democratic transition creates a political vacuum. The Army will always remain an option to facilitate this transition if need be to hold on to power as long as it deems fit as was the case in 2007.

(H) Future Prospect: Evolving Role

The Bangladesh Army would largely remain confined to its present role of securing the borders and as peacekeepers in the international arena. However, given the dynamics of Bangladeshi politics both the Awami League and the BNP would continue to try and keep the Army in good humour. Their modernisation bid is supported by the civilian government. The Awami League government allowed the Army to start the Trust Bank that basically caters to the Army. However, they are nowhere close to the Pakistan Army as far as their business interests are concerned. The Army remains averse to political interference in matters pertaining to their promotion and posting, etc.

The Army did not get into the political mess willingly on January 11, 2007. The Army-backed caretaker government took control when the state was almost on the verge of a civil war. General Moeen U. Ahmed, the Chief of Army Staff, had remarked: "The change of January 11 was therefore inevitable, unavoidable and formed part of 'reinvention' of the nation. The people accepted it and the international community has seen its logic and provided us with full support."[104] The intervention of January 11 also confirmed that the Army though was keen to have a larger say in the decision-making process, had been unable to do so given the resistance of political parties as well as the international community.

The division within the Army regarding its future role became apparent when in May 2008 General Moeen U. Ahmed transferred some of the important Generals who were instrumental in the formation of an Army backed caretaker government in January 2007. There are ideological divisions within the Army and there exists support for the two political parties. However, unlike in the post-liberation phase, the Army at present is united. The BNP also has a number of senior Army officers in its Advisory Council and Executive Council, whereas the Awami League has very few officers in the decision-making position of the party which further erodes its relationship with the military.[105] Army has posts reserved for it within the foreign service as well, a practice that had started during General Ershad's time and still continues.

The Bangladesh Army's future role will be more and more confined to seek peace and stability within its own border. The problems in the CHT continue to concern the Army as also the issue of fundamentalism that corrodes the societal fabric from within. The mutiny of BDR in February 2009 shook the Army and drew its attention to internal dissention within the paramilitary which is under the command and control of the Army. It is believed that this mutiny in which 57 Army officers were killed was aimed to destabilise and topple the newly elected government of Awami League by creating situation for Army's intervention. The coup attempt in December 2011 by 16 religiously motivated officers reveals the penetration of Islamists represented by radical outfits like the banned *Hizb ut-Tahrir*.[106] As has been stated earlier, elements within the Army and some retired officers are not happy with the 15th constitutional amendment that made secularism as part of the Constitution and Bangladesh's growing relations with India.

As the political relationship between Bangladesh and India has seen a dramatic improvement in recent times, the contact between the armies of the two countries has increased. The main architect of the caretaker regime, Army Chief General Moeen U. Ahmed visited India in 2008. The relations between the two countries improved during the caretaker government which had Army's blessings. The Bangladesh Government since 2008 has been inviting Indian Army personnel and has felicitated many of them for their contribution to the liberation war. Good relations between the two countries and increased interaction between the armies to a large extent will address their apprehensions and threat perceptions relating to India. Already the two countries have approved modalities and have agreed to jointly patrol the more than 4,000 km long border. The two countries had held joint military exercises or *Operation Sampriti.*

In the recent past, there have been high level exchange of visits by political leaders and chiefs of armed forces of the two countries. In 2010, General Abdul Mubeen, the then Bangladesh Army Chief, visited India and also visited Leh. The Indian air chief also visited Dhaka in January 2010. Dhaka has handed over leaders of the United Liberation Front of Assam (ULFA) who had taken shelter in Bangladesh signalling a major change in attitude. Dhaka is now contemplating to extradite Anup Chetia who has been in Bangladesh's custody since 1997. This change in approach with the change in political climate would help the two militaries in forging cooperative relationship to face the common challenge of terrorism.

The 2008 elections and successful transfer of power show that the Bangladesh Army would not like to involve itself in politics and also at the same time would not remain a mute spectator. Their future role would depend on the willingness of the political parties to not to involve the Army in day to day politics. As long as the two parties nurture a pathological hatred for each other, Army would be remain a major player and arbitrator of political conflict.

NOTES

1. Interestingly, Sheikh Mujibur Rahman was aware of the pattern of voting in the cantonment in the 1973 election. It was overwhelmingly anti-Awami League. See Anthony Mascarenhas, *Bangladesh: A Legacy of Blood*, Hodder and Stoughton, London, 1986, p. 34.
2. The personnel for *Jatiyo Rakkhi Bahini* were largely drawn from the *Mujib Bahini.* Mujib wanted to create this paramilitary force to aid civil administration which the army perceived as a counter-force being raised to reduce its importance in the affairs of the state. The army did not like the signing of 1972 Treaty that linked Bangladesh's security to that of India. Added to this was Mujib's close association with India which made the army believe that his decisions are influenced by India. It may be stated here that Mujib's decision could have sprung from the former East Pakistan's experience with Pakistan.
3. Harun-ur-Rashid, "U.S.-Bangladesh Defence Relations", *Asian Affairs*, p. 54, at http://www.cdrb.org/journal/2002/2/3.pdf
4. Haroon Habib, "Looking for a Strategic Umbrella", *Frontline*, 15 (16), August 1-14, 1998, at http://www.frontlineonnet.com/fl1516/15160550.htm
5. Alex Perry, "Deadly Cargo", *Time*, October 14, 2002, at http://www.time.com/time/magazine/article/0,9171,364423-2,00.html
6. Begum Khaleda Zia in her address to officers in the cantonment before handing over power to the caretaker government had lauded army's role in protecting democracy.

President Iajuddin Ahmed also lauded the army for its strong and positive role during the anarchic situation on January 11 in his address in an Army headquarters selection board meeting in Dhaka Cantonment on August 5, 2007. See "Army Saved Country from Anarchy on 1/11", *The Daily Star*, August 6, 2007, at http://www.thedailystar.net/2007/08/06/d70806011310.htm.

7. For example, the government's decision not to join the Asian Highway in 2006 and not to sign the BIMSTEC free trade agreement earlier in 2004 came under criticism and the government was accused of following its own political interest rather than the interest of the country.
8. Article 67 of the Bangladesh Constitution stipulates that any MP who remains absent for 90 consecutive days will lose his seat. The current *Jatiya Sangsad*, which began its journey on January 25, 2009, has been witnessing a very poor presence of the opposition. Till September 2012, the House has had 319 sittings, of which the opposition boycotted 266 and joined only 53. Leader of the Opposition and BNP chief Khaleda Zia joined only eight sittings. The opposition last joined the House on March 20, 2012 and then began a fresh boycott, which still continues. See Shekhawat Liton and Rashidul Hasan, "Key Issues, No Critical Voice", *The Daily Star*, September 12, 2012, at http://www.thedailystar.net/newDesign/print_news.php?nid=249422. Khalida's political opponent Sheikh Hasina as opposition leader attended 135 sittings in the fifth parliament (1991-95) and 45 sittings in the eighth parliament (2001-06). See Shakhawat Liton, "BNP Sets Sangsad Boycott record", *The Daily Star*, March 16, 2012, at http://www.thedailystar.net/newDesign/news-details.php?nid=226513
9. 473 local and 25 foreign NGOs were registered during the rule of the alliance government. See, "NGOs under Scanner for 'Funding militancy'", *The Daily Star*, March 19, 2009, at http://www.thedailystar.net/newDesign/news-details.php?nid=80287.
10. For elaborate discussion on this issue, see Smruti S. Pattanaik, "Islamic Extremism and the Terror Network in Bangladesh" in K. Warikoo (ed.) *Religion and Security in South and Central Asia*, Routledge, London, 2011.
11. "122 Outfits Involved in Terrorism", *The Daily Star*, April 2, 2009, at http://www.thedailystar.net/newDesign/news-details.php?nid=82385.
12. "We are very afraid after this", *BBC News*, March 28, 2009, at http://news.bbc.co.uk/2/hi/south_asia/7969558.stm
13. August 6, 1999 at a function organised by Udichi, Jessore; October 8, 1999 on Ahmediyas in Khulna; June 15, 2001in the AL office, Narayanganj; January 20, 2001 in the Communist Party of Bangladesh rally in Paltan Maidan in Dhaka; April 14, 2001 in the Pohela Boisakh celebration at Ramana Park, Dhaka; June 3, 2001in Baruyarchar, Gopalganj; September 23, 2001 in the AL rally in Bagerhat; September 26, 2001 in the AL election rally at Sunamganj; September 28, 2002 in the Cinema and circus pandals in Satkhira; December 6, 2002 in the cinema halls in Mymensingh; January 17, 2003 in Faila Pir Shrine at Sakhipur in Tangail; May 21, 2004 in the Shah Jalal Shrine in Sylhet; August 21, 2004 in the AL rally at Bangabondhu Avenue in Dhaka; January 16, 2005 cultural function in Bogra; January 27, 2005 AL rally, Habiganj. Total people killed in these incidents are 143. The attack on AL rally on August 21 is still being investigated. See "Most Cases of Bomb Blasts Remain Unresolved", *Financial Express*, August 18, 2005.
14. For example, a public opinion poll conducted by a magazine reflected that a total of 60 per cent of the respondents felt that a neighbouring country in the region has a hand in Bangladesh bomb blasts. 40 per cent ruled out this possibility, 32 percent said it is India, 11.48 said United States and 1.85 said it is Pakistan. See "Bomb Blast: People's Perception", *Probe*, October 14-20, 2005, p.14. Some feel that CIA, RAW and Mossad

are involved in helping the militants as these countries have specific interests (Author's interview with Ahmad Abdul Qader on September 7, 2007 in Dhaka). Some university teachers, party officials of the BNP and *Jamaat* said that India and the US could be helping the militants as it would pave the way for the US intervention, and since India and the US have become 'friends' it will advance India's interest in this country. Interaction with some faculty members in the Dhaka University and other organisations including the Press Secretary of *Islami Oikya Jote* and *alims* at Lalbagh Shahi Madrassa between May 26 and September 7, 2007 in Dhaka and Sylhet.

15. There are 473 local and 25 foreign NGOs were registered during the rule of the alliance government. See "NGOs under Scanner for 'Funding militancy'", *The Daily Star*, March 19, 2009.
16. There are about 2,479 local and foreign NGOs under the NGO Affairs Bureau; 55,000 under the Department of Social Welfare; 1.52 lakh under the Department of Cooperatives; 10,000 under the Office of the Registrar, Joint Stock Companies and Firms; 501 under Micro-Credit Regulatory Authority; 16,030 under the Department of Women and Children Affairs, and one lakh under the Department of Youth Development. See Syed Shukur Ali, "Reg of 550 NGOs cancelled. Most involved in irregularities, funding militancy", *The News Today*, March 21, 2011, at http://www.newstoday.com.bd/index.php?option=details&news_id=23086&date=2011-03-21
17. Zayadul Ahsan, "Foreign Funding, local business keep them going", *The Daily Star*, August 22, 2005, at http://www.thedailystar.net/2005/08/22/d5082201044.htm
18. These NGOs are Islamic Relief Organisation, Al Markajul Islami, Ishra Islamic Foundation, Ishrahul Muslimin, Al Forkan Foundations and Al Maghrib Eye Hospital. See "34 Islamic NGOs get over Tk 200cr from donors a year", *The Daily Star*, August 31, 2005, at http://www.thedailystar.net/2005/08/31/d5083101044.htm
19. "12 Years after CHT Accord, Still no Roadmap", December 2, 2009, at http://www.bdnews24.com/details.php?cid=2&id=148048
20. After the Awami League assumed power in January 2009, there was an increasing demand to implement the CHT accord which the government had signed in 1997. One of the clauses in the peace accord was withdrawal of the Army camps. There has been reoccurrence of violence in the CHT between the Chakmas and Bengalis. Interviews with Chakma students in Dhaka University in June 2007 and also with a leader of *Parbotiya Chattogram Jana Shanghati Samiti* on April 4, 2012. The interviews were done on the condition of anonymity.
21. For details, see Meghna Guhathakurta, "The Chittagong Hill Tract Accord and After: The Gendered Dimensions of Peace", *UNRISD Report*, 2004, pp. 6-7.
22. See Chakma Raja Debashish Ray's response to Dipu Moni's Statement in "RDR Says FM Statement Flawed", July 27, 2011, at http://bdnews24.com/details.php?id=201957&cid=2
23. See Haroon Habib, "A DeadlyCargo", *Frontline,* 21 (1), May 8-21, 2004, at http://www.frontlineonnet.com/fl2 110/stories/ 20040521000206100.htm. Also, see Ahmed Hussain, "Whose Arms Are They Anyway?", *The Daily Star, Weekend Magazine,* 1 (4), April 6, 2004.
24. For details, see Shafiqur Rahman, "Non-Traditional Threats to Security: Challenges for Bangladesh", *NDC Journal*, November-December 2005, pp. 1-21.
25. *Mastans* are musclemen patronised by the political parties.
26. The 2001 post-electoral violence can be attributed to the intolerant attitude towards the supporter of the Awami League and the way looting and arson provided economic incentive to the *mastans.* Capture of minority property under the vested property act is another instance.

27. M. Moniruzzaman, "Party Politics and Political Violence in Bangladesh: Issues, Manifestations and Consequences", *South Asian Survey*, 16 (1), 2009, p. 86.
28. "Human Rights Report 2011", *Odhikar Report on Bangladesh*, January 07, 2012, p. 46.
29. For details, see Shafiqur Rahman, "Non Traditional Military Threats to Security: Challenges for Bangladesh", *NDC Journal*, November-December 2005, pp. 1-24.
30. "Bangladesh Vision 2021", *Centre for Policy Dialogue*, 2007, p. 39.
31. See "Views of Bangladesh on Climate Change and its Possible Security Implications", September 8, 2009, at http://www.un.org/esa/dsd/resources/res_pdfs/ga-64/cc-inputs/Bangladesh_CCIS.pdf
32. For a detailed assessment on climate change, environmental degradation and its impact on security, see the report prepared by BIISS and Saferworld, "Climate Change and Security in Bangladesh: A Case Study", June 2009.
33. See M. Jashim Uddin, "Security Sector Reform in Bangladesh", *South Asian Survey*, 16 (2), 2009, p. 211.
34. "459 Blasts in 63 districts in 30 Minutes", *The Daily Star*, August 18, 2005, at http://www.thedailystar.net/2005/08/18/d5081801011.htm
35. M.G. Kabir and Shaukat Hassan, "Issues and Challenges facing Bangladesh Foreign Policy", *Bangladesh Society of International Studies*, Dhaka, 1989, p. 34. Also, see the account of Major (Retd.) Akhtar Ahmed, who after acknowledging the fact that many Indians lost their lives concludes India's sacrifice with a limited objective. See Akhtar Ahmed, *Advance to Contact: A Soldier's Account of Bangladesh War*, UPL, Dhaka, 2000, p. 220.
36. A.K.M. Abdus Sabur, "Bangladesh-India Relations: Retrospect and Prospects", Paper Presented in the International Conference on *Bangladesh and SAARC: Issues, Perspectives and Outlook* organised by BIISS, Dhaka, August 23-24, 1992, p. 4. However, for a different perspective on the 1972 Treaty, see Shahiduzzaman, "Alliance Reliability in the Post Cold War Context and Bangladesh's Military Strategy", Paper presented in the same international conference, p.5.
37. "Joint India-Bangladesh Exercise Continues Despite Dhaka Mutiny", *Hindustan Times*, February 26, 2009, at http://www.hindustantimes.com/India-news/NewDelhi/Joint-India-Bangladesh-exercise-continues-despite-Dhaka-mutiny/Article1-383824.aspx
38. "Bangladesh Army Chief on a Visit to India", Press Information Bureau, Government of India, November 29, 2011, at http://pib.nic.in/newsite/erelease.aspx?relid=77884
39. See "Framework Agreement on Cooperation for Development between India and Bangladesh", September 6, 2011, at http://meaindia.nic.in/mystart.php?id=100018197&pid=2294
40. Interaction with the BSF Officers at the BSF Academy Tekanpur, Gwalior, in August 2012. Also, see "Injuries to BSF Jawans on Indo-Bangla Border Increasing", *Outlook*, September 30, 2012, at http://news.outlookindia.com/items.aspx?artid=776820. According to this report, quoting statistics provided by the BSF, 57 Jawans were injured in 2010, and this number shot up to 147 in 2011. Till September 2012, this number stood at 98 and one soldier was killed. There were 93 deaths in 2009 in firing by the BSF which is now reduced to 16 till September 2012.
41. For details on border problems, see Smruti S. Pattanaik, "India-Bangladesh Land Boundary: Flawed Inheritance and Problematic Future", *Strategic Analysis*, 35 (5), 2011, pp. 245-71.
42. See Obayedul Hoque Patwary, "Bangladesh-Myanmar Relations: The Security Dimension", *Bangladesh Institute of Peace and Security Studies*, September 10, 2009, at http://www.humansecuritygateway.com/documents/BIPSS_BangladeshMyanmarRelations_SecurityDimension.pdf

43. The $255 million project of two metre gauge lines will connect Jhilongjha with Chittagong, the principal port city on one side, and on the other side, it will connect Ramu with Gundum near the Myanmarese border by December 2013. For the Bangladesh-Myanmar road link, it has been decided that under the first phase two kilometres of road will be constructed from Ramu to Gundum inside Bangladesh and 23 kilometres will be constructed between Taungbro and Baolibazar inside Myanmar. In the second phase, the Myanmar authorities will construct 110 kilometres of road link between Bolibazar and Kyanktow in Myanmar. There is a road link between Kyanktow and Kunming. The Chinese have agreed to help implement this project.
44. "Bangladesh: Political and Strategic Development and US interest", *CRS Report,* April 1, 2010, p. 1.
45. U.S. State Department, "Bangladesh", *Budget Justification Document 2011,* as cited in Bruce Vaughan, "Bangladesh: Political and Strategic Development and the Interest of the US", *CRS Report,* April 1, 2010, p. 13.
46. Emajuddin Ahmed, *Military Rule and the Myth of Democracy,* Gatidhara, Dhaka, 2000, p. 51.
47. Ibid., p. 44.
48. Ibid, p. 51.
49. Mizanur Rahman Sikdar, "Military in Bangladesh Politics: A Case Study of Ershad Regime", Unpublished Thesis, Department of Political Science, Dhaka University, 1997, p. 54.
50. Anthony Mascarenhas, no.1, p. 32.
51. The *Jatiyo Rakkhi Bahini* (Absorption in the Army) Ordinance, Ordinance number LII, 1975, at www.bdlaws.gov.bd/print_sections_all.php?id=505
52. IISS, *Military Balance,* London, 2010, p. 358.
53. Shahedul Anam Khan, "The Army's New Commander and New Commands", *The Daily Star,* July 5, 2012, at http://www.thedailystar.net/newDesign/news-details.php?nid=240894
54. AL has suffered the most during the military regimes. Sheikh Mujib, the Awami League leader, was killed at the hands of the army majors and later its front ranking leaders were killed in jail crippling the party for many years.
55. "PM opens Army HQs Selection Board", *The New Nation,* October 2, 2012, at http://www.thenewnationbd.com/newsdetails.aspx?newsid=10961
56. Email interview with Brig. (Retd.) Shahedul Anam Khan, September 27, 2012.
57. "Army Command to be Divided", *The Daily Star,* June 14, 2012, at http://www.thedailystar.net/newDesign/news-details.php?nid=238248
58. For details, see Smruti S. Pattanaik, "Analysing the failed coup in Bangladesh", *IDSA Comment,* January 23, 2012, at http://www.idsa.in/idsacomments/AnalysingthefailedCoupinBangladesh_SmrutiPattanaik_230112
59. Data sourced from a report submitted by Bangladesh government to the UN Convention on the Rights of Child on the involvement of children in the armed conflict. Report no. CRC/C/OPAC/BGD/1, July 14, 2005.
60. http://www.bangladeshnavy.org/career.html.
61. http://www.army.mil.bd/newahq/index5.php?category=22.
62. http://www.mod.gov.bd/responsibilities.html.
63. http://countrystudies.us/bangladesh/57.htm
64. Figures taken from http://articles.janes.com/articles/Janes-Sentinel-Security-Assessment-South-Asia/Defence-budget-Bangladesh.html
65. "Defence Budget up", June 7, 2012, at http://bdnews24.com/details.php?id=225998&cid=2
66. For a discussion on the defence budget and Bangladesh's threat perception, see Ishfaq

Ilahi Choudhury, "Some thoughts on the defence budget", *The Daily Star*, June 12, 2012, at http://www.thedailystar.net/newDesign/news-details.php?nid=237879
67. *Bureau of South and Central Asian Affairs*, March 2008, at http://www.state.gov/r/pa/ei/bgn/3452.htm.
68. Ibid.
69. It is considered at par with Harpoon missile of the US and can carry 165 kg war head. Sumit Sen, "Bangladesh Building Missile Arsenal", *The Times of India*, September 12, 2008, at http://articles.timesofindia.indiatimes.com/2008-09-12/india/27928053_1_anti-ship-missile-programme-strike-range
70. "Army Command to be divided", *The Daily Star*, June 14, 2012, at http://www.thedailystar.net/newDesign/news-details.php?nid=238248
71. "Integration of Defence Forces for Joint and Convergent Effects: Perspectives and Proposals", *Bangladesh Army Journal*, Issue 38, 2005, p. 44, at http://www.army.mil.bd/newahq/pub/doc/Army%20Journal-December2005(38th%20Issue).pdf
72. M. Mahbubur Rahman, "Bangladesh-China Defence Cooperation in the Twenty-First Century", Paper Summary, Round-table Discussion on Bangladesh-China Dialogue, *Bangladesh Institute of International & Strategic Studies*, March 14, 2010, at http://www.biiss.org/seminar_2010/papers/sop.pdf
73. Ruksana Kibria, "Strategic Implications of Bangladesh-China Relations", *The Daily Star*, 15th Anniversary Issue, February 19, 2006, at http://www.thedailystar.net/suppliments/2006/15thanniv/bangladesh&theworld/bd_world12.htm
74. Wendell Minnick, "Bangladesh Navy Tests Chinese Anti-Ship Missiles", May 14, 2008, at http://www.defensenews.com/story.php?i=3528643.
75. Malladi Rama Rao, "Dynamics of China-Bangladesh Relations", *Policy Research Group*, January 24, 2010, at http://policyresearchgroup.com/regional_weekly/hot_topics/540.html
76. "Bangladesh to purchase anti-armor and anti-ship missile from china", February 15, 2010, at http://www.defenseworld.net/go/defensenews.jsp?id=4149&h=Bangladesh%20purchase%20anti-armor%20anti-ship%20missile%20from%20china
77. Wendell Minnick, no. 74.
78. "Bangladesh to Purchase Missiles from Europe, Turkey", September 15, 2008, at http://www.defenseworld.net/go/defensenews.jsp?n=Bangladesh%20to%20Purchase%20Missiles%20from%20Europe,%20Turkey&id=1194
79. "Army Command to be divided", *The Daily Star*, June 14, 2012, at http://www.thedailystar.net/newDesign/news-details.php?nid=238248
80. Wendell Minnick, no. 74.
81. Siva Govinda Samy, "Bangladesh Air Force Eyes Upgrade and New Aircraft", August 19, 2009, at http://www.flightglobal.com/news/articles/bangladesh-air-force-eyes-upgrades-and-new-aircraft-331222/
82. "Army to be Split into Eastern Western Command: A.K. Khondoker", *New Age*, June 14, 2012, at http://newagebd.com/detail.php?date=2012-06-14&nid=13724
83. The UN spokesperson said if Army is seen as participating in the controversial January 22 elections, its role in peacekeeping would be reconsidered.
84. Speech of Foreign Minister of Bangladesh, Dipu Moni, on "Foreign Policy of Bangladesh: Priorities and Challenges and Issues of Bangladesh-China Relations" in Beijing, June 20, 2011, at http://www.mofa.gov.bd/index.php?option=com_wrapper&view=wrapper&Itemid=135.
85. http://www.ambafrance-bd.org/article.php3?id_article=382
86. Roland Buerk, "The Cream of UN Peacekeepers", *BBC News*, January 18, 2006, at http://news.bbc.co.uk/2/hi/south_asia/3763640.stm

87. See "Defence Pact Okayed to Train up Kuwaiti Army", *The Daily Star*, February 1, 2004, at http://www.thedailystar.net/2004/02/01/d4020101044.htm.
88. Interview with Col. (Retd.) Oli Ahmed, who was also a close associate of Gen. Zia, on August 27, 2007.
89. Zillur Rahman Khan, "Leadership Crisis in Bangladesh", UPL, Dhaka, 1984, p. 104, as cited in Emajuddin Ahmed, *Military Rule and the Myth of Democracy*, p. 55.
90. Mascarenhas, no.1, p. 17.
91. Armed Forces Division, at http://www.afd.gov.bd/
92. For details regarding the meeting between prime minister and the army offiicers in Sena kunj in Dhaka Cantonment, see the video (in Bangla) "Open Secrets of BDR Mutiny: Sena Kunj Exclusive, Part 3, (translated by the author), at http://www.youtube.com/watch?feature=endscreen&v=a6wt4wt2HNE&NR=1
93. Interview with a retired army officer whose relative was dismissed from the service. Interview in Dhaka, April 2, 2012.
94. "Bangladesh: Back to the Future", *International Crisis Group*, Asia Report 226, June 13, 2012, p.15.
95. Ibid. Quoted from the ICG report.
96. "China to help build deep sea port", *The Daily* Star, June 23, 2011, at http://www.thedailystar.net/newDesign/news-details.php?nid=191209
97. Hasan Jahid Tusher, "Army to get 44 tanks", *The Daily Star*, June 27, 2011, at http://www.thedailystar.net/newDesign/news-details.php?nid=191737
98. See the exclusive interview with China's Ambassador to Bangladesh, Li Jun, July 19, 2012, at http://www.thedailystar.net/newDesign/news-details.php?nid=242607
99. Borhanuddin Ahmad, *The Generals of Pakistan and Bangladesh*, Academic Publishers, Dhaka, 1993, p. 159.
100. General Ershad had proposed that Bangladesh cannot afford a large Army. He had called for combining the role of nation-building and national defence into a single concept of 'total defence.' Arguing further, he had said that rather than letting able-bodied trained soldiers sitting idle in the barracks, they should be engaged in a productive manner as Bangladesh has economic constraints to building sufficient fire power.
101. *The Guardian,* October 7, 1981, as cited in "Bangladesh Army to Seek Greater Role in Politics", *Defence Journal*, Karachi, 8 (5), 1982, p. 32.
102. See "UN Warned army against Coup", *The Daily Star*, September 7, 2011, at http://www.thedailystar.net/newDesign/news-details.php?nid=201433
103. Kamal Ahmed, "Bangladesh Army's Advancing Business Interest", *BBC News*, August 15, 2010, at http://www.bbc.co.uk/news/world-south-asia-10801268
104. "Army Chief Feels Need for Constitution Review", *The Daily Star*, July 11, 2007, at http://www.thedailystar.net/2007/07/11/d7071101011.htm
105. For military's political role, see author's earlier paper on "Reemergence of Military and Prospects of Democracy in Bangladesh", *Strategic Analysis*, 32 (6), November 2008, pp. 975-995.
106. "Army foils bid to topple govt", *The Daily Star*, January 20, 2012, at http://www.thedailystar.net/newDesign/news-details.php?nid=219131.

APPENDIX I

Army Chiefs of Staff

Name and Rank	*Appointed by*	*Tenure*
M.A.G. Osmany (General)	Bangladesh Government-in- Exile	December 1971-April 1972 (commander-in-chief of armed forces)
K.M. Shafiullah (Colonel)	Sheikh Mujibur Rahman	April 1972-August 1975 (dismissed after coup)
Ziaur Rahman (Major General)	Khondakar Mushtaque Ahmed	August-November 1975 (dismissed in November 3 coup)
Khaled Musharraf (Brigadier)	Self	November 3-7, 1975 (ringleader of short-lived coup; killed on November 7)
Ziaur Rahman (Major General)	-Do-	November 7, 1975- November 1980
Hussain Muhammad Ershad (Major General, later Lieutenant General)	Ziaur Rahman	December 1980-August 1985
Atiqur Rahman (Lieutenant General)	Hussain Muhammad Ershad	September 1, 1986-August 1990
Lt. Gen. Nuruddin Khan		August 1990-June 1994
Lt Gen Abu Saleh Muhammad Nasim		June 1994-June1996
Lt. Gen. Mahbabur Rahman	CTG	June 1996-December 1997
Lt. Gen. Mistafizur Rahman	Sheikh Hasina	December 1997-December 2000
Lt Gen M. Harun ur Rashid	Shiekh Hasina	December 2000-June 2002
Lt Gen. Hasan Masud Chowdhury	Begum Khaleda Zia	June 2002-June 2005
Gen. Moeen U Ahmed	Begum Zia	June 2005-June 2009
Gen. Md Abdul Mubeen	Sheikh Hasina	June 2009-June 2012
Gen. Iqbal Karim Bhuiyan	Sheikh Hasina	June 2012 to present

Source: http://lcweb2.loc.gov/frd/cs/bangladesh/bd_appen.html#table18 (and newspaper reports and other sources).

APPENDIX II

Defence Budget (In constant, 2010, US$ million)

Year	*1998*	*1999*	*2000*	*2001*	*2002*	*2003*	*2004*	*2005*	*2006*	*2007*	*2008*	*2009*	*2010*	*2011*
US$ m	823	852	888	888	861	864	881	893	961	1,011	999	1.166	1,298	1,367
Percentage of GDP	1.3	1.3	1.3	1.2	1.1	1.1	1.1	1.0	1.0	1.0	1.0	1.1	1.1	—

Source: http://milexdata.sipri.org/result.php4

APPENDIX III

Arms Procurement

Supplier/ recipient (R) or licenser (L)	*No. ordered*	*Weapon designation*	*Weapon description*	*Year of order/ licence*	*Year(s) of deliveries*	*No. delivered/ produced*	*Comments*
1	*2*	*3*	*4*	*5*	*6*	*7*	*8*
China							
R: Bangladesh	4	F-7M Airguard	Fighter aircraft	(1996)	1999-2000	4	FT-7BG version
	(21)	HN-5A	Portable SAM	(2000)	2001	21	HN-5JA1 version
	(114)	Red Arrow-8	Anti-tank missile	(2000)	2001	114	
	20	Type-83 122mm	Towed gun	(2003)	2004	20	
	1	Crotale	SAM system	(2004)	2007	(1)	FM-90 version; for DW-2000 frigate
	(250)	QW-2	Portable SAM	2004	2007	(250)	
	(10)	C-802/CSS-N-8	Anti-ship missile	(2005)	2008	(10)	For 1 Jianghu (Type-053 or Type-510) frigate
	(54)	D-30 122mm	Towed gun	(2005)	2006-2007	(54)	Type-96 version
	(100)	PL-7	SRAAM	(2005)	2005-2007	(100)	For F-7MG combat aircraft
	(14)	PL-9	SRAAM	(2005)	2006-2008	14	For F-7MG combat aircraft
	(20)	R-440 Crotale	SAM	(2005)	2007	(20)	FM-90 version; for DW-2000 (Bangabandhu) frigate
	16	F-7MG	Fighter aircraft	(2006)	2006	16	$44-118 m deal; F-7BG version

	(300)	Type-59G	Tank	(2009)	2010-2011	(55)	Bangladeshi Type-59 and Type-69 tanks rebuilt to Type-59G in Bangladesh with kits from China
	(2)	FM-90	SAM system	(2010)	2011	(2)	
	(75)	FM-90	SAM	(2010)	2011	(75)	
	(60)	C-802/CSS-N-8	Anti-ship missile	(2011)			For 6 CSOC-46m FAC
	16	F-7MG	Fighter aircraft	2011			F-7BGI version; delivery 2012
	3	Type-654	ARV	2011			
	44	Type-96G	Tank	2011			BDT12 b ($160 m) deal; delivery 2012-2013
L: Bangladesh	7	CSOC-46m	FAC	(2011)			Incl 5 produced in Bangladesh; delivery possibly from 2012
France							
R: Bangladesh	4	PA6	Diesel engine	(1998)	2001	4	For 1 DW-200H (Bangabandhu) frigate from South Korea
Germany (FRG)							
R: Bangladesh	1	ASO-90	ASW sonar	(1998)	2001	1	For 1 DW-2000H Type (Bangabandhu Class) frigate from South Korea
	2	Do-228MP	MP aircraft	2011			Do-228NG version; delivery 2013

(Contd.)

1	*2*	*3*	*4*	*5*	*6*	*7*	*8*
Italy							
R: Bangladesh	2	Compact 40L70	Naval gun	(1998)	2001	2	For 1 DW-2000H (Bangabandhu) frigate from South Korea
	(10)	Otomat-2	Anti-ship missile	(1998)	2002	(10)	For DW-2000H (Bangabandhu) frigate
	1	Super Rapid 76mm	Naval gun	(1998)	2001	1	For 1 DW-2000H (Bangabandhu) frigate from South Korea
	16	Grifo	Combat ac radar	2006	2006	16	Grifo-MG version; for 16 F-7MG combat aircraft from China; possibly from Pakistani production line
	2	A-109K	Light helicopter	2010	2011	2	
Netherlands							
R: Bangladesh	1	DA-08	Air search radar	(1998)	2001	1	For 1 DW-2000H (Bangabandhu) frigate from South Korea
	1	MIRADOR	EO search/fire control		(1998)	2001	1 For 1 DW-2000H Type (Bangabandhu Class) frigate from South Korea
	1	Variant	Air/sea search radar	(1998)	2001	1	For 1 DW-2000H Type (Bangabandhu Class) frigate from South Korea
	1	LIROD	Fire control radar	(1999)	2001	1	For 1 DW-2000H (Bangabandhu) frigate from South Korea; LIROD-2 version

Pakistan							
R: Bangladesh	(230)	Red Arrow-8	Anti-tank missile	(2001)	2001-2004	(230)	Baktar Shikan (Green Arrow) version
	19	T-37B	Trainer aircraft	2003	2004-2005	(19)	Ex-Pakistani; T-37C version
Romania							
R: Bangladesh	9	RN-94	APC	(2004)	2005	9	Ambulance version
Russia							
R: Bangladesh	8	MiG-29S/Fulcrum-C	FGA aircraft	1999	1999-2000	8	$115-124 m deal; incl 2 MiG-29UB version
	(96)	R-73/AA-11 Archer	SRAAM	1999	1999-2000	(96)	For MiG-29S combat aircraft
	2	1L-117	Air search radar	2000	2001	(2)	$15 m deal
	78	BTR-80	APC	2001	2001-2002	78	$16 m deal (financed by UN); for use by Bangladeshi UN peacekeeping forces
	3	Mi-8MT/Mi-17/Hip-H		Helicopter		2004	2007 3 BDT78 m ($1.3 m) deal; Mi-171 armed version
	60	BTR-80	APC	(2005)	2006	60	For use by Bangladeshi UN peacekeeping forces; financed via UN
	(80)	BTR-80	APC	2011			Incl ambulance and ARV version; possibly BTR-80A IFV version

(Contd.)

South Korea							
R: Bangladesh	1	DW-2000H	Frigate	1998	2001	1	$100 m deal; Bangladeshi designation Bangabandhu
	2	Sea Dolphin	Patrol craft	2000	2000	2	Ex-South Korean; aid
Turkey							
R: Bangladesh	(22)	Cobra	APV	2006	2007-2008	(22)	
UK							
R: Bangladesh	5	Island	OPV	2002	2002-2004	5	Ex-UK; Bangladeshi designation Kapatakhaya
	2	Castle	OPV	2010	2010	2	Ex-UK; $4 m deal; Bangladeshi designation Bijoy.
Ukraine							
R: Bangladesh	(47)	6TD	Diesel engine	(2011)			For 44 Type-96G tanks and 3 Type-654 ARV from China
USA							
R: Bangladesh	4	C-130B Hercules	Transport aircraft	1999	2000	(4)	Ex-US; $15 m deal; modernized before delivery
	4	TPE-331	Turboprop	2011			For 2 Do-228 MP aircraft from Germany

Source: SIPRI Arms Transfers Database.

Transfers of major conventional weapons: Sorted by Supplier. Deals with deliveries or orders made for year range 2000 to 2011

Note: The 'No. delivered/produced' and the 'Year(s) of deliveries' columns refer to all deliveries since the beginning of the contract. Deals in which the recipient was involved in the production of the weapon system are listed separately. The 'Comments' column includes publicly reported information on the value of the deal. Information on the sources and methods used in the collection of the data, and explanations of the conventions, abbreviations and acronyms, can be found at http://www.sipri.org/contents/armstrad/at_data.html. The SIPRI Arms Transfers Database is continuously updated as new information becomes available.

Chapter Three

The Royal Bhutan Army

Anand Kumar

Introduction: The Security Environment of the Country

Geo-political/strategic Significance of the Country

Bhutan, a tiny landlocked country, is strategically located between China and India. It controls several key Himalayan passes. Bhutan shares its land boundary with India on three sides and China on one side. The Indian states sharing borders with Bhutan are Sikkim, West Bengal, Assam and Arunachal Pradesh. Though the initial delineation of the Indo-Bhutanese border was done through the *Treaty of Peace* (1865) signed between Bhutan and British India, it was between 1973 and 1984 that a detailed delineation and demarcation was made. However, several small sectors, including the middle zone between Sarbhang and Geylegphug and the eastern frontier with the north-eastern Indian state of Arunachal Pradesh, remained unresolved.

The strategic location of Bhutan allows it to act as a buffer state between India and China in some parts of the eastern Himalayas. Similarly, eastern Bhutan adjoins the vital Indian Army defences in Arunachal Pradesh, which is still claimed by China. Here too, a Bhutan friendly to India ensures that the Indian Army defences in this region are not outflanked from the West in case of any Chinese military operation. The north-east India is attached to the mainland with a narrow strip known as Siliguri Corridor. Bhutan figures on the north of this corridor and helps India to keep this area secure unlike Bangladesh from where forces inimical to India have been allowed to operate.

Historically, Bhutan's foreign relations were limited to contacts with Tibet, India and Britain.[1] In 1975, Bhutan and four other landlocked Asian countries (Afghanistan, Laos, Mongolia and Nepal) were granted a special status as "least developed landlocked Asian countries" by the United Nations

Economic and Social Commission for Asia and the Pacific (ESCAP) in coordination with the United Nations Conference on Trade and Development (UNCTAD) and the United Nations Development Project (UNDP). Despite their intentions to assist Bhutan and other such countries in dealing with international transit problems, Bhutan declined to work with them probably because it wanted to pursue a foreign policy of isolation. The most significant international participation of Bhutan was in the 1980s when it became member of the South Asian Association for Regional Cooperation (SAARC). The Indo-Bhutan relations were greatly influenced by developments in Tibet which made China appear as a serious external threat to the Bhutanese security as well.

Geographical Terrain

Bhutan is a landlocked country with an area of 47,000 square kilometres and a land boundary of 1,075 kilometres (China 470 kilometres, India 605 kilometres).[2] The climate varies; tropical in the southern plains; cool winters and hot summers in the central valleys; with severe winters and cool summers in the Himalayas. The terrain is mostly mountainous with some fertile valleys. The lowest point is Drangme Chhu (97 metres) and the highest point is Kula Kangri (7,553 metres). The arable land in Bhutan is 2.98 per cent of the total landmass of the country. Violent storms from the Himalayas are the source of the country's name which translates as 'Land of the Thunder Dragon'. There are frequent landslides during the rainy season.

Threat Perceptions—Key Domestic and External Challenges

Bhutan's independence was recognised by the *Treaty of Punakha* which was signed on January 8, 1910.[3] According to this Treaty, external affairs were to be guided by India. India agreed not to interfere in Bhutan's internal affairs. With independence in 1947, India became the *de facto* protector of the Himalayan Kingdom and Bhutan signed a political treaty with independent India in 1949, much before it stepped out of its self-imposed isolation in early sixties. This treaty, at least in theory, required Bhutan to consult India in the conduct of its external relations.[4] However, the formal diplomatic relations between the two countries at ambassadorial level was established only on August 8, 1978. India is a major donor for Bhutan and finances all its five-year plans. The entire military budget of Bhutan is funded by India.

The threat perception of Bhutan or its national security perception has evolved in four stages.[5] Initially, Bhutanese national security perceptions were greatly influenced and shaped by geopolitical events in Tibet, especially with the Chinese integration of Tibet in 1951. This compelled it to sign a joint defence agreement with India in 1965.[6] The Chinese take over of Tibet also forced Bhutan to close its frontiers with Tibet and go for a closer relation with India. To reduce the chances of Chinese encroachment, Bhutan began a modernisation programme. Under this programme, land reforms were completed and slavery and serfdom were abolished. Judiciary was separated from the executive branch of government. The modernisation programme was mostly funded by India and included construction of roads linking the Indian plains with central Bhutan. During Jigme Dorji's reign, *Dzongkha* was made the national language. In 1966, Jigme Dorji Wangchuck made Thimpu the year round capital.

In the second stage, Bhutan started apprehending threat from the Indian side, especially after India annexed Sikkim in 1975.[7] Probably, Bhutan as a small country felt that it can also meet the same fate. Bhutan began perceiving its bilateral relations with India politically risky and uncertain.

Bhutan's apprehension of India further increased in the third stage after India involved itself in the Sri Lankan domestic conflict and deployed the Indian Peace Keeping Force (IPKF). This made Bhutan re-assess its threats from the south, which led to a gradual re-orientation of its foreign policy imperatives. Thus, Bhutan started to look beyond its neighbourhood and established bilateral diplomatic relations with other countries.

In the fourth stage, since the early 1980s, the armed struggle in Darjeeling and the separatist movements being waged in north-east India bordering Bhutan have enhanced its security concerns. Bhutan committed a national security blunder by allowing the United Liberation Front of Assam (ULFA) and Bodo insurgents of Assam to enter its territories.[8] Though Bhutan subsequently acted against these groups in December 2003 under *Operation All Clear*, reports indicate that they have once again become active inside Bhutan.[9] Also, groups like north Bengal-based Kamtapur Liberation Organisation (KLO) are operating in tandem with Nepalese Maoists which can pose threat to Bhutanese Government in times to come. Moreover, after the Bhutanese crackdown in 2003, several of these groups have turned anti-Bhutan.

On November 12, 2008, a Bhutanese national Tenzing G. Zangpo and self-styled home secretary of National Democratic Front of Bodoland (NDFB) Sabin Boro were arrested from a rented house in Guwahati.[10] Zangpo is a senior leader of the Druk National Congress which was formed by Bhutanese exiles in Nepal. Their interrogation revealed that the ULFA and the NDFB have been helping the Bhutanese Maoists who wanted to topple the government. Tenzing is believed to have told the police team that the ULFA and the NDFB were actively supporting the Bhutanese Maoists by supplying them with explosives.[11] This regrouping of Indian and Bhutanese insurgents prompted both the countries to think of a similar operation like the one carried out in December 2003.[12]

A major threat to internal security of Bhutan emerged in the late 1980s when Nepalese liberation movements emerged. In 1988, some ethnic Nepalese in Bhutan revived their protest against alleged discrimination. They demanded exemption from government decrees aimed at enhancing Bhutanese national identity. By early 1991, the press in Nepal was referring to insurgents in southern Bhutan as "freedom fighters." Supporting the government activities were expatriate Nepalese political groups and their supporters in Nepal and India. Thousands of Nepalese fled Bhutan. Even high-level Bhutanese Government officials of Nepalese origin resigned from their positions and moved to Nepal. These refugees are staying in seven camps in the south-eastern part of Nepal. Reports have indicated that Maoists have become active in the refugee camps of Nepal.

Origin/Evolution of the National Army

The Royal Bhutan Army (RBA) was organised as a regular military force in the 1950s, with the encouragement of India and in response to the Chinese takeover of Tibet. Following the establishment of a national militia in 1958, the government announced a new conscription system and plans for raising a well-equipped standing army of 2,500 troops. All able-bodied men were given military training and by 1963 a standing army was established. A reorganisation in 1968 led to an increase in the size of the Army to 4,850 troops, with a programme aimed at recruiting 600 additional troops per year.

In 1997, Bhutan decided to expand the RBA, a lightly armed infantry force with a strength estimated to number about 6,000, to meet the challenge posed by anti-Indian insurgents—the ULFA and the Bodo Liberation Tigers Force (BLTF)—operating in the country's eastern region. The RBA has raised many new wings since 1997, each of which is equivalent to an under-sized infantry battalion, but it is not clear whether the figures provided by government sources represent the overall intake. Each of the additionally trained wings is in different stages of training and acclimatisation and will be deployed for counterinsurgency duties, primarily along the eastern border areas. In mid-2000, the RBA was composed of 7,000 men, backed by a growing militia. Its present strength is estimated to be about 10,000.

Military Doctrine/Strategic Thought of the National Army

Three types of eventualities are envisaged in the Bhutanese concept of national security: security from external threats; the strategic environment and unsettled periphery and; internal factors such as externally induced domestic upheavals that could unsettle its core national values.[13] Thus, the security concerns of Bhutan are related to maintaining the sovereignty of the Bhutanese state and its territorial integrity. The RBA is meant to protect the sovereignty and territorial integrity of Bhutan.

External threats and the strategic environment have been dealt with under the section related to threat perception. The unsettled periphery for Bhutan means north-east India where a number of states like Nagaland, Manipur, Tripura and Assam are facing insurgency. This in turn also poses a security threat to Bhutan.

Structure/Formation of the National Army

Organisation: The supreme commander of Royal Bhutan Army is the *Druk Gyalpo*, the ruler of Bhutan. Regular administrative functions are carried out by the Chief Operations Officer with the rank of a Major General. Prior to 1981, the Chief Operations Officer was a Colonel. Organisationally, the army headquarters ranks as a ministry and is immediately subordinate to the council of ministers. The Army Headquarters are at Thimpu while the training centre is at Tenchholing. There are four Operational Wings: Wing 1 is at Changjukha (Geylegphug), Wing 2 is at Damthung, Wing 3 is at Goinichawa, and Wing 4 is at Yonphula. Organised into companies, platoons and sections, the troops are assigned to the wings deployed primarily in border areas. The Army also operates hospitals in Lungtenphug, Wangidphodran, and Yonphula. Members of the Royal Body Guards (an elite VIP protection unit commanded by a lieutenant colonel) have completed counter-insurgency and jungle warfare training in the Mizo Hills in India, the Indian College of Combat, and the Indian Military Academy.

Military Branches: The Bhutanese defence structure comprises the Royal Bhutan Army and Militia. There are five military branches, namely, the Royal Bhutan Army, National Militia, Royal Bhutan Police, Royal Body Guards and Forest Guards (Paramilitary). The Royal Bhutan Police (RBP), assisted by the Royal Bhutan Army (including those assigned to the Royal Body Guards), and a national militia maintain internal security.

Militia: Historically, the government had raised militia forces during the period of theocratic rule (1616-1907) at times of crisis. They were commanded by a *dapon* (arrow chief in Dzongkha). In modern times, a 5,000-strong militia was raised in 1958 as part of the defensive strategy against China. Militia personnel were trained by Army officers trained at the Indian Military Academy. Their primary function was to act as a first line of defence along the frontiers with China. Following an Indian inspection tour in 1961, the Bhutanese government was advised to step up militia recruitment. In 1967, the militia was reorganised on a national basis, with compulsory military training being given for three months each year for three years, to men 20-25 years of age. After the initial three-year training phase, militia personnel were placed on reserve status.

Para-Military Forces

Village security is a long-standing tradition. The present militia is controlled by the central government. Universal militia training by the Royal Bhutan Army was instituted in 1989. Uniformed Forest Guards are trained by the Royal Bhutan Army to ensure border security and to protect forests.

The Forest Guards

The Forest Guards, a uniformed government service with paramilitary capabilities, has been in existence since the early 1970s. Under the jurisdiction of the Department of Forestry, Forest Guards were trained in two six-month courses each year at the Forestry School. Small arms training are imparted by the Royal Bhutan Army. Besides guarding Bhutan's important forest resources, the Forest Guards provide border-security support to the Royal Bhutan Police.

Royal Bhutan Police (RBP)

Established on September 1, 1965, the Royal Bhutan Police (RBP) is not part of the armed forces. Its vision is "to make Bhutan the safest place to live and work in South Asia."[14] Its mission is to "work in partnership with the Bhutanese community to ensure safety, security and protection of lives and properties."[15] Since 1981, the recruits, grade six graduates and above, are trained at the police training centre in Jigmiling, Geylegphug District. The curriculum consists of weapons training, tae kwon do, physical training with and without arms, law, simple investigation techniques, turn-out drill, check-post duties, traffic control, public relations, and *driglam namzha* (traditional values and etiquette). The RBP is the only force that recruits women. A system of village defence committees is used for local patrolling in the border region. The RBP is subordinate to the RBA and is headquartered in each district and sub-district. Since the establishment of the police force, services of the Indian police advisers and instructors have been utilised.

Starting in 1975, Bhutanese instructors, trained in India for one year, began training recruits at the Zilnon Namgyeling Police Training Centre. Advanced training for selected police officers in criminology, traffic control, and canine corps has taken place in India and other countries. In 1988, following specialised training in India, a woman second lieutenant established a fingerprint bureau in Thimpu. Besides having access to training at the Indian Police Academy in Hyderabad, some students were also sent to the Police Executive Development Course in Singapore. Apart from performing standard police functions, members of the Royal Bhutan Police also serve as border guards and firefighters and provide first aid.

Strength of the Royal Bhutan Army

Royal Bhutan Army: 10,000
Supreme Commander: His Majesty
Chief Operations Officer: Maj. Gen. Batoo Tshering[16]

Forces

(i) *Royal Bhutan Army*[17]

No. 1 Wing-Tendu
No. 2 Wing-Damthang
No. 3 Wing-Goinchawa
No. 4 Wing-Yonphula
No. 5 Wing-Samchi
No. 6 Wing-Wangdi
No. 7 Wing-Paro
No. 8 Wing-Samchi
No. 9 Wing-Geylephug
No. 10 Wing-Deothang
No. 11 Wing-Rimte
No. 12 Wing-Wangdi
No. 13 Wing-Deothang
No. 14 Wing-Nanglam
No. 15 Wing-Thimpu (Rbg)
No. 16 Wing-Gelegphug
Training Wing-Tenchholing

(ii) *Independent Companies*—9 (Ha, Damthang, Gumchawa, Punakha, Kalikhola, Thimpu (2), Khkthang and Deothang)

(iii) *Special Forces*—6 companies

(iv) *Wangchuk Lo Dzong Military Training School*—Ha

(v) *Royal Bodyguards*—Three companies—Royal Palace (Thimpu)

(vi) *Forest Guards*

Equipment by type—Rifle (7.62 mm self-loading; some AK-47)

Machine guns (7.62 mm); Mortars (50mm)

(vii) *Army Aviation*—Dornier DO-28 1; Mil Mi-28 helicopters-7
(viii) *Royal Bhutan Police*
Police Training Centres—3 (Jigmiling, Geylephug and Zilnon Namgyeling)
(ix) *Airport Security Unit*—Paro

Source: Military Balance section in Col. (Retd.) Harjeet Singh (ed.) *South Asia Defence and Strategic Year Book*, Pentagon Press, New Delhi, 2008.

The Royal Bhutan Army now plans to reduce its strength to 8,000 and raise a militia. Bhutan thinks that the country is vulnerable to natural calamities like floods and earthquakes and the militia force would come handy and serve as an additional force to the armed forces in times of natural disaster.[18]

Civil-Military Relations

Civil-military relations in Bhutan are largely cordial. There was no possibility of a conflict with the civilian authority in the earlier regime as Bhutan was a kingdom. Even after it has turned into a democracy, the ruling political party, the *Druk Phuensum Tshogpa* (DPT), is made up mainly of the existing political elite and is staunchly loyal to the monarchy.[19] King remains the constitutional head and the structure of the Army has been inherited from the previous era. The Army remains loyal to the king.

Bilateral and Multilateral Defence/Security Co-operation

Since 1953, India and Bhutan have had extensive cooperation and have developed ties in various fields. India and Bhutan are also engaged in defence and security cooperation. In May 1961, the Indian Government had sent a team of military officers and men on a reconnaissance mission to Bhutan. Brig. J.S. Aurora, then BGS XXXIII Corps (later Lt. Gen. and Army Commander, Eastern Command, during 1971 War), had led the team of officers.[20]

On July 20, 1960, Brig. (then Col.) B.N. Upadhyay assumed the appointment of the first Commandant of Indian Military Training Team (IMTRAT), in Bhutan. His team of officers included Maj. A.N. Sudan, Maj. S.N. Gurung, Maj. P.N. Kackar and Capt. P.K. Chakraborti, RMO. An additional eleven officers joined the team by the end of the same year.

Institutes

- Wangchuk Lo Dzong Military School (WLDMS)
- Indo Bhutan Friendship Hospital (IBFH)

- Military Hospital, Haa

Wangchuk Lo Dzong Military School (WLDMS): The WLDMS was established on October 16, 1962 and commenced training with 22 officer cadets and 49 non-commissioned officers. The WLDMS conducts approx 70 to 75 pre-course capsules for about 30-35 different courses conducted at 20 separate training institutions in India. Initially, an officer from Royal Bhutan Army was attached to assist IMTRAT with training at the WLDMS. Two officers were subsequently posted to the School in 1974 for the first time and at present, one senior instructor, one assistant senior instructor, one directing staff coordination, demonstration company commander and a company officer are on the staff of WLDMS. The role of WLDMS is to impart military training to the personnel of Royal Bhutan Army and Royal Bodyguards.

Type of Training[21]

- Pre Courses
- Refresher Courses
- Promotion Cadres
- Miscellaneous Training.

Training Infrastructure[22]

- Sand Model Rooms
- Conference Hall
- Field Engineering Model Room
- Improvised Explosive Device
- Model Room
- Signal Model Room
- Computer Room
- Long Range
- Jungle Lane Shooting Range
- Rock Climbing Area
- Assault Course
- Unarmed Combat Pit
- Physical Training and Sports Training Area
- Field Engineering Demonstration Area
- Rural Insurgency Hide Out
- Urban Insurgency Mock Up
- Computer Training Lab
- Training Library

Indo Bhutan Friendship Hospital (IBFH): The foundation stone of Indo Bhutan Friendship Hospital was laid on July 4, 1970 by Lyonpo Dawa

Tshering, then Development Minister of the Royal Government of Bhutan. The hospital was inaugurated by Maj. Gen. T V Jeganathan, PVSM, AVSM, Commandant IMTRAT on April 27, 1973. The Hospital is organised into an OPD complex, an OT, ICU and a ward complex with 30 beds. The Hospital is staffed with several doctors.

Military Hospital, Haa: MH Haa provides state of the art facilities for Ultra Sonography, ECG, X-ray, Ventilator, Neo Natal Incubator and Pathology Lab. Facilities also exist for admitting limited number of civil patients. The Hospital extends all medical facilities to the civilian populace of Haa and adjoining areas free of cost. It treats approximately 100 civilian patients on a daily basis.

Mobile Clinic at Haa: A specially designed light commercial vehicle was dedicated by the Indian Ambassador to Bhutan, Dalip Mehta, on April 29, 1996. The vehicle has a minor OT, lab and a dispensary besides a portable X-ray unit and a dental chair. It is utilised to provide medical facilities to the civilians in far flung areas.

Detachments of IMTRAT in Bhutan

Headquarters of IMTRAT at Haa: Headquarters of IMTRAT is located at Haa Dzong at an altitude of 9100 ft above sea level. The Wangchuk Lo Dzong Military School and a military hospital are also located at Haa Dzong.[23]

Administrative Detachment at Phuentsholing: This detachment is located at Phuentsholing at a height of 755 ft. The small township of Phuentsholing is adjoining the Indian border town of Jaigaon, near Hasimara in West Bengal, with just the Bhutan gate separating the two.[24]

Detachment at Thimpu: This detachment is located at Thimpu, the capital of Bhutan, at a height of 7950 ft. A medical specialist, medical officers and a dental surgeon are also located at Thimpu in The Indo Bhutan Friendship Hospital (IBFH).[25]

Bhutanese officers have also been receiving training at the Indian military institutions. In 2005, the Bhutan King attended a course at the prestigious National Defence College (NDC) in New Delhi. He was the Guest of Honour at the NDC's golden jubilee celebrations in October 2010.[26] Maj. Gen. Batoo Tshering, the Bhutanese Army Chief, has received had training at the Indian Military Academy (IMA), Dehradun. In May 2011, The Royal Bhutan Army requested the Darjeeling-based Himalayan Mountaineering Institute (HMI) to rain its personnel in search and rescue missions during landslides and earthquakes in high altitude areas.[27]

Some of the recent high level visits by the top army officials of India and Bhutan are as:

- The Chief of Army Staff of the Indian Army, General J.J. Singh, visited Bhutan on a five-day goodwill visit in May 2005.[28]
- India's Chief of Army Staff General Deepak Kapoor visited Bhutan in June 2009.
- Chief of the Army Staff General V.K. Singh visited Bhutan from 7-11 June 2010. This was his first official overseas visit after taking charge.[29]
- The Bhutan Army Chief, Major General Batoo Tshering, visited New Delhi on a six-day goodwill visit in August 2010. This was his first visit since taking over as the Chief of Royal Bhutan Army in November 2005.
- From December 8-10, 2010, Gajraj Corps hosted a high level delegation of officers from the Royal Bhutan Army, led by Maj. Gen. Batoo Tshering, the Army Chief.[30]

National Army in People's Perception

There are three main ethnic, religious and linguistic groups and a dozen smaller groups in Bhutan. The Ngalungs or Ngalops (often called Drukpas) ethnic group live in the north-western region. They speak Dzonkha language and wear robe like dresses.[31] The second ethnic group is called Sharchops, who inhabit eastern and central region and practice Nyingmapa sect of Mahayana Buddhism and belong to Tibeto-Burmese ancestry. The third ethnic group is called Lhotshampas (meaning Southern Bhutanese) of Nepali origin. They live in six southern foothill districts, speak Nepali language, practice mostly Hinduism and have migrated from Nepal, and Darjeeling and Sikkim in India.[32]

People's perception of the Bhutanese Army varies according to the ethnicity of the people. Drupkas take national Army in high esteem. On the other hand, the same Army is looked with suspicion by the people of Nepalese origin as it was instrumental in driving away a large section of the Nepalese population from Bhutan.

Future Prospects

Bhutan being a small country is likely to keep a small national army meant largely for internal security purposes. Though some part of the Army is used to monitor the movement of the Chinese forces on its northern border, it is unlikely that the Bhutan would be preparing for meeting the military challenge from China. For the time being, Bhutan has managed to check the threat from the Indian insurgent groups who were earlier operating from its territory.

However, the insurgent groups are trying to regroup. What is worse, they are trying to ally with Maoists active in Nepal and Bhutan. These elements can create trouble for the nascent democracy in Bhutan.

However, the threat coming from the insurgents should not be very difficult to deal with if Bhutan chooses to make a common cause with India against them. Though the insurgent groups could pose a serious threat for Bhutan, after possible external threat from China, it is not likely to bring about any dramatic change in the Bhutanese Army.

NOTES

1. Col. (Retd.) Harjeet Singh (ed.), *South Asia Defence and Strategic Year Book*, Pentagon Press, New Delhi, 2008, p. 167.
2. Ibid, p. 160.
3. "1910—Treaty of Punakha signed", at http://www.bhutan2008.bt/en/node/198
4. Rakesh Chhetri, "The essence of Bhutanese foreign policy", *The Kathmandu Post*, January 30, 1998, at http://www.nepalresearch.com/publications/rakesh_1998.htm
5. Rakesh Chhetri, "National Security: A Bhutanese Perspective", *The Kathmandu Post*, December 25, 1997, at http://www.nepalresearch.com/publications/rakesh_1997.htm
6. Ibid.
7. Ibid.
8. Ibid.
9. "Militants regrouping to enter Bhutan: Assam government", *Bhutan News Service (BNS)*, August 4, 2009, at http://www.bhutannewsservice.com/main-news/militants-regrouping-to-enter-bhutan/
10. "Bhutan links to Assam serial blasts?", November 13, 2008, at http://www.timesnow.tv/NewsDtls.aspx?NewsID=20922
11. "ULFA, NDFB helping Bhutan rebels", *Assam Times*, November 18, 2008, at http://www.assamtimes.org/hot-news/2357.html
12. "Bhutan, India plan 2003-like ops against N-E rebel groups", *The Times of India*, August 27, 2009, at http://articles.timesofindia.indiatimes.com/2009-08-27/guwahati/28191675_1_royal-bhutan-army-ndfb-sarpang
13. Rakesh Chhetri, no. 5.
14. Royal Bhutan Police, at http://www.rbp.gov.bt/hist.php
15. Ibid.
16. Ministry of Foreign Affairs, Royal Government of Bhutan, at http://www.mfa.gov.bt/2011/10
17. Military Balance section in Col. (Retd.) Harjeet Singh (ed.), *South Asia Defence and Strategic Year Book*, Pentagon Press, New Delhi, 2008.
18. "Bhutan to reduce army strength, raise militia force", *The Times of India*, June 24, 2007, at http://articles.timesofindia.indiatimes.com/2007-06-24/rest-of-world/27977330_1_royal-bhutan-army-militia-rba
19. "Royalist Bhutan party sweeps polls", *The Telegraph*, March 25, 2008, at http://www.telegraphindia.com/1080325/jsp/foreign/story_9053937.jsp
20. See the website of the Indian Army, Indian Military Training Team (IMTRAT), Bhutan, at http://indianarmy.nic.in/index_imtrat.htm
21. Ibid.

22. Ibid.
23. Ibid.
24. Ibid.
25. Ibid.
26. "Army Chief begins Bhutan visit today", *The Hindu*, June 7, 2010, at http://www.thehindu.com/news/national/article448167.ece?service=mobile Also, see "His Majesty addresses NDC", October 22, 2010, at http://www.bhutanobserver.bt/his-majesty-addresses-ndc/
27. Vivek Chhetri, "Bhutan army to learn rescue tips at HMI", *The Telegraph*, May 5, 2011, at http://www.telegraphindia.com/1110505/jsp/siliguri/story_13940401.jsp#
28. "Indian army chief visits Bhutan", *Kuensel*, May 4, 2005, at http://www.kuenselonline.com/modules.php?name=News&file=print&sid=5394
29. "Army Chief begins Bhutan visit today", *The Hindu*, June 7, 2010, at http://www.hindu.com/2010/06/07/stories/2010060756421500.htm
30. "Bhutan Army Chief Visits Tezpur", *Snippets*, January 2011, at http://indianarmy.nic.in/Site/FormTemplete/frmTempSimple.aspx?MnId=odJUYBKdfjy7ie LiCZkUHg==&ParentID= RX5G38SbJoheyZ1UyXadPA==&flag=RkMAt1xPq9bv4bmSqonyJw==
31. People and Culture of Bhutan and Photo Collections, *Bhutan News Online*, at http://www.bhutannewsonline.com/people_culture.html
32. Ibid.

Chapter Four

Maldives' Security Dilemma and its National Defence Force

Alok Bansal

Maldives, strategically located in the central Indian Ocean, is the smallest state in South Asia. With a population of less than 400,000 people, it faces security dilemmas which are unique to this tiny Island-nation. The islands comprising Maldives stretch 800 km North to South, from South of Lakshadweep all the way to Chagos Archipelago, where the American base of Diego Garcia is located. The islands stretch 130 km from east to west and claim archipelagic status, which entitles them to a huge Exclusive Economic Zone (EEZ), disproportionately larger than its small area of approximately 298 square kilometres. The islands are located 640 km from the southern tip of the Indian land mass, 720 km from Sri Lanka and 384 km from Diego Garcia, which bestows upon the Island state a very strategically significant location. The Island of Minicoy in the Indian Union Territory of Lakshadweep is separated by Eight Degree Channel from Maldives and the northern-most island of Maldives is just 128 km from Minicoy. This central geo-strategic location bestows enormous advantages on Maldives under the United Nations Convention on the Law of the Sea (UNCLOS) III, but creates security dilemmas, as faced by other mini island-states of the Indian Ocean, like Seychelles and Comoros.[1]

Maldives comprise of approximately 1,200 islands located in 26 natural atolls. The exact number of islands varies, because new islands keep emerging in the coral atolls, while some get submerged. These atolls are spread over an area of 90,000 square kilometres. Because of their coral origins, islands are all flat with very little elevation and each island is circled by a shallow lagoon and a reef.[2] Geographically, the double rows of atolls that constitute Maldives are sharp ridges rising sharply from the deep oceans and have historically created enormous problems of navigation for the mariners. Of the numerous islands, only 198 are inhabited with permanent residents.[3]

Small island states have their own unique set of problems. They need to focus their meagre resources on tackling key security threats, which vary from state to state, based on their location, ethnicity, resources and susceptibility to external developments. Due to paucity of resources, the small states often rely on political and diplomatic tools rather than military or economic instruments. As for Maldives, it is regarded as "a classical case of a 'Micro State' which by all definitions is an atoll state." Its security problems have various dimensions and revolve around internal security, regional security and the global security system. Maldives today perceives three major types of threat—internal, external and environmental. Together, they define the security environment of Maldives.[4]

Internal Threats

Like in any other small country, internal threats pose a much greater potential of destabilisation in Maldives than any other bigger state. Until the implementation of recent political reforms and Maldives' transition to multiparty democracy, it was virtually impossible to correctly gauge the public sentiments. Lack of avenues to express dissent had contributed to the radicalisation of the society.

In keeping with the global trend, Islamic fundamentalism made its foray in the Island-state too. Maldives had its first brush with Islamist terrorism on September 29, 2007 when a bomb blast occurred in Male and injured 12 foreign tourists. Eight of those injured were Chinese nationals, whilst two were Japanese and two others were British.[5] On January 8, 2008, an Islamist hardliner attempted to stab the then President Maumoon Abdul Gayoom at Hoarafushi Island in North Thiladhunmathi Atoll.[6] Subsequently, on February 1, 2008, a moderate Islamic preacher, Dr. Afrashim Ali, was attacked in a mosque in Male after he led the Friday prayers.[7] These events in quick succession heralded the threat of radical Islam in hitherto peaceful and idyllic Island-nation.

The Maldivian Constitution bars the practice of any religion other than Sunni Islam. People have traditionally followed moderate *Shafi'i* school of Islam and the judicial system has been based on *Sharia*. Former President Gayoom, who was educated in Islamic jurisprudence in Egypt,[8] introduced religious education and brought in Egyptian clerics to enlighten his countrymen. Subsequently, the Saudi Government built an Islamic college and pumped huge funds in this regard into Maldives.[9] With the funds arrived conservative Wahabi Islam. Saudi Arabian funds and Pakistani seminaries have assisted in spreading Wahabism in Maldives.[10] Wahabis accuse government of propagating alcohol culture in the country through resorts; and they boycott state mosques as having been built with "alcohol money."[11] Before the process of democratisation began, the religious congregations provided the only legal avenue for dissent. Growing disenchantment with the government had increased the number of Islamic hardliners and has resulted in the emergence of numerous breakaway illegal mosques.[12]

After the bomb blast in Male in September 2007, the government banned the entry of foreign clerics. Wearing of veil by women in public places was banned and television stations were ordered not to show women with *burqa* on television.[13] Propagation of radical thoughts and religious gatherings without permission were banned. In the immediate aftermath of the bomb blast, the army and police raided an illegal Wahabi mosque in Male. Subsequently, they raided another illegal mosque in Himandhoo Island, fighting pitched battles with youth armed with iron rods and wooden planks.[14] The Island has been the centre of Wahabi resistance and an earlier mosque built by them was demolished by the government.[15]

However, the democratic reforms and the change of government consequent to the presidential elections led to considerable improvement in situation. The government released the radical clerics imprisoned by the previous government and removed the drastic restrictions imposed by the previous administration. The democratic environment under President Mohamed Nasheed's government initially prevented any further attacks by the Islamic militants. Islamic *Adhaalath* Party was included in the government and a council of scholars to adjudicate on Islamic matters was constituted. Controversial scholars were kept away from this council. Islamic interest free banking has also been introduced in Maldives to pander to the hardcore Islamic fringe. According to a recent report, girls in some islands are not being allowed to pursue education, while in some others people still pray separately as they believe that the prayers in government mosques will not be valid, as they have been built with the money received from the resorts, where alcohol is served. This showed that the Islamic radicalism was only temporarily down but not out and Maldives needed to address this problem or could face being overwhelmed by the rising tide of Islamic extremism akin to other countries of South Asia.[16]

The problem, however, erupted after a brief hiatus in May 2011 when Israeli national carrier *El Al* applied for flying to Maldives from December. The permission was granted to facilitate Israeli tourists to visit Maldives as well as to allow Maldivian pilgrims to visit Jerusalam. However, the *Adhaalath* Party, which was a constituent of the government, threatened to walk out, if permission was granted. In September 2011, *Adhalath* finally walked out of the government, protesting against its religious policies, especially on the issue of permitting Israeli flights. Although its president, Dr. Abdul Majeed Bari, continued to be the Minister of Islamic Affairs, he had to subsequently resign from the party leadership.[17] The radical Islamists had opposed monuments of various SAARC countries that were set up after the South Asian Association for Regional Cooperation (SAARC) summit in Addu Atoll in November 2011. The Pakistani monument was vandalised and an attempt was made to burn the Sri Lankan monument. Subsequently, Nepalese monument was 'stolen'. The other monuments are being guarded by the security forces. The Islamists have demanded removal of all monuments.[18] Subsequently, the United Nations High Commissioner for Human Rights, Navi Pillai's statement asking Maldives to end flogging for women convicted for adultery, further inflamed the radical Islamists in Maldives.[19]

On December 10, 2011, a silent protest by some 30 participants calling for religious tolerance was attacked by Islamists in which their leader and blogger Ismail 'Khilath' Rasheed had sustained head injuries. He was subsequently arrested without any charges. The Islamists wanted harsher punishment for those calling for religious freedom. Even the Chief Justice of Maldives Ahmed Faiz Hussein had expressed shock at the demand for religious tolerance.[20]

On December 23, 2011, an opposition rally led by *Adhaalath* Party to 'defend Islam' demanded removal of the SAARC monuments in Addu, condemned the UN human rights chief Navi Pillay's comments about Islamic *Sharia*, opposed the move to allow Israeli airlines to operate flights, demanded the closure of brothels (spas and massage parlours) in Male and reversal of decision to declare areas of inhabited islands as uninhabited in order to permit alcohol sales. A surprise element was that many of the participants in the rally were avowedly moderate and secular political parties. As many leading opposition members, who participated in the rally, run tourist resorts, the government decided to pre-empt them by closing down all massage parlours, which were accused of being brothels. The government also stated that it was considering a complete ban on alcohol and pork.[21]

The move was intended to prevent the opposition leaders with sizeable stakes in tourist resorts from using Islam to counter the government. However, it is fraught with danger and an analysis of developments in Pakistan shows that any accommodation of extremist view point not only provides respectability to the extremists, it also accelerates the process of radicalisation. Moreover, greater emphasis on Islam will bring out subtle difference in its interpretation. A committee of religious scholars convened by the government adopted a hawkish posture on most contentious issues, but what was more significant was that there was no unanimity on most issues.[22] Minor difference can snow ball into major confrontations in future. Maldives need to understand that tourism is a highly sensitive industry and no tourist goes to Swat valley in Pakistan despite its scenic beauty, although at one stage it was the prime tourist destination. In times to come, religious extremism might pose the gravest threat to Maldives' security.

After the coup on February 7, 2012, many of the rebels went and destroyed pre-Islamic Buddhist artefacts in the museum at Male. The whole coup against President Nasheed where he was forced to resign was led by Islamist forces and shows their influence. The fact that they could incite mutiny within the ranks of the police and the army indicates their reach. According to a report in *The Wall Street Journal*, increasing influence of hard line Islam was the main cause for the downfall of the democratically-elected Government of President Nasheed. The opposition in cohort with these radical elements was successful in propagating to the masses, including some members of the police and the military, that the president was undermining their faith. Nasheed was even accused of working in cohort with the Zionists to undermine the Islamic law.[23]

The country had also faced a secessionist movement in 1959. The southern most Addu Atoll, which had in the past enjoyed a special stature in the Maldives and had provided leadership in the resistance against Portuguese, had declared its independence. The Atoll had assumed greater significance because of the presence of British military bases on its soil. The Atoll in conjunction with two other atolls, under the leadership of Afif Didi, had then declared itself as United Suvadiva Republic. However, the breakaway republic was disbanded on September 30, 1963 and President Afif Didi was sent into exile, and soon thereafter, an agreement was reached between the British and the Maldives.[24] There have been trouble in Addu Atoll in the recent past but the new spirit of democracy had largely eradicated the discontentment within this volatile region. However, Addu Atoll was again in the forefront of disturbances that lead to the coup as well as the violent reaction to the change of regime. It was the demonstrations against monuments set up in Addu Atoll that brought the opposition together and forced the change of regime. It was also the arena for most of the violent protests in support of the ousted president after the coup. In view of its tumultuous history, the government in Male needs to show greater tact in dealing with the perceptions of population in Addu.

External Threats

Because of its location in the Indian Ocean astride the trade routes, Maldives has elicited enormous external interest. There are over 80,000 expatriates working in Maldives, who constitute over 25 per cent of its population and over half of the work force. Most of these, especially those involved in manual work, are Bangladeshis and they live in appalling housing and living conditions, and have often complained of inhuman treatment.[25] Bangladesh has raised its concerns about the matter with the Maldivian Government. This could provide fertile recruits for international terrorist organisations. Being a small state, any external non-state armed group can easily threaten the security of Maldives.

In 1988, People's Liberation Organisation of Tamil Eelam (PLOTE), a Sri Lankan Tamil militant group, could have almost taken over the state but for timely assistance by India. Many of the uninhabited islands provide ideal sanctuaries for terrorist groups. There were reports in the past that the Liberation Tigers of Tamil Eelam (LTTE), the Sri Lankan Tamil insurgent group, used some of these islands and the waters around them to tranship its consignments of arms and ammunition. There have been intelligence reports that the militant groups are using Maldives to send activists to southern Indian cities. The LTTE was also believed to be using that country to ferry arms and to send illegal migrants to work as spies.[26] After its decimation in Sri Lanka, the residual elements of the LTTE may seek to revive it in some uninhabited islands of Maldives. To counter any such eventualities, Maldives signed a memorandum of understanding (MoU) on intelligence sharing and an extradition treaty with Sri Lanka in 2007.

Its strategic position in the centre of Indian Ocean makes it an ideal location for overseas bases for external powers as well. During the Second World War, the United Kingdom (UK) built the southernmost Addu Atoll into a strategically important military base, especially as a link with Australia and the Pacific Ocean across the Indian Ocean. An airfield was constructed in the Gan Island and a radio-communication base on Hittadu Island in the Atoll. The bases were finally closed in 1976.[27] Of late, there have been reports that China is seeking a naval base in Maldives,[28] to monitor its shipping in the region. Even the US has an interest in Maldives and does not want Islamic radical elements to flourish in the islands and till the 2012 coup had hoped to project Maldives as a model for Islamic societies. Though Maldives does not have any territorial dispute with any of its neighbours, in the run up to the last presidential elections, some political parties had accused the government of not contesting a claim by the UK Government to all waters within 200 nautical miles of Chagos Archipelago, even though it intrudes into Maldivian waters by over 40 miles.

Maldives is a typical case of a miniscule state in the middle of the ocean with a small widely dispersed population and fairly limited financial resources. It will accordingly find it difficult to provide resources to counter threats emanating from overseas. It therefore needs a regional security framework that guarantees security without in any way undermining its sovereignty. It has accordingly sought an international security umbrella and managed to get a resolution passed by the United Nations General Assembly in 1989, which "appeals to the relevant regional and international organisations to provide assistance when requested by small states for strengthening their security."[29] In recent times, there have been many instances, where Somalian pirates have operated within Maldivian waters and abandoned pirate boats have been recovered in Maldives on numerous occasions. According to Admiral Robert Willard, head of US Pacific Command, the Somali pirates moving deeper into Asian waters posed the greatest security threat to Maldives.[30]

Environmental Security

One of the most significant existential threats to Maldives is that of deteriorating environment especially that of rising sea levels due to global warming. The Island-nation lives under the continuous threat of environmental catastrophe and fears being engulfed by the rising waters of the Indian Ocean. Maldives being coral islands are surrounded by reefs and lagoons and any threat to either of them poses grave danger to the islands. On an average, the islands are three to six feet above the mean sea level. As a result, a number of environmental issues impact on the very survival of the Island-nation.[31]

Reefs and corals are extremely vulnerable and can be destroyed by increasing pollution, which in turn makes the islands unstable. There have been occasions in the past when parts of some of the islands in Maldives have collapsed posing a grave danger to the population residing there. In many cases, coral reefs have been dredged for the construction activities. Extreme pressure on land has accentuated this problem. Maldives has been dependent on soil imported from India and Sri Lanka for its construction activities. Both the countries had stopped the export of their soil in the past, but India has subsequently allowed limited soil export. Large scale construction and reclamation have taken their toll on the reefs and lagoons and have led to unusually high tidal waves. In 1987, a large wave had caused widespread damage and destruction in Male including washing away of large tracts of reclaimed land.[32]

The gravity of the devastation that could be caused by the huge tidal waves can be gauged from the Tsunami that hit Maldives and parts of South and South-East Asia in December 2004. One third of total population was severely affected. Nearly 53 of the 199 inhabited islands had suffered severe damage, 20 islands were completely destroyed and 14 islands were completely evacuated. About 11,500 people were displaced. Over one-fifth of all tourist resorts had suffered extensive damage. A large number of fishing boats and nets were also destroyed.[33] Fishing and tourism being the two major components of the Maldivian economy, the fastest growing economy in South Asia contracted in the aftermath of tsunami and had registered a negative growth.

According to a recent report by the *International Panel on Climate Change* (IPCC), the Antarctic and Greenland ice sheets are melting faster than anticipated, as a result the sea level is expected to rise between 20 cm to 60 cm by 2100. This could lead to catastrophic flooding of countries like Maldives.[34] Besides, Maldives is also facing acute problems of coastal erosion, growing salinity, spreading of tropical diseases like Malaria and loss of coral ecosystem that supports the country's fishing industry. As a result, one of the first steps initiated by President Nasheed after his election victory was to create a sovereign wealth fund to be financed by tourism to buy a new homeland for the inhabitants of Maldives in India, Sri Lanka or even Australia.[35]

Maldives has also announced an ambitious programme to become the first country in the world to attain carbon neutrality by 2020. According to the plan, the fossil fuels could be virtually eliminated from the country. It also includes generation of electricity through renewable means and a transmission infrastructure that would include 155 large wind turbines and solar panels extending to half a square kilometre and a biomass plant using coconut husks. Battery banks would be set up to provide back-up when neither wind nor solar energy is available. The project not only covers homes and businesses, but even cars and boats, where diesel engines are being replaced by electrical engines run by batteries.[36] To draw global attention to the perils of global warming, President Nasheed held a cabinet meeting under water, where it signed a resolution calling for global cuts in carbon emissions.[37]

Maldives National Defence Force (MNDF)

The origin of Maldives defence forces lie in a police force that was established in 1933, but was subsequently disbanded. It was re-established in 1972 as a branch of security force called National Guards, which functioned under the Ministry of Public Safety. In 1979, the Ministry of Public Safety was renamed as the Ministry of Defence and National Security and the National Guards were called National Security Service (NSS). NSS continued to include the police force till 2004 when widespread protests against the head of the police force, Adam Zaheer, forced the then government of President Gayoom to separate the police force from NSS. The separation of police force entailed a change of mission and duties of NSS. The force was accordingly renamed as the Maldives National Defence Force (MNDF) on April 21, 2006.[38] Initially, an all male force, the MNDF began inducting women in March 1989 and women have since been a regular part of the force. The president of the country is the commander-in-chief and administers the MNDF through the defence minister. Maldives spends approximately 5.5 per cent of its GDP on defence.[39]

The MNDF is tasked with the responsibility of defending the security and sovereignty of the Maldives. Its primary task encompasses meeting all the internal and external security requirements of the Maldives, including protection of the EEZ and maintenance of peace and stability. It functions directly under the command, direction and guidance of the Minister of Defence and National Security and is headed by a Chief of Defence Force of the rank of Major General. It has five components namely the Coast Guard, Fire & Rescue Service, Infantry Services, Defence Institute for Training & Education (Training Command) and Support Services.[40]

The MNDF Coast Guard is the naval arm of the force and is the oldest service amongst the various components of the MNDF. It was officially established as a separate wing of the defence forces on January 1, 1980. Being an Island-nation, with 90 per cent of the country covered by sea and the remaining land mass scattered over a large area, of which the largest island does not measure more than eight square kilometres in area, most of the Maldives' security concerns lay within its maritime zones. This necessitates primacy of the Coast Guard within the MNDF. The main duties of the Coast Guard include search and rescue operations, naval deterrence, border control, maintenance of peace and security in the commercial sea lanes, and the protection of the country's EEZ.[41]

A concerted effort was made to strengthen the capabilities after the attack by PLOTE terrorists on November 3, 1988. Four Tracker II class, one Dagger class and one Cheverton class patrol craft were acquired from the UK. In 1998, two Coastal Surveillance Vessels and one Fast Landing Craft were built by the Colombo Dockyard.[42] After the Tsunami, an urgent need was felt for larger vessels with off-shore patrol capabilities, and to meet the immediate need, India donated *INS Tilangchang*, a Trinkat Class Fast Attack Craft of 46 metres length and in service with the Indian Navy to Maldives Coast

Guard. The ship was commissioned in the MNDF Coast Guard as *CGS Huravee*.[43] The Coast Guard subsequently commissioned a 35 m patrol craft on April 21, 2007 and a 42 m patrol craft on November 11, 2007. Both the ships were built by the Colombo Dockyard, Sri Lanka.[44]

The MNDF Infantry Services incorporate Quick Reaction Forces (QRF), Special Protection Group (SPG) and Special Forces (SF). These are organised into infantry heavy combat teams and combat groups with amphibious armoured vehicles and have the capability to be mobilised both at land and sea. QRF have been established at strategic locations and vulnerable areas and their tasks include conducting combat operations, counter-insurgency and counter-terrorism operations. It has also been tasked to assist the Coast Guard in maritime operations and civil authorities in crisis. Its other tasks are guarding key personalities, search and rescue operations and humanitarian and disaster relief activities. SPG also undertakes these activities but their primary task remains the protection of the president and visiting dignitaries. It was established after the abortive coup attempt of 1988. SF constitutes the elite cadres, which have been trained to perform their duties at any time and at any place. Their usage is envisaged in situations which are difficult for any normal infantry unit.[45]

The Training Command deals with the training and education of the MNDF personnel and is responsible for inculcating in them the values and expertise required for soldiering. It works towards preparing the force to meet new challenges and threats. The Defence Institute for Training and Education (DITE) is the main unit responsible for training and conducts institutional and individual training for all personnel. In addition, it is also responsible for training exercises and coordinates training activities of all units. Besides training at DITE, selected personnel are trained overseas. Joint training exercises with friendly countries are also conducted frequently to further hone the skills of the MNDF personnel.[46]

The Support Services are the backbone of the force and provide the necessary wherewithal for the MNDF to perform its task and are akin to the support arms in modern armies. Some sort of support services have existed in the force right from its inception and with the passage of time they have evolved to cater to the changing needs and demands of the MNDF. The major supporting units are:

(a) *Communication, Electronics and Information Technology Service (CEITS)*, which looks after all the communication needs of the force, including the IT requirements. It also looks after servicing and repairs of all communication equipment.

(b) *Project Planning, Implementation and Maintenance Service (PPIMS)*, which is responsible for designing and building new infrastructure for the MNDF and for maintaining the existing infrastructure. It also supervises the work of private agencies, wherever they are involved in any construction work for the MNDF.

(c) *Electrical and Mechanical Engineers (EME)*, which deals with the repair, maintenance and modification of all the electrical and mechanical equipment of the MNDF. Apart from this, they are also entitled for marine engineering, fibre glassing, air-conditioning, production of various metal structures, and to bring required modifications to the weapons used by the MNDF. They have the authority to check on any such item at any time which is entrusted to any unit of the MNDF.

(d) *Medical Service (MS)*, which is responsible for providing medical assistance to all the MNDF personnel, whether at sea or on land.

(e) *Transport Service (TS)*, which provides land and sea transport to the MNDF and is responsible for ensuring the prompt and efficient mobility of the force across the scattered island-nation.

(f) *Quarter Master Service (QMS)*, which is responsible for provision of all food and ration requirement and the issue of Q items for the MNDF. It provides most of the services to the force by contracting the responsibilities to private sector and is responsible for proper supervision of these contractors.

(g) *Band and Music Wing (BMW)*, which is a ceremonial detachment to accompany the force in ceremonial parades and all national ceremonies. It comprises of a brass band, a Western band, a pipe band, an orchestra band and a cultural band.[47]

Besides the above military components, the MNDF also comprises of Fire and Rescue Service (FRS), a non military component of the force, responsible for fire-fighting and providing rescue services to the public. The mutiny and division within the ranks of the MNDF during the coup on February 7, 2012 have raised serious questions about the training, cohesiveness and professionalism of the MNDF.

Foreign Cooperation

There have been numerous reports of various countries wanting to expand bilateral defence cooperation with Maldives. However, after closing of the facilities in Addu Atoll by the UK, Maldives has not had any worthwhile defence cooperation with any other country except India in recent past. During the visit of Maldivian defence minister to China in March 2009, the Chinese defence minister indicated China's desire to expand the bilateral defence cooperation and friendly exchanges between Chinese and Maldivian armed forces.[48] There have also been some speculation in the media about a

Chinese submarine base in Marao Island, but the Maldivian authorities have strongly denied both the existence of any Marao Island or any Chinese base in Maldives.

India's defence cooperation with Maldives has increased significantly since 1988, when Indian military assistance saved President Gayoom's regime from a coup launched by some dissidents backed by Tamil rebels from PLOTE. Even after the terrorist attack in September 2007, Indian intelligence agencies helped Maldivian authorities with the probe.[49] Maldives being strategically located, its infrastructure could be useful to India in patrolling the Indian Ocean. In 2001, India gifted radar to Maldives for surveillance and agreed to train the personnel in its operations. A memorial for Indian soldiers, who laid down their lives in Gan Island during Second World War, has also been constructed there. As mentioned earlier, India in 2006 gifted a fast patrol boat *INS Tillanchang* to the MNDF to enhance its capability to patrol its EEZ. Indian Coast Guard has been conducting a regular bilateral exercise with Maldives called *Dosti*. Indian armed forces also provide training to Maldivian armed forces personnel in various fields, including counter-insurgency.[50]

In February 2007, the then Indian Chief of the Army Staff, General J.J. Singh, had visited Maldives and discussed the modalities of mutual defence cooperation. He had met the president, the foreign minister and the defence minister and had also visited the newly established Maldives National Defence Forces Training Centre.[51] In February 2009, the then Indian Naval Chief, Admiral Sureesh Mehta, had visited Maldives and interacted with the Maldivian defence minister and chief of defence force for enhancing mutual cooperation.

Maldives has been strengthening its armed forces to meet the security challenges facing the country since 1988. The recent mutiny in the police and the dissensions within the ranks of the MNDF, which led to the forced resignation of President Nasheed, has brought into question the MNDF's professionalism. Probably it needs to enhance its selection and training process so as to emerge as an effective force capable of defending Maldives' national interests against both external and internal threats. However, being a mid-ocean mini state, it can never have a force strong enough to guarantee its security against any major external aggression or serious internal disorders. Maldives, therefore, would remain dependent on cooperation from the international community as well as the regional powers to ensure its national security.

However, the gravest threat that Maldives faces today is on the environmental front, as it fears being submerged to extinction by the rising sea levels. The environmental security has therefore assumed a salience and Maldives has initiated steps in this regard. However, unless it manages to convince the international community of the impending disaster, Maldives cannot do much in this field on its own.

NOTES

1. K.R. Singh, *Navies of South Asia*, Rupa & Co., New Delhi, 2002, p. 222.
2. Ibrahim Hussain Zaki and Regina Mulay Parakh, *Small States Security Dilemma: A Maldivian Perception*, Lancer Books, New Delhi, 2008, p. 35.
3. Ibid, p. 38.
4. Ibid, pp. 20-22.
5. Ajay Makan, "British campaign group 'partly responsible' for explosion: Maldives President", *Minivan News*, Online Edition, September 30, 2007.
6. "Maldives President survives bid on life", *The Hindu*, January 9, 2008.
7. Aiman Rasheed, "Attack on controversial preacher Dr Afrashim", *Minivan News*, February 2, 2008.
8. Philip Sherwell and Ben Leapman, "Has Islamic terrorism arrived on Maldives?", *Telegraph*, Internet Edition, October 1, 2007.
9. "Maldives militant move condemned", *BBC News*, October 18, 2007, at http://news.bbc.co.uk/2/hi/south_asia/7050820.stm (Accessed February 1, 2008).
10. "Maldives were 'warned of Islamic danger'", *The Telegraph*, Internet Edition, October 1, 2007.
11. Ajay Makan, "Police and Army lay siege to Himandhoo Mosque", *Minivan News*, Online Edition, October 6, 2007.
12. Ibid.
13. "Terrorists threaten tourist paradise", October 22, 2007, at http://www.news.com.au/travel/news/terrorists-threaten-tourist-paradise/story-e6frfq80-1111114696204
14. Ajay Makan, "Fundamentalism biggest threat to Maldives Security: Government Advisor", *Minivan News*, Online Edition, October 7, 2008. Also, see Chan Tau Chou, "Maldives faces social divide", *Al Jazeera*, November 6, 2007, at http://www.aljazeera.com/NEWS/ASIA/2007/11/2008525138440l955.html
15. Ajay Makan, no. 11.
16. "HRCM: Young girls being deprived of education in some areas of Maldives", *Haveeru Online*, February 26, 2009.
17. Ahmed Nazeer, "National Security Committee to forward resolution prohibiting Israeli flight operations", *Minivan News*, December 28, 2011.
18. Ahmed Nazeer, "Mosque, SAARC monument vandalized in Addu", *Minivan News*, November 20, 2011; Ahmed Adhshan, "MP Ali Waheed calls on Addu mayor to rmove SAARC monuments", *Haveeru Online*, December 25, 2011. Also, see "Maldives: Islam becoming an election issue?", *Daily Mirror*, December 28, 2011.
19. "Thousands demonstrate in Maldives for and against strict Islamic law", *The Seattle Times*, December 23, 2011, at http://seattletimes.com/html/nationworld/2017080027_apasmaldivesmuslimprotest.html
20. Eleanor Johnstone, "Calls for religious tolerance 'shocked the nation': Chief Justice Faiz", *Minivan News*, January 1, 2012.
21. Hussain Fiyaz Moosa, "Maldives 'considering' complete ban of alcohol and pork", *Haveeru Online*, December 28, 2011.

22. "Religious scholars oppose SAARC monuments, Israeli flights", *Minivan News*, January 1, 2012.
23. Tom Wright, "Islamism Set Stage for Maldives Coup", *The Wall Street Journal*, February 11, 2012.
24. K.R. Singh, no. 1, p. 225.
25. "Maldives: climate change threatens right to housing, says UN expert", February 26, 2009, at http://www.un.org/apps/news/story.asp?NewsID=30026&Cr=housing&Cr1=climate (Accessed March 9, 2009). Also, see "Lessons of the Post Tsunami reconstruction in Maldives are crucial to design international strategies for climate change adaptation", Press Release, February 26, 2009, at http://www.unhchr.ch/huricane/huricane.nsf/view01/E4E1B0832D3EC025C1257569005189C7?opendocument
26. "Maldives: The new terror hub?", August 26, 2007, at http://www.timesnow.tv/Newsdtls.aspx?NewsID=2261 (Accessed August 27, 2007). Also, at http://www.atolltimes.com/asia-and-region/127-maldives-the-new-terror-hub.html
27. K.R. Singh, no. 1, p. 223.
28. Satheesan Kumaaran, "Sri Lanka and Maldives fall victims to regional and international hegemonic powers", *The Island*, Internet Edition, February 27, 2008.
29. K.R. Singh, no. 1, p. 229.
30. "Somali pirates pose a great threat to Maldives-US Military", *Miadhu News*, February 20, 2011.
31. Zaki and Parakh, no. 2, pp. 45-48.
32. Ibid, p. 48.
33. Ibid, p. 56.
34. Robin Mckie, "Figures deliver stark warning of a flooded future", *New Zealand Herald*, March 9, 2009.
35. Frances Williams, "Climate is rights issue, says Maldives minister", *The Financial Times*, London, March 4, 2007.
36. Duncan Clark, "Maldives first to go carbon neutral" *The Observer*, March 15, 2009, p. 14.
37. "Maldives cabinet makes a splash", *BBC News*, October 17, 2009, at http://news.bbc.co.uk/2/hi/8311838.stm (Accessed January 15, 2012)
38. The official website of the MNDF, at http://www.mndf.gov.mv/about.asp (Accessed March 11, 2009).
39. See http://en.wikipedia.org/wiki/Maldives_National_Defence_Force (Accessed March 9, 2009).
40. Ibid. Also, see the official website of the MNDF, at http://www.mndf.gov.mv/about.asp (Accessed March 11, 2009).
41. The official website of the MNDF, at http://www.mndf.gov.mv/about.asp (Accessed March 11, 2009).
42. See "Maldivian Coast Guard", at http://en.wikipedia.org/wiki/Maldivian_Coast_Guard (Accessed March 9, 2009).
43. Ibid. Also, see Alok Bansal, "Onset of Multiparty Democracy in Maldives" in Ashok K. Behuria (ed.), *India and its Neighbours: Towards a New Partnership*, Institute for Defence Studies and Analyses, New Delhi, 2009, p. 31 and Mohammed Khalid, "India and the Indian Ocean—A Geo-Economic Dimension", *Journal of Indian Ocean Studies*, 15 (1), April 2007, p. 67.
44. See "Maldivian Coast Guard", at http://en.wikipedia.org/wiki/Maldivian_Coast_Guard (Accessed March 9, 2009).

45. The official website of the MNDF, at http://www.mndf.gov.mv/mndf_infantry.asp (Accessed March 9, 2009).
46. The official website of the MNDF, at http://www.mndf.gov.mv/about.asp (Accessed March 11, 2009).
47. Ibid.
48. Yang Yang, "China vows to Expand Military Cooperation with Maldives", February 19, 2009, at http://english.cri.cn/6909/2009/02/19/1361s455799.htm (Accessed March 17, 2009).
49. "Don't worry, no Al Qaeda in Maldives", *DNA* (Daily News & Analysis), December 2, 2007.
50. "India to train Maldivian army in counter terrorism", *The Times of India,* Internet Edition, November 13, 2007.
51. "Indian Army chief concludes visit", *Minivan News,* Internet Edition, February 17, 2007.

Chapter Five

The Nepal Army at the Crossroads

Nihar Nayak

As an institution, the Nepal(ese)[1] Army (NA), which until 2006 was known as the Royal Nepal Army (RNA), has played an important role in the evolution of Nepal as a modern state. The NA has evolved as a professional force over time, and it is at the crossroads due to massive political transformation in Nepal since the abolition of monarchy in 2008. While Nepal is transiting from monarchy to democracy, the Army has found it challenging to adapt to the evolving political situation. It is natural especially because as an institution, its objectives, structure and functions were decided by the erstwhile ruling classes.

Professionally, the NA has contributed to the maximum number of UN peacekeeping operations. It is also important to note that the NA has largely functioned under civilian authority since the beginning of political transition in 2006, and has supported the peace process by integrating the Maoist combatants in its command structure. Although the NA had initially taken some rigid position on the integration issue, later it agreed to cooperate with the civilian government. The NA is not known to have tried to take advantage of the fragile political situation in the country for its own aggrandisement, unlike the armies of some other South Asian countries, such as, Pakistan and Bangladesh.

I. Origin/Evolution

The earliest name given to the Army of Nepal was the Gorkhali Army or *Tilanga* (1559). It was renamed as Nepal Army by Prime Minister Chandra Shamsher Jang Bahadur Rana (1901-29). Later King Mahendra (1955-72) added the prefix 'Royal' to it and renamed it as Royal Nepal Army (RNA) in 1962. After the passing of the new Nepal Army Act, 2006 on May 18, 2006, the term 'Royal' was dispensed with and the Army was called 'Nepal Army' or *Nepali Sena*. To avoid confusion, the term 'Nepal Army' is being used uniformly to connote the Army of Nepal.

The Army of Nepal was formed as an organised force in 1559, making it the one of the oldest armies in South Asia. During King Prithivi Narayan Shah's reign (1768-1775), it acquired modern weapons for its military campaigns beyond the so-called Gorkha State and the physical limits of the modern Nepalese State.[2] According to Gen. (Retd.) Ashok K. Mehta, the Royal Nepalese Army (RNA)—the predecessor of the present Army—"traces its origin to 1748 when the first army unit, *Shri Nath Gan*, was raised under the order of King Prithvirajnarayan Shah."[3] The NA had participated in the two World Wars and impressed the British commanders.

During the democratic movement of 1950, the NA supported the Rana rulers. It was named as Royal Nepalese Army (RNA) under King Mahendra's regime in 1962. The Army played a major role in curbing democratic movements in the 1990s and in April 2006. The RNA was always identified as the King's Army rather than an Army for the protection of the common people. After the abolition of the monarchy in May 2008, it has remained under civilian control. It has been observed that the Nepal Army has always maintained its loyalty to the "executive authority"[4] despite changes in name and structure.

Although the primary objective and purpose of the RNA, like any other army in the world, had been to preserve and protect Nepal's territorial integrity against external aggression, it regarded the King as above the State and his protection as its ultimate duty. During the 1990s, almost all the prime ministers of Nepal faced the brunt of the palace-NA nexus while deploying the Army against the Maoists. Former Prime Minister G.P. Koirala, in an interview to the *British Broadcasting Corporation* (BBC) on May 6, 2005, disclosed that "When the Maoists had influence in only two places in [Nepal], we repeatedly told [King] to use the military against the Maoists...But the military was reluctant to go and the King was hesitant to move."[5]

2. Nepal's Security Environment

The dissolution of the Constituent Assembly (CA) followed by political stalemate has complicated the political transition in Nepal and has also adversely affected its economy. Nepal has no legitimate government or legislature since May 27, 2012. The public order is also in bad shape. Around the world, there is a growing perception that Nepal is becoming a failed state.

The country has been facing multiple challenges. Some of the key issues begging serious attention are: atrocities by the Maoist combatants who have been disqualified from joining the army; presence of illegal armed groups in the Terai region; turf wars between the youth wings affiliated to various political parties;[6] human rights violations; intra-party factional conflicts; wide divergence of views on national issues; high inflation; criminalisation of the India-Nepal border; food deficit in the western and mid-western districts; poor communication infrastructure; frequent road blockades and general strikes by various trade unions and political parities, intra-party conflicts, etc.

There is once again talk of achieving political goals by unleashing a class struggle. The All Nepal National Independent Students Union-Revolutionary (ANNISU-R) leaders declared on October 2, 2012 at Tribhuvan University that the student wing of the Communist Party of Nepal-Maoist (CPN-Maoist) was ready to lead the people's revolution through a series of student uprising. They also criticised the neo-revisionism in the Unified Communist Party of Nepal-Maoist (UCPN-Maoist) party and emphasised on achieving their political goal by unleashing a class struggle.[7]

The split in the UCPN (Maoist) and formation of the CPN-Maoist has not only complicated the differences between the political parties, but has also emerged as a serious public order issue. The central committee of CPN-Maoist on September 5, 2012 passed a resolution that it would unleash another round of armed struggle if its peaceful struggle did not help it to come to power. It also decided to form people's governments both at the local and central levels.[8] Although the top leaders of CPN-Maoist have been saying that armed struggle is not their immediate goal, according to some media reports, the party has formed a military wing on lines of the earlier People's Liberation Army (PLA). It has asked Netra Bikram Chand, who also heads its youth wing, to look into this aspect. Initially, it was trying to accommodate the former Maoist combatants in the new structure by taking advantage of their grievances against the UCPN (Maoist). The reports also indicate that the party has already collected some weapons, which were not submitted before the United Nations Mission in Nepal (UNMIN), for training purposes. It has also formed military divisions by appointing formed commanders.[9] It submitted a charter of 70-point demands to the government on September 5, 2012, warning that it would launch people's uprising followed by armed struggle if these demands are not addressed. As part of its demands, on September 26, 2012, it imposed a ban on the movement of Indian vehicles, playing of Indian movies and music in Nepal.[10] Indian traders on the India-Nepal border region complained before the Indian authorities that the CPN-Maoist cadres have been attacking and looting their goods trucks.[11]

Nepal has also become vulnerable to ethnic tensions especially in the eastern, far western and Terai region after the failure of the CA on the federalism issue. The ethnic groups and Madhesis suspect that there could be a grand strategy by the upper-caste ruling elites not to have ethnic-based federalism. On this issue, many Janajati leaders have abandoned their parent parties—the NC and UML—to form their own parties focusing on ethnic federalism. Some Janajati groups have also made tactical alliances with the UCPN (Maoist) and Madhesi-based political parties.[12] The NA is the only organisation that can take on a possible secessionist movement originating from this ethnic divide.

Nepal's Geo-political/Strategic Significance

As a landlocked country between China and India, Nepal has benefited from its geographical location, especially because of the counterbalancing efforts of these two countries. Nepal has turned their competitive quest for influence (in Nepal) to its advantage. According to Kunda Dixit, "Nepal [Monarchy] played China and India off against each other, getting aid from each and letting the Chinese build highways right down to the Indian border. The King uses that fear to tweak India and it works brilliantly."[13] It is often surmised that the political violence lingered for thirteen years in Nepal because of the machinations of major powers like the US, the UK and China. Any future political system in Nepal would be influenced directly or indirectly by these major powers. India, therefore, has strong stakes in the ongoing political transformation in Nepal.

Nepal alone in South Asia has an open border with India, around 1,800 km long. It also has topographical similarities along the northern borders of India. In these conditions, according to a senior Indian Army officer with whom this author interacted (on July 24, 2012), India is vulnerable to Chinese attacks during a conflict situation. The Chinese Army can negotiate the Himalayan barriers in Nepal without much resistance. India has developed physical defences on the borders with China except in the sectors adjoining Nepal. Given the security infrastructure that China has built in Tibet in the last fifteen years, India's vulnerability has increased further *vis-à-vis* China. Any political turmoil in Nepal would also have a major spill over effect in India.

Of particular concern to India is Pakistan's presence in Nepal. Pakistan has three major agenda items in Nepal, which are succeeding because of the open border and anti-India sentiments fomented by certain regimes in Nepal. Pakistan's first agenda is to use Nepal as a launching pad for spreading militancy/terrorism in India. Pakistan has also been using the open border to supply fake Indian currency via Nepal with the objective of destabilising the Indian economy. Pakistan's third agenda item is to establish linkages with the Muslim population living in the Terai region and spread anti-India sentiments there, which can be leveraged for sustained use by Pakistani intelligence in future for asymmetric war against India. The Muslim-dominated districts of Nepal are reportedly getting regular funding from some Gulf counties and Pakistan's Inter-Services Intelligence (ISI) is reportedly handling these funds.[14] There is also an overwhelming apprehension in India's security establishment of a possible linkage between the Nepalese Maoists, especially the Mohan Vaidya faction, and the Indian Naxalites. Political victory of the Maoists, who have branded India as expansionist power, could embolden the Indian Naxalites to harbour similar aspirations of radical political change in the country.

The growing triangular relationship between Pakistan, China and some groups in Nepal is viewed with serious concern in India. Massod Khalid, Additional Secretary in the Pakistan Ministry of Foreign Affairs, and in-charge of South Asia, had reportedly stated that "both Nepal and Pakistan attach greater importance to the relations with that giant neighbour [China] to the north."[15] China's newfound interest in protecting Nepal's territorial integrity also signals a change for proactive engagement with Nepal to minimise/reduce India's negative influence. On November 4, 2008, Liu Hong Chai, the International Bureau Chief of the Chinese Communist Party who met some Nepali journalists in Beijing, said, "We assure the Nepali people that any foreign conspiracy to disintegrate Nepal will be appropriately dealt with by China."[16]

For India's growing need for energy and water, Nepal with its snow-fed rivers could be a major source. Jo Johnson has observed that "as the lower riparian country, India has a strategic interest in ensuring the stability of the Himalayan sources of some of the subcontinent's most vital rivers, among them the Ganges."[17] Since China has a similar interest, Nepal will benefit by bargaining with these two competitive entities. A former Chinese Ambassador to Nepal, Zeng Xuyong, has said, "China will provide and actively cooperate in the energy development of Nepal in the future. The Chinese assistance can be either grant or BOT based."[18] Hiranyala Shrestha has observed that future water resources cooperation between Nepal and China could be in terms of "construction of a bypass from Brahmaputra through the Arun River which can permanently solve the water dispute of this region."[19]

For China, Nepal is a geographical and cultural barrier between Tibet and Tibetan refugees living in India. China feels insecure over India's leverage in Nepal as well as the presence of the US, UK and the EU. China has always looked for a credible nationalistic force in Nepal for political stability, hence its support for the monarchy as long as it lasted. Successive kings in Nepal served the Chinese interests well by taking strong measures against Tibetans and anti-China movements in Nepal.

Other than China and India, the US also has strategic interests in Nepal. During the Cold War, the US identified Nepal as a strategic location to prevent the spread of communism to South Asia. When the Maoists began their armed struggle in 1996, the US declared that it had "a strong interest in helping the people of that country overcome the serious political problems they face, and the developmental problems from which much of their current political crisis derives."[20] Washington also considered Nepal as the ideal listening post to monitor not just communist China but the whole of South Asia as well. Bruce Vaughn observed that "American foreign policy interests in Nepal seek to prevent the collapse of Nepal which, should it become a failed state, could provide operational or support territory for terrorists."[21]

Terrain

Nepal broadly comprises three kinds of terrains: Mountain, Hill, and Terai. They run parallel east to west as continuous ecological belts, occasionally bisected by river systems. The government divided them into development sectors within the framework of regional development planning. There are also three major river systems that run from East to West: Kosi, Narayani (Gandak in India) and Karnali.[22]

Threat Perceptions

Though Nepal's frontiers have always been regarded by India and China as valid international boundaries, the country's geo-strategic position between China's restive Tibetan population and the Indian heartland places it in a vulnerable position. Gen. (Retd.) Ashok Mehta in response to a query—whether the Royal Nepalese Army (RNA) factored in any external threat, either from China or India—observed that its deployment in the 1970s in the Terai region indicated that the main threat, as perceived by the Nepal Army, would be from the south—that is India.[23]

According to the RNA's strategic review report in 1988, the RNA was expected to fight both external and internal security challenges:

> India and China were identified as the external threats. Against India, the RNA was to fight a series of prolonged battles for up to fifteen days. In the case of China, taking tortuous terrain into account, the delay in action—to keep the enemy at bay—was to last for twenty days, during which time Nepal would seek UN assistance and mediation.[24]

In accordance with the perception of the report that India was the biggest threat, Nepal purchased air defence guns from China in the late 1980s. Most importantly, Nepal also frequently changed the size of its troop formations. During the Maoist insurgency, one RNA document alleged that India was providing support to the Maoists and suggested that Nepal should take assistance from the US and the UK to counter this threat.[25]

Nepal currently does not have a military doctrine. Earlier, the Army used to prepare reports on "threat" perceptions based on its internal circulations.[26] Nepal-based security analysts have been seriously urging for a military doctrine as a means of providing clear guidance and orientation to the Army. A doctrine will help it formulate a strategy, recruitment, logistic arrangements and arms and weapons procurement.

Domestic Challenges

Other than ethnic conflict, illegal armed groups and periodic extremist movements, the harsh topography and inclement weather remains a major challenge to the stability of Nepal. The NA is the only organisation which can provide logistical support to the civilian government in the mountainous region. Troops have to march over precarious trails subject to washouts, landslides, avalanches of boulders, ice and snow. Supply drops by helicopters and airplanes, which are critically short in the NA, can be made only in favourable weather and in the restricted areas accessible to troops. In the lowlands, ground movement is virtually impossible during the wet season.[27]

The NA will face the difficult task of remaining apolitical if the country undergoes prolonged political turmoil in future. There is already a trust deficit between the NA and the political parties. Some of the latter still consider the NA as a potential threat to democracy, and argue that it still supports the monarchy. The non-Maoist parties believe that modernisation and restructuring of the Army under a Maoist movement could be utilised by them to capture power. Second, the Army may face internal disturbances if the regularly recruited NA personnel discriminate against the around 1,459 former Maoist combatants recently integrated into the Army. A major concern could also be adherence to basic principles of human rights. For example, despite protests to the NA by civil society and human rights groups over Col. Raju Basnet's history of human rights violations, on October 3, 2012, the NA promoted him to the rank of brigadier general.

3. Military Doctrine/Strategic Thought

In the absence of any written and well-spelt-out military doctrine, the NA maintains an operational doctrine for tactical purposes. The NA enunciated its duty and responsibility for the first time in June 2002 as defender of Nepal's territorial integrity, sovereignty and independence.[28] Providing assistance to the civilian government in the maintenance of internal security was stated to be its second priority.

According to Chiran Thapa, a military expert, "Nepal shall:

- refrain from branding any state as an enemy
- not employ the instrument of force in its interstate relations
- not pre-emptively deploy its military against any state
- not join any military alliance unless Nepal's national interest is imperilled
- not allow the stationing of foreign troops within its territory
- maintain a military force capable of conducting defensive operations
- consistently train its military to engage in both conventional and asymmetric warfare
- strictly adhere to the charter of the UN and international laws
- continue with its commitment to assist in maintaining international security.

Under this doctrine, the following acts constitute threats which will prompt a military response:

- incursion into Nepali territory by any hostile foreign armed force
- armed assault against the Nepali population or the Nepali armed forces by any organised armed group
- armed insurgency aimed at undermining the authority of the state."[29]

As peacetime activities, the NA has decided to engage its forces in humanitarian assistance, disaster relief operations, nature-conservation activities and international peace-making efforts. Some scholars and retired army officers argue that the NA should refrain from infrastructure-building activities as it is likely to affect its combat performance.

Although, the NA until recently was rated as a ceremonial force and the king's Army, major doctrinal changes in its outlook are expected in the coming years. In the absence of the monarchy and given the commanding position of the Maoists in the Nepalese polity, the NA is likely to focus more on national security and modernisation programmes, and seek assistance from external forces, other than India. The civilian government would prefer minimum use of the NA in internal security matters.

4. Structure and Formation

The NA was restructured over time keeping in view the political changes taking place at the domestic and regional levels. Post-1950, the NA experienced the first major restructuring in 1955. King Mahendra in 1959 introduced the Army Act, keeping the NA under direct control of the King.

Despite the 1990 Constitution and formation of the National Security Council (NSC), the Army maintained its loyalty towards the monarchy due to the preponderant influence of the King(s) in the Nepal polity. In fact, all major changes in the NA until 2006 were conducted under the 1959 Army Act. King Gyanendra increased its strength and modernised it further in 2001. A new Army Act[30] replaced the 1959 Act on May 18, 2006 after the reinstatement of Parliament in April 2006.

The Interim Constitution (IC) of 2007 has a separate section on the Army. Under Article 144(A1), the President of the country shall be its supreme commander. Under Article 144(A3), the President on the recommendation of the Council of Ministers shall control, mobilize and manage it in accordance with the law. The Council of Ministers shall, with the consent of the political parties and by seeking the advice of the concerned committee of the Legislature-Parliament, formulate an extensive work plan for its democratisation and implement it. In other words, ultimately, the Council of Ministers is the highest decision-making body which will be responsible for the Army's overall development excepting the operational technicalities, which lie with the COAS. If the COAS makes a proposal on Amy restructuring or modernisation, the cabinet has to take the consent of the political parties and the concerned committee of the Legislature/ Parliament before implementing it. This provision is there because of the transition phase. The provisions related to other political parties' consent may not be there in the final version of the Constitution.

There is a National Defence Council (NDC) to make recommendations to the Council of Ministers about mobilisation, operation and use of the Army. It comprises six members—Prime Minister (Chairman), Defence Minister, Home Minister, and three other ministers nominated by the Prime Minister. The Defence Secretary is its secretary. The NDC is mostly a recommendatory body and the Council of Ministers may not abide by its recommendations. Interestingly, in its earlier form—National Security Council (NSC), under the 1990 Constitution, the COAS was a member of the NSC.[31]

Command Structure

The NA is organised into six divisions—Far-Western, Mid-Western, Western, Central, Eastern, and Valley—with separate Aviation, Parachute, and Security brigades as well as brigade-sized directorates encompassing air defence, artillery, engineers, logistics, and signals. In addition, approximately 3,400 of the Gurkha forces serve in the British Army and 40,000 serve in the Indian Army.[32] The NA divisions are according to the five development regions plus

Kathmandu Valley. This reorganisation was designed to improve its capacity to fight the Maoist insurgency. The current structure of the Army was decided during King Gyanendra's time. In 2002, its strength was increased from around 45,000 to above 100,000. The day-to-day affairs of the Army are currently conducted under the Nepal Army Act, 2006.

Each division is headed by a major general and comprises a number of brigades. Each combat division has combat brigades, combat support units and combat service support units. As of 2006, the Army had 15 combat (Infantry) brigades.[33] However, other sources indicated that the NA has got around 24 brigades, including two special brigades. As part of the Comprehensive Peace Agreements, the top political parties agreed to form a new directorate to accommodate the former Maoist combatants in 2011. The directorate is headed by a major general.

Chain of Command

The COAS is a four-star general, who leads the Nepal Army. Assisting him and accountable to him are the Chief of General Staff (CGS) and Chief of Staff (COS), both three-star generals (Lieutenant General). The CGS handles operation, training and intelligence and provides seamless architecture of integrative training, operation and intelligence systems within the Army. The COS is accountable for UN peacekeeping operations, nature conservation and wildlife preservation, National Cadet Corps (NCC) and various welfare schemes in the army. There are four directorates, seven thematic departments, an office of Principal Staff Officers (PSOs) and six divisions under the direct command of COAS. There are four directorates, seven thematic departments, an office of PSOs and six divisions under the direct command of COAS.[34] (Appendix-4)

The Inspector General (IG) inspects the operational readiness of the Army. The Adjutant General (AG) ensures that the human resources development is both quantitatively and qualitatively optimised and utilised to its full potential. It is responsible for recruitment, records, pay and services, posting and promotions of all Junior Commissioned Officers (JCOs) and Non-Commissioned Officers (NCOs), ceremonies, legal and medical services. It also formulates directives that ensure effective regimentation is maintained at parades and ceremonies, and that adequate functional discipline is adhered to. The Quarter Master General (QMG) deals with logistic matters. It is responsible for acquiring suitable accommodation, rations and clothing, provision and procurement of military aircraft, management and maintenance of fuel, transport and transfer of personnel and shifting logistics. The Master General of Ordnance (MGO) is responsible for planning, procurement and maintenance of weapons, ammunition, equipment and clothing. The IG, AG, QMG and MGO are headed by two-star generals.[35]

The Military Secretary (MS) looks after the career graph of officers and their postings. The department also conducts career courses for officers and arranges for their course training outside the country. The Directorate of Research and Development (R&D) conducts research on the latest military hardwar. The Directorate of Defence Production (DDP) is responsible for the production of ammunition and explosives and uniforms. The Directorate of Development and Construction (DDC) is responsible for construction of infrastructure. The Directorate of Public Relations (DPR) is responsible for public relations and media work. The Department of Administration and Finance looks after finances. The MS, Directorate of Research and Analysis, DDP, DDC, DPR, and Department of Administration and Finance are all headed by one-star generals (Brigadier General rank).[36]

Restructuring Proposal

The NA for the first time placed a proposal for restructuring in May 2012 before the Parliamentary State Affairs Committee (SAC) by indicating that the "current structure was 'obsolete' and incompatible with the international models."[37] Prime Minister Baburam Bhattarai endorsed the plan and observed that the NA had been following a 47-year-old structure when its strength was around 18,000. The SAC directed the government to have a consensus among political parties on the issue. The dissolution of the CA on May 27, 2012 delayed the restructuring plan. The proposal was again presented by the new COAS, General Gaurav Shamsher Rana, on September 25, 2012. In brief, the NA proposal is to create two additional posts of lieutenant generals, six major generals, 10 brigadier generals, 14 colonels and 50 lieutenant colonels.[38] The plan might be delayed further due to the absence of a constituent assembly and parliament, widening of the differences between the political parties on contentious issues, and non-existence of SAC.

Air Power

Nepal has no separate Air Force but has several aircrafts in the 11th Brigade, also known as the Nepal Army Air Wing, which was established in 1979. The main objective of this wing is transport, flying paratroopers and assistance during natural disasters. Scattered around the country are thirty-six airfields that can support military operations. Many of them are configured only for short-take-off-and-landing operations. During the operations against the Maoists, Nepal acquired several types of aircraft—Mi-17, M28 Skytruck, ALH Lancer, Dhruv, Puma, Alouette, Skyvan, M-28 and HS-748. The UK delivered two Islanders and two Mi-17s free of charge. China delivered an MA-60 (a Y-7 derivative).[39] As part of the NA modernisation process, some military experts in Nepal, of late, have suggested that taking into consideration topography of Nepal and nature of future warfare, the NA should strengthen its Air Wing by acquiring VTOL (vertical-take-off-and-landing) and STOL (short-take-off-and landing) aircrafts.

Ethnic Composition

There are around 100 ethnic/caste groups in Nepal as they have been identified in the 2001 census. Only six of these groups have more than 5 per cent of the national population; only 18 groups have a population size greater that 1 per cent. The table 1 indicates that Chhetris dominate in the Nepal Army with 43.64 per cent of the total manpower. Dalits and minority groups have less than 1 per cent representation in the NA. After Madhesi uprising in 2007 and their demand for representation of Madhesis in the NA, the government had decided to introduce reservation of certain percentages of Madhesis in the NA. So far, the NA has reservation for five different ethnic communities—Magar, Gurung, Tamang, Kiranti/Limbu and Madhesi.[40]

Table 1: State of Castes/Ethnic Inclusion in Nepalese Army

S.N.	*Caste/Ethnic Groups*	*Population (2011 Census)*	*% of Total Population*	*Representation in NA*	*% of Total Representation*
1.	Chhetri	3,593,496	15.80	39,824	43.64
2.	Brahmin	2,896,477	12.74	7,634	8.36
3.	Magar	1,622,421	7.14	6,444	7.06
4.	Tamang	1,282,304	5.64	5,473	6.00
5.	Newar	1,245,232	5.48	6,035	6.61
6.	Tharu	1,629,691	7.17	4,343	4.76
7.	Gurung	543,571	2.39	3,145	3.45
8.	Thakuri	334,120	1.47	2,967	3.25
9.	Kami	895,954	3.94	2,488	2.73
10.	Rai/Sunuwar	635,151	2.79	2,687	2.94
11.	Sanyasi	199,127	0.88	2,058	2.25
12.	Dhamai/Dholi	390,305	1.72	1,900	2.08
13.	Sarki	318,989	1.40	1,034	1.13
14.	Gharti	117,568	0.52	1,257	1.38
15.	Kumal	99,389	0.44	763	0.84
16.	Hajam/Thakur	98,169	0.43	707	0.77
17.	Limbu	359,379	1.58	434	0.47
18.	Majhi	72,614	0.31	325	0.36
19.	Teli/Yadav/Rajput	304,536	1.34	260	0.28
20.	Darai	14,859	0.07	142	0.16
21.	Sherpa/Thakali	1,80,558	0.74	120	0.13
22.	Dusad/Paswan	158,525	0.70	124	0.13
23.	Danuwar	53,229	0.23	104	0.11

S.N.	Caste/Ethnic Groups	Population (2011 Census)	% of Total Population	Representation in NA	% of Total Representation
24.	Muslim	971,056	4.27	12	0.01
25.	Mechhe/Tatma	3,763	0.02	47	0.05
26.	Jirel	5,316	0.02	52	0.06
27.	Thami	22,999	0.10	10	0.01
28.	Chepang	52,237	0.23	09	0.01
29.	Pahari	11,505	0.05	33	0.04
30.	Raji	2,399	0.01	06	0.006
31.	Others	00	00	821	0.9

Source: Nepal Army, Nepal. Data as of April 1, 2009.[41]

As far as top official ranks are concerned, except former NA chief General Chhatra Man Singh Gurung, all COASs have been Chhetries or Thakuris, though Magar, Gurung, Rai, Limbu and Brahmin ethnic groups have a substantial number of soldiers. Officers from the Shah, Rana and Thapa clans monopolise the senior posts. Prakash A. Raj has observed that in 2004 only 13 out of 53 senior officers of the RNA belonged to Janajatis,[42] to which most of the Maoists belong, especially the Kham Magar ethnic group.

Table 2: Ethnic Affiliation of Senior Army Officers
Brigadier General and Above

Caste/Ethnic groups	National %	N A %
Chettri (including Ranas)	15.80	38.10
Brahmin (Hill)	12.74	7.90
Magar (Hill Ethnic)	7.14	7.90
Tharu (Terai Ethnic)	6.75	0.00
Tamang (Hill Ethnic)	5.64	1.60
Newar	5.48	6.30
Muslim	4.27	0.00
Kami (Dalit caste)	3.94	0.00
Yadav (Terai caste)	3.94	0.00
Rai (Hill Ethnic)	2.79	3.20
Gurung (Hill Ethnic)	2.39	15.90
Damai (Dalit caste)	1.72	0.00
Limbu (Hill Ethnic)	1.58	9.50
Thakuri	1.47	9.50

Source: Prakash Nepali and Phanindra Subba, "Civil-Military Relations and the Maoist Insurgency in Nepal", *Small Wars and Insurgencies*, 16 (1), March 2005, p. 100.

Defence Expenditure

Nepal has consistently increased its military budget since 2001. In the early 1980s, Nepal spent less than one per cent of its GNP on defence (US $30.353 million in 1983–84).[43] As indicated in Table 2, since 2001 the government has allocated more money for defence modernisation than for the social sectors.

Table 3: Military Expenditure* of Nepal since 1996
Start of Financial Year: July

Year	*In local currency (m. rupees)*	*In constant (2010) US$ m.*	*As percentage of gross domestic product*
1996	2,358	74.5	0.8
1997	2,583	79	0.8
1998	2,995	80.1	0.8
1999	3,486	86.7	0.9
2000	3,817	95.3	0.8
2001	5,882	123	1.1
2002	7,420	164	1.3
2003	8,255	183	1.5
2004	10,996	218	1.6
2005	11,745	241	1.7
2006	11,136	226	1.6
2007	11,389	210	1.4
2008	14,712	219	1.3
2009	17,811	244	1.4
2010	19,491	255	1.4
2011	19,101	241	NA

*Figures for these countries do not include spending on paramilitary forces.
Convention: US$ m. = Million US dollars; NA = Data not available, th. = thousand; m. = million; b. = billion
Military expenditure figures in local currency is presented according to the financial year of the country in question. Figures in constant US dollars and as a share of GDP are presented by calendar year.
Source: The SIPRI Military Expenditure Database 2011.

Integrating the eligible Maoist cadres into the NA would raise the defence budget further, cutting into long-term development programmes. Downsizing of the NA after integrating the PLA cadres will be a hard option, considering the disaffection it will cause among those retrenched. In fact, the NA proposal on creating senior positions only will cost the government an additional (Nepalese Rupees) NRP 120.5 million per year. The government has already spent a total NRP 9.61 billion for management of the Maoists combatants since November 2006.[44]

5. Weaknesses

The first and foremost weakness of the NA is its poor public image, despite its cooperation in the peace process and its willingness to function under civilian control. It is still considered as an anti-people force dominated by upper-caste hill Chhetris and Brahmins. There are also a large number of allegations of human rights violations by the NA personnel during the counterinsurgency operations against the Maoists. NA officials have also been accused of human rights violations during their deployment as part of the UN peacekeeping force in Africa.

Second, the NA lacks war experience. Its structure itself is not intended for any major war. Its experience in counterinsurgency operations has also not been quite effective. Third, there are allegations of mismanagement of Army welfare fund and corruption. Fourth, the NA is not an inclusive organisation. Dalits, women and Madhesis and marginalised groups are under-represented in it. Many officers of the NA are not in favour of a separate battalion for Madhesis. Last but not least, the military budget is inadequate.

6. Civil-Military Relations

Civil-military relations in Nepal have varied from regime to regime. In 1960, after King Mahendra took over power, dismissing the first popularly elected government of the Nepali Congress headed by B.P. Koirala, he introduced the party-less *Panchayat* System. He tightened his personal control over the military by weeding out overly ambitious officers and cultivated the loyalty of the remnants by taking a personal interest in the careers of senior officers. Some former Army officials went on to become heads of departments in the crucial home and defence ministries and enabled the palace to tighten its grip over the civil administration.

The process of broadening the ethnic and social base of the officer corps, which started with the military reforms of 1952 and opened recruitment in the Army to all eligible citizens, also gathered pace. This development enabled the monarchy to accommodate and co-opt newly educated members of under-represented groups, such as the hill people, into the system and widen its support base as well as balance the different caste and ethnic groups. Overall, Mahendra's regime witnessed a different kind of civil-military relations under an authoritarian regime.

In the 1990s, the issue of control over the Army was to some extent resolved by providing the king with the authority to mobilise the Army on the recommendations of a National Security Council (NSC), comprising the prime minister, the defence minister, and the army chief, which theoretically gave the civilian government the upper hand. This arrangement enabled the monarchy to retain its hold on the military, by requiring its consent on key issues pertaining to the Army.[45]

Many civilian leaders, belonging to the two major political parties, the Nepali Congress and the Communist Party of Nepal (Unified Marxist Leninist), do not identify themselves with the role of the Army in the country's history, as their parties were formed to represent the interests of those constituencies that were not part of the original establishment. They have shown little interest in national security issues. Also, due to different historical memories, they have strongly identified themselves with the history of the struggles conducted under the leadership of their respective parties. The interaction between the political leadership and the Army has been very weak, as the key leaders of the major parties are not conversant with military ethos and security affairs. All the army chiefs so far have had aristocratic/ military family background and have been traditionally linked to the monarchy. The senior officers have exerted a disproportionate influence in Nepalese politics and have given a conservative orientation to the military as well as a strong sense of historical continuity. There have been occasions when the NA refused to obey the orders of the elected government. For example, when the civilian government decided to engage the NA in counterinsurgency operations in 2001, the latter created a problem by demanding an all-party consensus and declaration of emergency.[46]

The ethnic and caste composition of the leadership structure of these institutions also differs significantly and is an important element in the power equation. The Ranas, Thakuris, Chhetris and hill ethnic groups have a tradition of valuing military attributes and dominate the military leadership structure. On the other hand, the top leadership of both major political parties consists almost exclusively of hill Brahmins, especially from Eastern Nepal, with caste-based occupations of priest and astrologer.[47]

In a major policy change in recent times, the Army has expressed its willingness to work under the elected civilian government in the post-conflict period since May 2006. Although, internally, many senior Army officials were not happy with the mainstreaming of the Maoists, they desisted from openly expressing their opposition to it. Maj. Gen. Shiva Ram Pradhan, representative of the NA in a joint monitoring committee that is overseeing the management of the arms and soldiers of the state army as well as the Maoists' guerrilla PLA, had stated: "The army will obey the commands of any government that has the mandate of the people."[48] Initially, the NA had reservations over the political decision on the integration of Maoist combatants. It feared that it might get politicised due to the integration of politically indoctrinated Maoist combatants. The Army argued at the time that politically indoctrinated combatants should undergo two years of a capsule course of political debriefing before joining it.[49]

The Army's relations with the elected government deteriorated further, on account of the differences between the Maoist-led government and the then COAS, General Rukmangath Katawal in 2008. The differences emerged because the COAS unilaterally decided on fresh recruitment to the Army, extension of the services of eight Brigadier Generals and withdrawal of the NA personnel from the national games, disregarding the directives of the Ministry of Defence on all these issues. The government sacked the COAS.

In protest to the reinstatement of General Katawal by President Ram Baran Yadav, the Prime Minister resigned. The hidden revolutionary agenda of the Maoist-led government *vis-à-vis* the intentions of the Nepali Congress and UML to use the Army as insurance were at the bottom of this rot.[50]

7. Bilateral and Multilateral Defence/Security Cooperation

Nepal receives periodic military assistance from India, China, the US, the UK, Pakistan and some European countries. The new Maoist government got military assistance worth Rs. 62.5 million from China in September 2008. The military relations and cooperation between China and Nepal have experienced continuous growth. China had given military assistance of $989,000 to Nepal in 2005. The agreement was reached during the visit of the then COAS, General Pyar Jung Thapa, to China.[51] Nearly all the former Army Chiefs and Defence Secretaries of Nepal have visited China. The Defence Minister and the General Chief of Staff of China have also visited Nepal. Since 1998, the NA has been sending officers and soldiers to study in Chinese military universities. Around 21 officers and soldiers went to China for training in the academic year 2006-07. China has also been sending military officers to participate in the adventure training programmes organised by the NA since 2002.[52]

India suspended its military assistance to Nepal immediately after King Gyanendra's dissolution of parliament and takeover of power in February 2005. In June 2006, India agreed to sort out issues relating to defence cooperation and military supplies at a joint committee meeting between the two countries.[53] As a result, India delivered a shipment of non-lethal military supplies to Nepal on July 6, 2006. The shipment included jeeps, bullet-proof vests, bunker protection devices and concertina barbed wire.

The US Pacific Command (USPACOM) coordinates US military engagement and security assistance with Nepal through the Office of Defense Cooperation. Cumulative US military assistance to the NA has consisted of $22.56 million in grant assistance, which includes Foreign Military Financing (FMF) since 2002, annual professional and technical training provided under the International Military Education and Training Program (IMET), additional training provided under the Counter Terrorism (CT) Fellowship approximately $200,000 annually), and approximately $5.6 million for Global Peace Operations Initiative (GPOI) funding to increase the pool of international peacekeepers and promote interoperability. Every year a number of NA officers attend US military schools, conferences and seminars, such as those provided by the National Defense University (NDU), Marshall Center, and the Asia Pacific Center for Strategic Studies (APCSS).[54]

8. Prospects

The successful completion of the programme of integrating the former Maoists in the NA by September 2012 has restored confidence both within the NA and the government about a positive future. The NA itself expects the government to support its proposal for restructuring the Army. Considering the geo-political situation, the NA's strength may be decreased gradually in the interests of economy. It looks like the NA is going to be a highly mechanised army with modern technology. It may build a strong air defence regiment with technical assistance from other counties and may improve its signal command with latest sophisticated electronic devices.

Integration of the PLA in the NA is expected to improve the Army's military capability since the PLA is adept in guerrilla warfare. Integration would, thus, contribute to augmenting the NA's capability in unconventional warfare, and would subsequently lead to improvisations in its doctrine, tactics, and strategies. Besides, since the PLA cadres have a broader understanding of politics, their integration would help the NA in understanding its role and responsibility in a democratic setup.

Moreover, since the PLA has worked with the common masses, this integration would establish a new relationship between the common masses and the NA. This will positively impact the legitimacy of the NA.

NOTES

1. The Army of Nepal has been named as the 'Nepal Army' or '*Nepali Sena*' (in Nepali language) by the Interim Constitution of Nepal 2006 (see http://www.nic.gov.np/download/interim-constitution.pdf). However, the website of the army uses the term 'Nepalese Army' (http://www.nepalarmy.mil.np). The current article uses the term 'Nepal Army' as per the nomenclature adopted by the Interim Constitution of Nepal.
2. Narahari Acharya, "The Nepalese Army" in Bishnu Sapkota (ed.), *The Nepali Security Sector: An Almanac*, Brambauer Publishers, Hungary, 2009.
3. Ashok K. Mehta, *The Royal Nepal Army, Meeting the Maoist Challenge*, Rupa, New Delhi, 2005, p. 31.
4. Narahari Acharya, no. 2, p. 122.
5. Ashok K. Mehta, no. 3, p. 51.
6. The Young Communist League of the UCPN (Maoist), Youth Force of CPN-UML, Tarun Dal of Nepali Congress, All Nepal National Independent Students Union-Revolutionary (ANNISU-R) of the CPN-Maoist and the Nationalist Youth Front of Rastriya Prajatantra Party (RPP-Nepal).
7. "ANNISU-R 19th conference kicks off", *myrepublica.com*, Kathmandu, October 2, 2012.
8. For more information, see "Maoist Outlook" (Organ of the Communist Party of Nepal-Maoist), 1 (1), August 2012.
9. For more information, see "CPN-M 'forming' war-era military structure", *ekantipur*, October 2, 2012.
10. "CPN-Maoist ban Indian number plate vehicles", *myrepublica.com*, September 26, 2012.

11. "Anti-Maoist stir on Indo-Nepal border, security beefed up", *The Times of India*, October 2, 2012.
12. On August 16, 2012, UCPN (Maoist), Joint Democratic Madhesi Front and around twenty small parties, including some Janajati parties, established the Federal Democratic Republic Alliance (FDRA) for formation of ethnic-based federalism and the new constitution. On October 1, the Madhesi Janadhikar Forum-Nepal (Upendra Yadav), Rastriya Madhes Samajbadi Party (Sarat Singh Bhandari) and around five Janajati parties formed the Federal Democratic Alliance. The following day, the Royalists formed the Desbhakta Loktantrik Morcha.
13. Jo Johnson, "Nepal's Kingdom of Discontent", *Financial Times*, January 2, 2006. Kunda Dixit is editor of *Nepal Times*.
14. Author's interaction with Nepalese leaders during a research trip to Nepal in June 2011 and interaction with a senior Government of India official in New Delhi in October 2012.
15. Yubanath Lamsal, "Steady Growth of Nepal-Pakistan Ties", *The Rising Nepal*, May 21, 2008.
16. "We will not tolerate any foreign interference in Nepal: China", *The Telegraph Nepal*, November 5, 2008.
17. Jo Johnson, "Kingdom of Discontent: Maoists Enter the Mainstream to Threaten Nepal's Monarchy", *Financial Times*, January 3, 2006.
18. Hiranyalal Shrestha, "Water Resource in Nepal-China Relation", *The Telegraph Nepal*, May 7, 2008.
19. Ibid.
20. Donald Camp, "United States Interests and Goals in Nepal", Statement before the U.S. House of Representatives Committee on International Relations, Washington DC, March 2, 2005, at http://2001-2009.state.gov/p/sca/rls/rm/2005/42910.htm. Camp was Principal Deputy Assistant Secretary for South & Central Asia in the US State Department.
21. Bruce Vaughn, "Nepal: Background and US Relations", *Congressional Research Service, Report for Congress*, Library of Congress, February 2, 2006, p. 17. Vaughn is an analyst in Southeast and South Asian Affairs, Foreign Affairs, Defense, and Trade Division in the US Congressional Research Service.
22. "Nepal-Geography", Country Studies Section, at http://www.mongabay.com/reference/country_studies/nepal/GEOGRAPHY.html
23. Ashok K. Mehta, no. 3, pp. 33-34.
24. Ibid, p. 39.
25. Ibid, p. 40.
26. Trailokya Raj Aryal, "Nepal and its defence doctrine", *South Asia Monitor*, September 10, 2012, at http://southasiamonitor.org/detail.php?type=n&nid=3858
27. "The Security Environment, Nepal", at http://www.mongabay.com/history/nepal/nepal-the_security_environment,_nepal.html
28. Ashok K. Mehta, no. 3, p. 33.
29. Chiran Jung Thapa, "Nepal's Military Doctrine", *News Blaze*, September 21, 2008.
30. For more information, see Nepal Army Act 2006, at www.lawcommission.gov.np
31. Article 145(d)(4) of the Interim Constitution 2007, Republic of Nepal.
32. "Background Note: Nepal", *US Department of State*, at http://www.state.gov/r/pa/ei/bgn/5283.htm (Accessed December 3, 2008).
33. Narahari Acharya, no. 2.
34. Ibid. Also, see Chain of Command, at http://cyberyana.free.fr/army2000/nepal/chainofcommand.php.html (Accessed October 10, 2012)
35. See Organisation, Nepal Army, at http://www.nepalarmy.mil.np/organisation.php. Also, see Chain of Command, at http://cyberyana.free.fr/army2000/nepal/chainofcommand.

php.html (Accessed October 10, 2012)

36. Nepal Army official documents, at http://www.nepalarmy.mil.np/organisation/combatsupport.php?hdng=combatsupport&pg=1 (Accessed October 10, 2012).
37. "PM backs Army's structure re-do proposal", *ekantipur*, May 8, 2012.
38. Ibid.
39. "Nepal Army Air Wing", at http://www.scramble.nl/np.htm (Accessed October 10, 2012).
40. "Inclusiveness, Nepal Army", at http://www.nepalarmy.mil.np/inclusiveness.php?
41. As per data provided on the website of the Nepal Army, at http://www.nepalarmy.mil.np/inclusiveness.
42. Prakash A. Raj, *The Dancing Democracy*, Rupa & Co., New Delhi, 2006, pp. 46–47.
43. Prakash Nepali and Phanindra Subba, "Civil-Military Relations and the Maoist Insurgency in Nepal", *Small Wars and Insurgencies*, 16 (1), March 2005, p. 87.
44. As of October 2012, a total of NRP 15.02 billion (State NRP 9.61 billion and Peace Fund NRP 5.41 billion) was spent for the management of former Maoist combatants since November 2006. For more details, see "Rs 15.02b spent for mgmt of ex-PLA", *myrepublica,* October 6, 2012.
45. Lt. Gen. (Retd.) Bala Nanda Sharma, "Civil-Military Relations: Strengthening Democracy in Nepal", Paper Presented at a High Level Seminar organised by Ex-Police Organisation and FES in Kathmandu on April 24, 2009. Also, see Prakash Nepali and Phanindra Subba, "Civil-Military Relations and the Maoist Insurgency in Nepal", *Small Wars and Insurgencies,* 16 (1), March 2005.
46. Nepali and Subba, no. 43.
47. Ibid.
48. "Nepal Army Ready to Work under Maoist Government", April 15, 2008, at http://72.14.235.132/search?q=cache:0Ef9haxAHMUJ:news.webindia123.com/news/Articles/Asia/20080415/932671.html+Nepal+army+under+Maoist+government&hl=en&ct=clnk&cd=3&gl=in
49. N.P. Upadhyaya, "Will Nepal Army Exhibit Flexibility?", *The Telegraph Nepal,* September 10, 2008, at http://www.telegraphnepal.com/news_det.php?news_id=4040 (Accessed July 17, 2009).
50. For more information, see S. D. Muni, "The civil-military crisis in Nepal", *The Hindu,* May 6, 2009.
51. "China Gives $989,000 Military Aid to Nepal", *Times of India,* October 25, 2005, at http://timesofindia.indiatimes.com/World/Rest-of-World/China-gives—989000-military-aid-to-Nepal/articleshow/1274264.cms
52. "Nepal-China Relations", Embassy of The People's Republic Of China in the Federal Democratic Republic of Nepal, September 5, 2007, at http://www.chinaembassy.org.np
53. "India, Nepal to discuss resumption of military supplies", June 6, 2006, at http://www.india-defence.com/reports-2059 (Accessed July 17, 2009).
54. "Background Note: Nepal", U.S. Department of State. For more information, see at http://www.state.gov/r/pa/ei/bgn/5283.htm

APPENDIX 1

List of Battalions in the Nepal Army

1. Shree Sher Battalion
2. Shree Kali Prasad Battalion (Engineers)
3. Shree Vajra Dal Company
4. Shree Keval Jung Company
5. Shree Nanda Buksh Company
6. Shree Chandi Dal Company
7. Shree Bhimkali Company
8. Shree Bhairav Nath Battalion (Paratroopers)
9. Shree Devi Dal Battalion
10. Shree Surya Dal Company
11. Shree Gorakh Buksh Battalion
12. Shree Chandan Nath Company
13. Shree Shardul Jung Company
14. Shree Indradhoj Battalion
15. Shree Shivadal Company
16. Shree Samar Jung Company
17. Shree Rana Simha Dal Company
18. Shree Birdal Company
19. Shree Kali Jung Battalion (Engineers)
20. Shree Narsimha Dal Company
21. Shree Aridaman Company
22. Shree Durga Bhanjan Company
23. Shree Kalidal Battalion
24. Shree Durga Buksh Battalion
25. Shree Raj Dal Battalion
26. Shree Barakh Battalion
27. Shree Bhawani Buksh Battalion
28. Shree Jwala Dal Battalion
29. Shree Tara Dal Battalion
30. Shree Batuk Dal Battalion
31. Shree Bhawani Dal Battalion
32. Shree Rana Shardul Battalion
33. Shree Rana Sher Battalion
34. Shree Jabar Jung Battalion
35. Shree Shreenath Battalion
36. Shree Kali Buksh Battalion (Engineers)
37. Shree Barda Bahadur Battalion
38. Shree Sabuj Battalion

39. Shree Purano Gorakh Battalion
40. Shree Devidutta Battalion
41. Shree Naya Gorakh Battalion
42. Shree Bhairavi Dal Battalion
43. Shree Singh Nath Battalion
44. Shree Shreejung Battalion
45. Shree Ranabhim Battalion
46. Shree Naya Shree Nath Battalion

APPENDIX 2

List of Divisions

Far Western Division-Headquarter at Dipayal

Mid-Western Division-Headquarter at Surkhet

Western Division-Headquarter at Pokhara

Mid Division-Headquartered at Suparetar

Valley Division-Headquarter at Kathmandu

Eastern Division-Headquarter at Itahari

APPENDIX 3

Training Establishment

The Nepal Army has many specialised army-level academies and schools under the Directorate General of Military Training (DGMT). Those are:

1. Nepal Army Command and Staff College, Shivapuri.
2. Nepal Army School, Nagarkot.
3. Military Academy, Kharipati.
4. Nepal Army Recruit Training Centre, Trishuli.
5. Nepal Army Jungle Warfare School, Amlekhgunj.
6. Nepal Army High Altitude and Mountain Warfare School, Mustang.
7. Nepal Army Intelligence School, Kharipati.
8. Nepal Army Logistics School, Chhauni.
9. Birendra Peace Keeping Operation Training Centre, Panchkhal.
10. The Nepal Army Para Training School, Maharajgunj.
11. Specific to Arms and Services Schools

APPENDIX 4

Important Military Appointments

Sl.No.	*English Terminology*
1.	Chief of Army Staff (COAS)
2.	Chief of the General Staff (CGS)
3.	Chief of Staff (COS)
4.	Inspector General (IG)
5.	Adjutant General (AG)
6.	Quarter Master General (QMG)
7.	Master of General Ordinance (MGO)
8.	Military Secretary (MS)
9.	Military Assistant (M.A.)
10.	Director General of Military Operation (DGMO)
11.	Director General of Military Training (DGMT)
12.	Director, Directorate of Public Relation(DPR)
13.	Director, Directorate of Military Operation (DMO)
14.	Director, Directorate of Planning and Policy
15.	Director Military Intelligence (DMI)
16.	Director, Directorate of Research and Development (R&D)
17.	Director, Directorate of Peace Keeping Operation(DPKO)
18.	Director, Directorate of Welfare and Planning
19.	Director, Directorate of National Parks and Wild life Preservation
20.	Director, Directorate of Defence Production
21.	Director, Directorate of Development and Construction
22.	Director, Directorate of Artillery
23.	Director, Directorate of Engineer
24.	Director, Directorate of Signal
25.	Director, Directorate of Air Defence
26.	Director, Directorate of Electrical and Mechanical
27.	Chief, Human Rights Division
28.	Division Commander
29.	Brigade Commander
30.	Battalion Commander
31.	Company Commander
32.	Platoon Commander
33.	Section Commander
34.	Commandant, Nepal Army Command and Staff College
35.	Commandant, Jungle Warfare School

Sl.No.	*English Terminology*
36.	Commandant, Mountain Warfare School
38.	Commandant, Military Intelligence School
39.	Commandant, Electrical and Mechanical School
40.	Commandant, Para Training School
41.	Commandant, Military Academy
42.	Commandant, Recruit Training Centre

Source: Nepal Army (www.nepalarmy.mil.np)

Chapter Six

The Army of Pakistan: Dominant by Default

Ashok K. Behuria and Sumita Kumar

Introduction

Pakistan was established as an independent state on August 14, 1947; it was carved out of British India as a homeland for Muslims of the Indian Subcontinent. It is situated at the confluence of Central, Southern and Western Asia. It shares its border with Iran on the south-west, with Afghanistan on the west and north, and with India, on the east and south-east. It is bordered by the Arabian Sea to the south. Pakistan has attracted the attention of the world for its strategic location and has sought to take advantage of it ever since its creation. During the Cold War years, the first military ruler of Pakistan, Ayub Khan, had exaggerated the threat from the erstwhile Soviet Union to seek US help. Pakistan received $1.8 billion in military and economic aid and entered into military alliances with the US during 1948-66.

It was in fact called the 'most allied ally' of the US. The Soviet threat became real indeed with the invasion of Afghanistan in December 1979 and turned Pakistan into a frontline state. The ensuing Afghan *jihad* years saw Pakistan playing a critical role in the defeat and withdrawal of the Soviet forces from Afghanistan. The end of the Cold War did not lessen the strategic importance for Pakistan. The unintended consequences of the Afghan *jihad* in the shape of the rise of the Taliban in Afghanistan and the 9/11 attacks by Al Qaeda on the US soil catapulted Pakistan to the centre stage of Global War on Terrorism (GWOT) led by the US. Pakistan has remained central to American strategy in the region ever since. The geo-political situation of the region in which Pakistan is located has remained quite critical over the years and has lent Pakistan immense strategic relevance primarily because of the role it has played in determining the overall direction of regional politics.

While Pakistan's geo-strategic importance has attracted continued international attention over the years, the nature of international engagement (primarily militaristic) has ironically retarded the growth of democratic and accountable governance in the state. The Army of Pakistan has overshadowed other state institutions and evolved as an institution of disproportionate strength and importance. An overdeveloped army with an under-developed statecraft has had negative consequences for the state and society.

This paper seeks to trace the evolution and growth of the Pakistan Army, identify its strengths and weaknesses and develop a futuristic assessment of its role and its ability to contribute to the stability of the Pakistani state at a critical juncture of its history.

Origin and Evolution of the Army

The Pakistan Army was carved out of the British Indian Army on June 30, 1947. The division was on the basis of population and Pakistan got six armoured, eight artillery and eight infantry regiments (India in comparison received 12 armoured, 40 artillery and 21 infantry regiments). The Pakistan Army had only one Division (the 7th). The 8th and 9th Divisions were raised in 1947; the 10th, 12th and 14th Divisions were raised in 1948. The 15th Division was raised in 1950. At some point before 1954, 6th Division was raised and the 9th Division was disbanded. The 6th Division was disbanded at some point after 1954 as the US assistance was available only for one armoured and six infantry divisions.

Pakistan has always alleged that the division of assets including those related to the military was unjust and India's hesitation in releasing its share from the Reserve Bank of India (RBI) has been cited ever since as proof of India's unwillingness to accept Pakistan as an independent and sovereign country.

Evolution of the Army

In the initial years after partition, the Army in Pakistan was largely influenced by the British, given that the shortfall of Pakistani officers was made up by the retention of British officers in various capacities including in senior positions and in the technical branches.[1] Further, at the time of its establishment, its cadres were from the former British India Army. A number of officers had served in the Second World War and some were trained at Sandhurst. However, later, the American influence on the Army became more predominant as many Pakistani military personnel received their training in the US. While the first two generations of the Pakistan Army were largely influenced by the British and American training, the third generation of officers mainly comprised those who had received their training from military institutions within Pakistan. They were less exposed to the American thinking and their outlook was largely shaped by the outcome of the 1971 war with India.[2]

At the time of partition, assets between Pakistan and India were divided in the proportion of 36:64, and given the disparity in size and population, Pakistan received comparatively fewer stores, supplies and facilities.[3] Initially, the Pakistan Army retained the organisational structure of the British Indian Army which was 'based on static rather than operational considerations'[4] but it was slowly re-organised in keeping with operational requirements. While before partition, the concentration of forces of the British India Army as well as the logistic infrastructure and cantonments were established keeping in mind the threat from Russia through Afghanistan in the context of the 'Great Game' being played between Britain and Russia, but post-partition, forces and infrastructure had to be aligned in order to meet the perceived threat from India.[5] To overcome the disparity with India, Pakistan became dependent on foreign aid, equipment and training. After Pakistan joined Western-led multilateral military alliances like the South East Asia Treaty Organisation (SEATO) in 1954 and the *Baghdad Pact* (later Central Treaty Organisation or CENTO) in 1955, American military equipment and training were introduced into the Pakistan Army which resulted in major changes in the Army's structure.

Pakistan was helped to equip an additional armoured division, four infantry divisions, one armoured brigade group, and support elements for two corps by the Americans. Not only did the Pakistan Army receive equipment and training from the Americans, but it was also introduced to American military doctrine and strategy. While hardly any changes were made in the infantry, the armour, artillery and other technical branches were heavily influenced by American practices.[6] After the 1971 war, as the perceived security threat from India increased, Pakistan began looking towards other countries as well, especially China, to bolster its defence preparedness. The Pakistan Army's force size grew in response not only to the loss of its territory in the 1971 war with India, but also to the presence of Soviet armed forces in Afghanistan in the 1980s.[7] The attempt to acquire some sort of military parity with India led Pakistan's leadership to accord priority to defence expenditure. It is estimated that between 1947 and 1959, up to 73 per cent of the total government spending was demarcated for defence purposes, with the average during those years being 60 per cent.[8]

At the time of partition, Muslim representation in the British Indian armed forces was estimated to be 30 per cent in the army, 40 per cent in the navy and 20 per cent in the air force.[9] Muslims constituted 24 per cent and Hindus 48 per cent of the officer cadre, and 34 and 56 per cent respectively in other ranks.[10] Pakistan was to get approximately 150,000 army personnel including officers, out of the total British Indian Army personnel numbering about 461,800. Over the years, the Pakistan Army has grown in size and attained its present strength of about 550,000. The propensity of the Punjabis (holding immense land and industrial assets) to dominate the ethnic composition within the Army drew recriminations from the less represented ethnic groups, given the overarching role of the Army in the politics and governance of Pakistan. In terms of representation from the various provinces of Pakistan, it was estimated that Punjab contributed 70 per cent, the North-West Frontier Province (NWFP, now Khyber Pakhtunkhwa) 14 per cent, Sindh 9 per cent, and Baluchistan 3 per cent to the 1979 cadre. In addition, Pakistan occupied Kashmir (PoK) contributed 1.3 per cent.[11]

On the one hand, the Pakistan Army was organised keeping in view the antecedents of the British Indian Army, on the other, soon after independence, it began to acquire Islamic ideological strains. The concept of *jihad* was used even as early as 1947-48 to mobilise the tribesmen who were involved in the incursions into Kashmir.[12] Over the years, religious feelings were incited and continued to be used to garner support for a response to the perceived Indian threat. The nexus between the military and the religious leaders/parties became strong during the Afghan *jihad* against the Soviet Union and was subsequently responsible for inciting unrest and terrorism within Kashmir and later in other parts of India. It is generally believed that it was during General Zia-ul Haq's tenure as chief that the Army acquired a more Islamic orientation.

Strategic Thought[13]

The beliefs of the officers of the Pakistan Army in the arena of domestic politics as well as foreign policy are largely shaped by what they are taught at their military institutions of learning like the Pakistan Military Academy at Kakul, the Staff College at Quetta and the National Defence College at Islamabad. Other factors like social disposition, ethnic background as well as their ideological leanings also determine their attitudes.[14] Right from the start, the Pakistan Army has employed Islamic symbolism to motivate its personnel. The motto of the Pakistan Army remains essentially Islamic, and to certain extent sectarian in character. It lays emphasis on *iman* (the belief that Allah is the only God and Muhammad was his last prophet), *taqwa* (fear of Allah, righteousness and good conduct) and *jihad-fi-sabilillah* (fight in the cause of Allah).[15]

Pakistan's strategic thinking has been influenced by a number of factors which include its self-image, its geography and its history. In the years soon after independence, the leadership in Pakistan perceived that the country was weak compared to India, and believed that it faced an existential threat from India. This was perhaps understandable given the sheer discrepancy in the size, population and resources of the two countries. Pakistan's inability to establish a stable democratic system in the years soon after independence allowed space for the repeated intervention of the Army. Every time the military leadership assumed power, it claimed to have been propelled by circumstances and in the larger interests of the country. Policy decisions made even in the early years allocated a major share of the budget to the military which increased the likelihood of it exercising a disproportionately higher influence within the state.

The Pakistani political as well as military leadership constantly relied on the refrain of 'the Indian threat' to perpetuate their hold on power. While Pakistan focused on India as its principal threat and launched wars against it in 1947 and 1965, the real threat to its integrity came from within. Ethnic contradictions within the country and the dominance of the Punjabis within the power structure provided a fertile ground for the movement for secession in East Pakistan. While the secessionist movement may not have achieved success without India's help, yet there was obviously an indigenous demand and capability that existed within East Pakistan. Pakistan continues to blame India for the loss of its eastern wing and its leadership has remained steadfast to its aim of avenging the Pakistani defeat in the 1971 war.

Pakistan's strategic thinking can be said to have been mostly dominated by the Army given that it has had a continuous role in governance, sometimes direct, at other times indirect. This was because ideological as well as ethnic divisions in addition to administrative and security problems gave the bureaucracy and military the chance to acquire a preponderant position in the power structure. The lack of a strong social base and an organised political leadership also allowed the military to play a larger role in governance. The Pakistan Army has been preoccupied with finding a military solution to Kashmir and has adopted an aggressive attitude towards India. This is evident in the *lashkar* invasion of October 1947 and the attack on India in 1965. Pakistan adopted a strategy to destabilise India by covert means by supporting Punjabi separatists through the 1980s and then sponsoring terrorism in Jammu and Kashmir from the late 1980s. The Kargil operation in 1999 was launched with the aim of acquiring Indian territories around Kargil so as to force India to resolve the Kashmir issue on terms that would be favourable to Pakistan. In the last decade also, India continued to bore the brunt of terrorist attacks on areas of significant political, economic and scientific value not just in Kashmir but in other parts as well.

Pakistan's behaviour with Afghanistan can also be said to be marked by aggression. Such behaviour was legitimised by concepts like 'strategic depth' which paved the way for expansionism in Afghanistan, by giving support to the anti-Soviet *Mujahideen*, and later by training and providing support to the Taliban. *Jihad* has been an essential element of Pakistan's strategic thinking and has been used to mobilise people to fight in Afghanistan, Kashmir and other places in India. One of the most important analyses of the Holy Quran, which provided pointers for the Army to wage war against the enemy, was by Brigadier S.K. Malik in the late 1970s in his book *The Quranic Concept of War*. This book highlighted the importance of waging *jihad* on multiple fronts in order to attain policy objectives and was commended by General Zia-ul Haq.[16] Pakistan has believed that it would be able to wrest Kashmir from India and destabilise India through sub-conventional warfare.

To offset India's advantage in terms of conventional forces, Pakistan adopted the strategy of "offensive defence" *vis-à-vis* India. Stephen P. Cohen believes that this was apparent in the 1965 war wherein it was understood that a 'short, sharp war' would enable Pakistan to meet both its military as well as political objectives. The Pakistan Army has relied on offensive ripostes as part of its overall defence plans and this has been openly enunciated at times, but most recently by Shuja Nawaz in his book *Crossed Swords*,[17] which has drawn wide acclaim. At the same time, Pakistan has relied on 'irregulars' to achieve its military objectives and this type of warfare involving the use of 'irregulars' was suggested as a possible answer to Pakistan's security predicaments in Ayub Khan's time.

Over the decades, it is obvious that not only have 'irregulars' been used by Pakistan against India as in 1947 when Pashtun tribesmen were sent into Kashmir or in 1965 when guerrillas were trained and inducted across the ceasefire line, but that 'irregulars' have then been reinforced by regular army troops in order to try and consolidate any gains made. But whether this strategy has made Pakistan achieve its objectives, remains doubtful. Even in Kargil in 1999, which was primarily an army operation, forces were initially sent into India in the guise of "Islamic militants".

Having acquired nuclear capability in 1987, and feeling quite secure in the knowledge that India would not retaliate with conventional war due to the nuclear deterrent, Pakistan began implementing its plan of achieving its strategic goals initially in Kashmir, and later in the rest of India through low intensity conflict or proxy war. Pakistan has extensively used non-state actors on targets within India and the links between the Pakistan establishment and militant organisations like the *Lashkar-e-Taiba* (LeT), the *Jaish-e-Mohammad* (JeM) and the *Harkat-ul Mujahideen* (HuM) are well documented. Nuclear weapons too are an important element in Pakistan's strategic thinking. Pakistan's nuclear programme is essentially Indo-centric and even though Pakistan claims that India's 1974 peaceful nuclear explosion provided the impetus for its nuclear programme, it is obvious that it was Pakistan's defeat in the 1971 war that provided the impetus for Zulfiqar Ali Bhutto's decision to go nuclear. While a comprehensive nuclear doctrine is yet to be enunciated, certain principles of Pakistan's nuclear policy are apparent given the various statements made by the Pakistani leadership from time to time. The stated policy is that of 'minimum deterrence', yet it is not clear as to what 'minimum deterrence' implies. It follows a principle of nuclear retaliation in case of a preventive or pre-emptive strike, and does not subscribe to the 'no-first use doctrine'.

Pakistan's strategic location, which led to its alliance with the US both in the Cold War context as well as in the aftermath of the bombing of the World Trade Center in New York in September 2001, has also shaped its security perceptions. Pakistan's proximity to China also became a factor giving space to China to be a major player in Pakistan's security strategy. Pakistan has relied on the US and China for augmenting its conventional and nuclear weapons capability.

Structure of the Pakistan Army

There are about 620,000 active-duty personnel in the Pakistani armed forces. Of these, the Pakistani Army numbers 550,000. Military service in Pakistan is voluntary for two years in all services. The Pakistani Army is commanded by the Chief of Armed Forces (COAS), who operates from the General Headquarters, Rawalpindi, close to Islamabad, the capital of Pakistan. He is assisted at the level of lieutenant general by eight principal staff officers. They include the Chief of General Staff (CGS), who is responsible for the functioning of Military Operations and Intelligence Directorates; the Chief of Logistics Staff (CLS); the Adjutant General (AG); the Quarter-Master General (QMG); the Inspector General of Training and Evaluation (IGT&E); and the Military Secretary (MS). In 2008, the incumbent COAS, Pervez Kayani, added two more Principal Staff Officers (PSOs) positions to include the Inspector Generals of Arms as well as Communications and IT.

The Army has three commands. It was reported first in April 2007[18] that Pakistan Army will have three new commands (like the Pakistan Air Force or PAF) to improve the operational efficiency and working of its land forces. The three proposed commands were, i.e., Northern, Southern and Central Commands, which would be responsible for the administrative arrangements of the corps falling under their respective commands. As per the news reports in April 2010, the Chief of the Army Staff, General Ashfaq Parvez Kayani, visited army's Northern Command to witness logistic and operational activities of the troops conducting second phase of Exercise *Azm-e-Nau III*.[19]

The Pakistan Army is organised into ten corps. The Army Strategic Forces Command corps has been the latest addition and was established in February 2000 to the already existing nine operational corps, and it is responsible for the training, deployment and activation of nuclear missile assets. In 2006, the government set up separate commands in its three services equipped with nuclear weapons and missiles capable of retaliating for any first nuclear strike. A corps is usually commanded by a lieutenant general and has army divisions under its command. It consists of the infantry, mechanised, armoured, artillery and anti-tank divisions and brigades. Apart from these regular corps, there are two other corps responsible for anti-aircraft artillery operations and for air defence for the Army. Of these, the XI Corps headquartered at Peshawar is active in the counter-insurgency operations.

Most of Pakistan's ground units are deployed along the Indian border. The X1 and XII Corps, earlier deployed along Pakistan-Iran border, are now used to reinforce units stationed in Kashmir and along the Indian border. The V Corps in Karachi performs a peace time internal security role in Sindh Province; it is also assigned to protect the Indus Highway, an essential north-south byway, during wartime. The X Corps headquartered in Rawalpindi is stationed along the Line of Control (LoC) in Jammu and Kashmir sector, including the Siachen Glacier region and other strategic high altitude passes. The IV (Lahore), XXX (Gujranwala) and XXX1 (Bahawalpur) Corps are responsible for the defence of Punjab. The I (Mangla) and II (Multan) Strike Corps are supposed to be the Pakistan Army's primary counter-attack force during wartime. In October 2008, the Pakistani military suspended the construction of a new army headquarters in Islamabad for economic reasons. The new complex was scheduled to be completed in 2012 at the cost of $763 million.

Ethnic Composition

As the data culled from various sources indicate, Punjabis and Pakhtuns compose almost 85-95 per cent of the Pakistan Army. The lopsided ratio of these two ethnic groups is the legacy of the British recruitment policy during the colonial years. The British believed that the Punjabis, the Pathans and the Gurkhas were martial races and hence this had direct impact on the recruitments into the British Indian Army. This trend continued even after the formation of Pakistan. The majority of the recruits into the Pakistan Army continued to come from Punjab and the NWFP, that too from select districts like Kohat, Peshawar, Campbellpur (now Attock), Rawalpindi, Jhelum and Gujrat. After the secession of East Pakistan, the leadership realised the need to make the Army more representative and Article 39 of the Pakistan Constitution promulgated in 1973 mentioned clearly that the state "shall enable people from all parts of Pakistan to participate in the armed forces of Pakistan." However, Punjabis and Pakhtuns dominate to this day.

The Army reportedly launched a ten-year recruitment plan (2001-11) with a view to redressing the ethnic imbalance and to increase the representation of Pakhtuns from 13.5 per cent to 14.5 per cent, that of Sindhis from 15 to 17 per cent, and that of the Baloch from nearly nil to 4 per cent and the numbers of persons from 'Azad Kashmir' and Gilgit Baltistan (earlier Northern Areas) from nil to 9 per cent of the force. Punjabis would still have dominant presence and constitute the balance of 55.5 percent. By 2007, it was reported in an Information Brief published by Inter Services Public Relations Directorate that the presence of Punjabi officers had been reduced to 57 per cent (from the earlier estimated 71 per cent in 2001).[20] However, these figures could be misleading because they tend to reflect recruitments from the provinces rather than recruitment on the basis of different ethnicities.

While it may be true that there has been a general lack of enthusiasm for joining the Army among other ethnic groups including Bengalis (in the undivided Pakistan), this lopsided over-representation of the two major ethnic groups and especially the Punjabis has been cited as a deliberate attempt by the ruling Punjabi elite to perpetuate its hold on power.

Defence Budget

The Pakistan military has traditionally utilised a large share of government revenues over the years. A comparative estimate (SIPRI figure) with India suggests that it has consistently spent a greater percentage of its GDP on defence even if there has been a drop in expenditure over the years.

Pakistan's quest for parity with India has sustained such expenditure pattern. The trend analysis by *Jane's Defence Budgets 2010* shows that Pakistan will continue to spend around 3 per cent of its GDP on defence in the years to come.

The Pakistan Government allocated Rs. 442 billion ($5.27 billion) towards defence in its annual budget in June 2010 and it was increased to

Table 1: Ethnic Composition of the Pakistan Army

	Population (%) Census figures	*% in Army Figures by independent analysts*	*% Officers Figures by independent analysts*	*ISPR figures 2007 (May not be according to ethnicity)*	*Targets set by Army by 2011 (May not be according to ethnicity)*
Punjabis +Seraikis	44.15 + 10.53	65-72	65-75	57	54
Pakhtuns	15.42	13-15	15-22	13.5	14.5
Mohajirs	7.57	4-8	11-15		
Sindhis Balochis Brahui, Kashmiri, Hindko	14.1 3.57 4.66	1-2	2.5	15 * 3.2*	17 4
Azad Kashmir and Gilgit-Baltistan		N.A.	N.A.	9.11	9
Minorities	3.84	N.A.	N.A.	0.72	1

* May include other ethnic groups residing in Sindh.
The data given has been collected by IDSA Research Team from various sources.

Table 2: Economic Indicators and Defence Budget—Pakistan*
(All figures are in Billions US$ and based on constant values for the current year)

Title	*2008*	*2009*	*2010*	*2011*	*2012*	*2013*	*2014*	*2015*
GDP	156.4	162.3	167.3	173.9	181.6	190.3	198.6	207.3
GDP Growth (%/yr)	5.951	3.740	3.072	3.962	4.453	4.774	4.360	4.373
Inflation (%/yr)	20.3	13.6	12.0	8.7	6.7	6.0	6.0	6.0
Total Defence Budget	3.937	4.133	4.313	5.273	5.715	6.002	6.256	6.497
Total Defence Budget as % GDP	2.517	2.547	2.579	3.032	3.146	3.154	3.150	3.134

Title	*2007*	*2008*	*2009*	*2010*	*2011*	*2012*	*2013*	*2014*
GDP	147.6	156.4	162.3	167.3	173.9	181.6	190.3	198.6
Defence Budget	3.921	3.937	4.133	4.313	5.273	5.715	6.002	6.256
Total Defence Procurement	1.188	1.195	1.258	1.313	1.609	1.752	1.834	1.909
Army Budget	1.686	1.811	1.901	2.027	2.478	2.629	2.701	2.753
Navy Budget	0.627	0.610	0.620	0.690	0.844	0.943	0.960	1.001
Air Force Budget	0.922	0.925	1.013	1.009	1.266	1.429	1.501	1.564
Defence-Wide Budget[21]	0.686	0.591	0.599	0.587	0.686	0.714	0.840	0.938
Other expenditures								
RDT&E	0.217	0.205	0.213	0.217	0.262	0.283	0.309	0.330
Military Personnel	1.237	1.263	1.326	1.395	1.706	1.844	1.921	1.990
O&M	0.980	0.992	1.045	1.091	1.337	1.453	1.519	1.578
Other	0.300	0.282	0.292	0.298	0.358	0.383	0.419	0.449

*Actual figures till 2010 and projections for other years based on current trends.
Source: *Jane's Defence Budgets 2010.*

Rs. 495 billion ($5.73 billion) in June 2011. There was a 22 per cent increase (from 2009) in 2010 and an 11.7 per cent nominal hike (from 2010) in 2011. The budgeted estimate includes salaries, operating expenses, 'physical assets' and 'civil works.'

According to the budget figures for 2011-12, Rs. 206.5 billion ($2.46 billion) will be spent on employee related expenses, Rs. 128.3 billion will be spent on operating expenses, Rs. 117.6 billion ($1.4 billion) will be spent on physical assets (the likely source of procurement funds) and Rs. 42.6 billion ($0.5 billion) will be spent on civil works. The Army will receive the largest portion of the expenditure with Rs. 236.3 billion ($2.8 billion); the Air Force will be allocated Rs. 106.1 billion ($1.3 billion) while the Navy will receive Rs. 51.6 billion ($0.6 billion).[22]

It has to be mentioned here that due to Pakistan's involvement in the counter-insurgency operations the US has been providing an additional $ 1.34 billion of military aid every year since 2002. Between 2002 and 2010, Pakistan has received an estimated $18.5 billion of military and non-military economic assistance from the US. Pakistan receives substantial military aid from the US through Foreign Military Financing (FMF), which is used to buy military equipment, and Coalition Support Fund (CSF), to pay for military operations for Pakistan's participation in the War on Terror. The FMF comes through the US State Department (within the international affairs budget), and CSF is provided by the US Department of Defence (DoD) and appropriated through supplemental spending requests. These two sources have added some $7.9 billion to Pakistan's military budget since 2001.

Apart from this, the World Bank programme also provided Pakistan with $6.5 billion during 2006-09. In October 2009, the *Kerry-Lugar Bill* provided Pakistan with an additional $7.5 billion of non-military aid until 2015. There is a suspicion that Pakistan may use these funds for acquisition of modern defence equipment. In recent years, Pakistan has in fact been focussed on procurement of modern weaponry, and has concluded purchase agreements with many countries.

As far as expenditure is concerned, 30 per cent of the defence budget is being spent on defence procurement, 6 per cent on research, development, training and evaluation and about 31 per cent on personnel. Since 2008, there has been a significant increase in the pay of the military personnel which has had an inflationary impact on the operating costs. As per *Jane's* estimates, the operating costs stood at $1.07 billion in 2007. They increased to $1.15 billion in 2009 and $1.41 billion in 2010. They are projected to reach $1.61 billion by 2013.

Other Issues

Pakistan began recruiting women for combat officer positions in 2006. The first batch of 30 females was placed in mechanical and engineering positions, though women will also be allowed to serve in other front-line capacities. Pakistan is the only Islamic country to have women serving in ranks as high as major general in its Army.

Pakistan conducted a number of missile tests in 2006-07, including successful tests of its cruise missile, Babur; its longest range ballistic missile, Shaheen II; and short-range ballistic missile, Hatf II Abdali. Additionally, Pakistan has been able to produce Hatf III Ghaznavi strategic missiles domestically with smuggled missile technology from North Korea. It has also been assisted substantially in its indigenisation programme by China. Pakistan completed a number of tests of its long and short-range Hatf missiles in 2007 and 2008.

Future Plans

Pakistan also managed to produce about 300 Al-Khalid tanks in its armoury at a factory in Taxila in 2007. It has also been able to upgrade its T-59 tanks to the Al-Zarar standard, which includes new weaponry, fire control and armour. The US supplied 115 M109A5 howitzers in December 2005 at Pakistan Army's request. In 2004, the US and Pakistan embarked on a $235 million project to help build Pakistan Army's aviation capability. During the first phase of the project (2004-07), Pakistan leased the helicopters while the US provided the resources, funding, training and support to help Pakistan establish a strong and reliable helicopter fleet. The US is expected to deliver a total number of 20 refurbished AH-1 Cobra attack helicopters to Pakistan. Of these, eight were delivered in February 2007 and four more were delivered in October 2007. The US has also equipped Pakistan Army with night operations capable equipment to help the latter in its counter insurgency operations. By October 2007, the US had formally transferred 25 Bell 412 helicopters to Pakistan, which Pakistan is using under a long-term lease. The major acquisitions from the US are indicated in a recent US Congressional Research Service (CRS) report.[23]

Civil-Military Relations

Pakistan Army and Internal Politics

The political instability following the formation of the state, the lack of political consensus on critical issues and the ineffective leadership after the early deaths of Muhammad Ali Jinnah and Liaqat Ali Khan, came in the way of the drafting of the constitution and establishment of a democratic system of governance in Pakistan. The initial years also witnessed sectarian conflict (anti-Ahmadiya movement) on a massive scale which brought Pakistan Army to the forefront of the efforts to maintain law and order and even to take over the administration at municipal levels in certain areas. Simultaneously, the bureaucratic apparatus at the level of the central government assumed lot of significance because of inability of the political leadership to take charge at the helm of affairs. They could not evolve a mechanism for settling differences on various issues like nature of the state, power sharing between the centre and the provinces, as well as other institutions of governance.

The constitution, which was finally adopted after almost 11 years of deliberation, could not satisfy the ruling military-bureaucratic elite and inevitably the Army, perhaps the most well organised of all institutions by then. The Pakistan Army for the first time took over the reins of political power in October 1958. The following 13 years of military rule widened the gulf between the two wings of Pakistan and resulted in the secession of the eastern wing in 1971. After a brief interlude of about six years, when the ruling democratic political leadership proved incapable of handling its differences with the opposition, the Army intervened in July 1977 and continued to rule for 11 years till 1988.

The democratic politics of next 11 years (1988-99) were a familiar tale of corruption, favouritism, repression and autocracy by those in power on the one hand, and confrontational politics by the opposition parties on the other. Taking advantage of the polarisation in politics, the Army again intervened in 1999 and continued to rule till 2007. Interestingly, though the Army has been hailed as the saviour by a wide section of the people in Pakistan each time it has assumed power, it is equally true that it has had to relinquish power because of popular protest as well. Unfortunately, the people of Pakistan have had to choose between a venal political class and a vainglorious military leadership over the years. The inherent weakness of the Pakistani society and polity—a deeply entrenched feudal elite unwilling to allow socio-economic transformation to throw up a responsive and responsible political leadership—has perpetuated the hold of the Army as an institutional balancer by default. The military's domination over politics has been a typical feature of the Pakistani state and given the nature of irresponsible and self-aggrandising politics in Pakistan, this trend is unlikely to change in future.

Civil Military Interaction

The role of the Army has been the most crucial factor in the evolution of Pakistan since its creation. The military's authority has permeated all sectors of life in Pakistan. It has spread its tentacles around state institutions, the economy and society at large, incorporating these into its spheres of influence. This enables the military to exercise a high level of dominance in the governance of the country. The overarching control which allows the military to accrue to itself immense direct benefits can be considered to be the prime motive behind the military's literally perpetual presence in Pakistan's politics, overt or covert. Such gains do not allow the military to let go the reins of government and step back from exercising power.

The military has wide-ranging corporate interests through which it has established an overwhelming presence in the national economy.[24] It is the efficient functioning of these that is of foremost importance for the military due to the attendant benefits which percolate to the military. The appointment of military personnel to civilian jobs was used to increase its influence over the civil administration, and at the same time created opportunities for the military to gain materially. The military's reliance on other dubious means to gain wealth has become apparent from time to time. Some well-known cases have given insights into the military's linkages with corruption, including defence-related kickbacks and the drugs trade. The military has also been able to use the lack of transparency in the defence budget to its advantage.[25]

The military withdrew from active politics after General Zia-ul Haq's death due to the severe criticism of its political role in the preceding years. However, the Army's position of pre-eminence could hardly be doubted as it continuously exerted influence from behind the scenes. The period from 1988 till General Pervez Musharraf's takeover in 1999 was uniquely governed by what is popularly known as the 'troika', a reference to the three centres of power in Pakistan, comprising the army chief, the president and the prime minister. It saw the constantly changing balance of power between the members of the 'troika'. Whether during the military regimes (1958-69, 1969-71, 1977-88, and 1999-2008) or when it played an indirect role during democratic periods, it has been a dominant factor in the formulation of economic, foreign and defence policies as well as internal security issues.

The Army has assumed power on four occasions in the history of Pakistan. Each time, the Army's justification was that the country was moving inescapably towards chaos due to political and economic mismanagement and corruption of the incumbent government. The explanation for military rule centred round the argument that the Army being the most organised and disciplined institution was the only one capable of setting things right and dealing effectively with internal and external problems. However, an analysis of the specific situations in which the Army has seized power at different periods of history suggests otherwise. For instance, the primary reason given by General Musharraf for the 1999 coup was the intention to safeguard the 'integrity, sovereignty and unity' of the country. However, it is apparent that the coup was a response to what was perceived by the military as unwarranted interference by the political leadership in the dominant role that the Army was playing in the affairs of the state, and which it perceived to be constituting a threat to its professional/institutional interests. Firstly, Nawaz Sharif was responsible for getting the Eighth Amendment to the Constitution—Article 58(2b)—which had allowed the Army to exercise influence over the political leadership *via* the president—repealed. Secondly, Nawaz Sharif successfully removed Jehangir Karamat as the Army Chief, when the latter advocated an institutionalised role for the Army in the decision-making process. Thirdly, Nawaz Sharif's promise to the then US President Bill Clinton that Pakistan would withdraw its troops from across the LoC, was a blow to the Army. The Army did not take kindly to the fact that the blame for Kargil was being heaped on it. All these tensions culminated in the attempted dismissal of General Musharraf as the Army Chief in October 1999. This was unpalatable to the Army high command and was the breaking point in the already acrimonious relationship between the military and Nawaz Sharif, the then prime minister.

While Musharraf forcibly took over the reins of the country with the promise to bring about wide-ranging reforms within the country, his achievements are questionable. While Musharraf lambasted his political predecessors for indulging in tyranny, dishonesty and cronyism, he manipulated the political parties in Pakistan to suit his own purposes. He engineered a split in the Pakistan Muslim League-Nawaz (PML-N) by cultivating the dissident faction of the PML. He also tried to eliminate major political opponents by amending the Political Parties Act of 1962 in order to oust, convict and disqualify rival politicians. While the National Accountability Bureau (NAB) was criticised for being selective in its functioning, the National Reconstruction Bureau (NRB) faced criticism for accommodating a large number of Army personnel. The referendum of April 2002 was criticised for certain 'irregularities' which allowed the verdict to be in Musharraf's favour. Article 58(2b) was restored. The National Security Council (NSC) faced criticism due to its composition and the fact that it allowed the Army to further consolidate its position.

Terrorism, extremism and sectarianism were major threats to the internal security and stability of the country. This was underscored by the attacks and assassination attempts targeting senior military and government officials including Musharraf. However, the efforts made by Musharraf to clamp down on militant organisations were widely regarded as being temporary and cosmetic. These were aimed more at curbing inter-sectarian terrorism within the country rather than beyond the borders of Pakistan. While the Pakistani establishment maintained the façade of flushing out militants from the Federally Administered Tribal Areas (FATA), yet many Taliban and Al Qaeda elements were allowed safe passage. While the various indicators of the economy did show improvement during his rule, the stabilisation of the domestic economy could perhaps be attributed to the assistance received from international aid donors. Musharraf's attempts to introduce grassroots democracy by holding local government elections were criticised for a number of irregularities that allowed the PML-Quaid-e-Azam (PML-Q) candidates to come to power. His promises to bring about provincial harmony are belied by the massive anti-government feeling within Balochistan at the time and the crisis created by the killing of the veteran Baloch leader Nawab Akbar Khan Bugti.

The overwhelming support for the return to democracy from the civil society, especially the lawyers' movement which led the anti-Musharraf tirade finally resulted in the elections of 2008, and the return to power of a duly elected government.

The restoration of democracy after nine years engendered high hopes that the newly elected government would be able to provide effective governance. It was assumed that post-elections, the Pakistan People's Party (PPP) would work together with the other mainstream party, the PML-N, to enforce democratic norms, which would ensure a limited role for the Army. However, relations between the leadership of the two parties remain fraught with tension and mistrust. Indications are that the current government headed by the PPP will complete its full five year term, various problems notwithstanding. To that extent it would seem to be a big achievement, as the previous governments of PPP and PML leadership were never allowed to finish their full term due to disagreements with the Pakistan military on various domestic, foreign and security issues. The current leadership's success can partly be attributed to the understanding within the Army, that public opinion would not be amenable to an overt role for the Army in governance. Hence, the Army has continued to play an important role in matters of foreign policy and internal security, more or less in coordination with the government. Its position of importance is also ensured given the significance that the US attaches to its relationship with the military, in its War on Terror.

There continues to be an uneasy co-existence between the political leadership and the Army. Stark differences on issues of national security and policy remain. President Asif Ali Zardari soon after assuming power made the statement that Pakistan will review its nuclear policy with regard to 'No-First Use' and made a plea for betterment of relations between India and Pakistan. Yet, he has not been able to follow this up with any concrete proposals. On the other hand, statements emerging from the military leadership continued to stress the Indo-centric nature of their military preparedness. In addition, there has been enough evidence linking the Pakistani establishment to the Mumbai blasts of November 2008. Also, the response of the civilian government and the military to the Mumbai blasts was quite divergent. Prime Minister Syed Yousuf Raza Gilani's proposal to send the Inter Services Intelligence (ISI) chief to India for consultations soon after the attacks was shot down by the military.

In an earlier incident, the civilian government was unsuccessful in its attempt to place the ISI under the ministry of interior. The effort to bring the agency under the political control of the government was aborted rather quickly. Further, the *WikiLeaks* expose underscored the lack of trust between the civilian and military leadership. This was revealed by the president in his verbal communication with foreign visiting dignitaries wherein he expressed his fears that he would be removed from office by the Army, or that he was kept in the dark about critical information. The Army chief, on the other hand, revealed his thinking regarding the removal of the president as well as his concerns regarding corruption and mis-governance.

At the same time, circumstances dictate that both the political and civilian leadership work together on crucial national security matters. There have been significant instances, when the military leaders have given briefings to the political leadership apprising them about the counter-terrorism efforts in FATA. Also, both the political and military leadership are present in meetings of the Pakistan-US strategic dialogue.

The killing of Osama bin Laden by the US Special Forces within Pakistan followed by the terrorist attack on Mehran Base evoked sharp criticism against the military and raised doubts about the credibility and efficiency of the Army. The extent to which the Army suffered loss of credibility can be gauged from the fact that this incident has been compared to the same loss of face that the Army suffered in the aftermath of the 1971 war, when Pakistan lost East Pakistan. As people expressed discontentment with the handling of Pakistan's national security strategy, the Army chief felt compelled to reassure his men, as he made a round of various garrisons. That the Army felt the pressure was obvious. Yet, the civilian government showed itself incapable of capitalising on the anti-Army wave. Ironically, the parliamentary resolution in the aftermath of the US action in Abbottabad, called for a review of the US-Pakistan relationship rather than questioning how Osama bin laden and his family lived in the vicinity of a well-known military academy without the knowledge of/or with the connivance of the Pakistan military. Further, in the resolution adopted on May 13, 2011 at the end of the joint session of parliament, the members declared full confidence in the defence forces.

Army in People's Perception

The popular perception of the Army in Pakistan has changed with changing times. In fact, the Army has taken full advantage of popular disillusionment with the political conditions from time to time. The first coup by Ayub Khan was welcomed by the people because it offered them some promise of stability. The first seven years of intense political bickering over fundamental issues of statecraft had tried the patience of the people who saw in Ayub a plausible alternative to the ineffectual political class. The second coup of July 1977 by Zia-ul-Haq, was again, in many ways, a culmination of the politics of self-aggrandisement by Zulfiqar Ali Bhutto, who sought to overreach himself and became so dictatorial that he made a mockery of constitutional democracy which he had himself initiated. The Army, thoroughly discredited by its defeat in 1971 at the hands of India, was provided an opportunity to reinvent itself and its usurpation of power was again welcome by a section of the people as a natural consequence of failure of political leadership. The third coup by Musharraf in October 1999 was similarly a reaction to the efforts of a democratically elected government led by Nawaz Sharif to assume dictatorial powers by steamrolling all opposition to his rule by undemocratic means. Musharraf was hailed as a saviour by some politicians in the opposition when he dismissed the civilian government and took charge as the 'chief executive' of Pakistan.

This is not to suggest that the military dictators are liked by the people of Pakistan. While military dictators have been welcome as alternatives to the civilian political leadership at certain critical junctures of Pakistani history, the fact remains that there have been popular protests against these dictators when they seek to perpetuate their hold on power by manipulating the system. All of them have tried to legitimise their rule through popular referendums or even sham elections. However, they have ruled by force rather than popular will. Popular protest against military rule has been very common in Pakistan despite violent reprisals by the military.

The Army is likely to retain its significance in Pakistan because of the following reasons: the failure of Pakistan to evolve as a democracy; the inability of the political leadership to win the confidence of the people; the gradual consolidation of the Army as a vital institution and an important pillar of the state; and the perpetuation of the irrational fear of India. Despite popular disillusionment with military dictators, the people tend to look at the Army as the only institution that can keep the country together.

Relations with India

An important factor legitimising Army's dominant role in Pakistani state structure has been the obsession of the Pakistani ruling elite with idea of India as an implacable enemy eternally conspiring to destroy Pakistan and reunite it into the so called 'Akhand Bharat'[26] (undivided India). The perennial sense of enmity with India cultivated carefully through propaganda and a selective drumming up of history has succeeded in over-exaggerating the importance of the Pakistan Army as an existential necessity in the Pakistani psyche. This explains why the military has retained its popularity despite the fact that it has led Pakistan to unnecessary confrontations with India and to summary defeats at the hands of the Indian Army.

Since its formation in 1947, Pakistan has waged three major wars with India in 1947, 1965 and 1971, apart from the low intensity Kargil war of 1999. All these wars were started by Pakistan[27] and ended in huge reverses for the Pakistan Army. Pakistan has had an insecurity complex *vis-à-vis* India right since 1947, and since the war in 1971, which resulted in dismemberment of Pakistan, this has been coupled with a desire for vengeance. Pakistan has unleashed an asymmetric war (through armed non-state actors) against India right since 1947, initially aimed at wresting Kashmir from India, but later with the express aim of keeping India internally engaged. Since late 1980s, when Pakistan went nuclear,[28] Pakistan has used this strategy even more consistently. The most visible face of this asymmetric war was its subversive strategy in Punjab and Jammu and Kashmir during the late 1980s.

Pakistan's sponsorship of militancy in Jammu and Kashmir especially since 1988-89, has been termed variously as 'proxy war' and 'cross-border terrorism' by Indian analysts. This strategy continued even through the Kargil invasion, the 9/11 attacks and subsequent pressure on Pakistan to snap its links with *jihadi* elements. Following militant attack on the Indian Parliament on December 13, 2001, Musharraf assured India that he would rein in *jihadi* elements in Pakistan. There was a drop in infiltration across the LoC after 2002 and militancy in Kashmir declined. However, this did not mean that Pakistan gave up its strategy of using the non-state actors to weaken India. The series of bomb attacks in various cities of India since 2004-05 (Surat, Jaipur, Mumbai, Bangalore, Hyderabad and the capital city of Delhi) and the 26/11 Mumbai attacks suggest that this asymmetric war has now spread beyond Kashmir and the basic strategy of Pakistan military has been to pose an internal security challenge to India and weaken its capacity for any possible external aggression directed especially against Pakistan.[29] Pakistan's close association with the US in the decade long Afghan War (1979-89) and the ongoing War on Terror (2001-till date) has added considerably to the capacity of the Pakistan Army to wage such a prolonged asymmetric war against India.

Future Prospects

Pakistan Army is very likely to remain the most dominant institution by default in future. It is a tightly knit professional group, with a political world-view of its own, that has largely defined the national interest of Pakistan for a long time. The political forces have failed to throw up a reliable alternative to the Army and are unlikely to do so in future, primarily because they are a divided lot and have no clear vision or moral authority to legitimise their hold on Pakistani society and the state. They have squandered away several historical opportunities (the last being the popular upsurge against Musharraf's rule), to unite and redefine statecraft, to limit the role of the Army in politics and foreign policy and rein in rogue elements/departments within the Army. The Army has, in the meanwhile, reasserted itself as the protector of national interests and has managed to win over popular trust and confidence as the only institution that can hold Pakistan together. In the face of the worsening internal as well as regional security situation, the Army has assumed centre-stage in Pakistani politics once again. It will continue to dictate Pakistan's security and foreign policy in future and the civilian governments are unlikely to take any step to curtail the Army's powers and provoke it thereby.

This is not to deny however that the Army is free from trouble. Due to the blow back of the Afghan *Jihad* of the 1980s and the Taliban assertion of the 1990s, Pakistani society as a whole has been unmistakably radicalised and it has had its influence on the Army as well. The increasing attacks on military facilities since mid-2008 indicate that Pakistani armed forces have been penetrated by *jihadi* forces, such as the Al Qaeda and its affiliates. Thus, in spite of the efforts of the high command to purge the armed forces of *jihadi* malcontents, a large number of subalterns view radical forces as natural allies and share their perspective of converting Pakistan into an Islamic Emirate. In the aftermath of the US withdrawal from Afghanistan, these elements may assert themselves and build pressures from within and force the top leadership to Islamicise the Army further. This would spell disaster for both Pakistan and the region. If the Sunni-Wahhabi orientation of the most assertive radical forces in the Af-Pak region is allowed to have its way then the region may witness a sectarian holocaust followed by inter-state tensions which will destabilise South and South-Central Asia and pose a threat to international peace.

Another plausible scenario could be that Pakistan Army would retain its professionalism even if it accommodates jihadist philosophy to certain extent. However, this *jihadi* temper will certainly be used against India as a natural unifier and a diversionary tactic to keep both Army and Pakistan together. Short of direct military engagement, the Army may take recourse to its familiar strategy of encouraging subversive forces within India and complicate the internal security situation in India to keep it internally engaged. Thus, in either case, the security concerns of India will increase manifold. In any case, the Army would retain its importance and influence in Pakistan and remain a critical factor in the regional security calculus.

Notes

1. Stephen P. Cohen, *The Pakistan Army,* Oxford University Press, Karachi, 1998, p. 7.
2. Professor Stephen Cohen has demarcated the officers of the Pakistan Army into three generations. For a detailed analysis, see Stephen P. Cohen, *The Pakistan Army,* Oxford University Press, Karachi, 1998, pp. 55-74 and Stephen P. Cohen, *The Idea of Pakistan*, Oxford University Press, New Delhi, 2005, pp. 99-109.
3. Stephen P. Cohen, no. 1, p. 7.
4. Maj. Gen. Fazal Muqeem Khan, *The Story of Pakistan Army*, Oxford University Press, Karachi, p. 47, as cited in Pervaiz Iqbal Cheema, *The Armed Forces of Pakistan*, Oxford University Press, Karachi, 2006, p. 52.
5. Pervaiz Iqbal Cheema, *The Armed Forces of Pakistan*, Oxford University Press, Karachi, 2006, p. 57.
6. Stephen P. Cohen, *The Idea of Pakistan*, Oxford University Press, New Delhi, 2005, p. 102.
7. Shuja Nawaz, *Crossed Swords: Pakistan: Its Army, and the Wars Within*, Oxford University Press, Karachi, 2008, Introduction, p. xxxvii
8. Owen Bennett Jones, *Pakistan: Eye of the Storm*, Yale University Press, London, 2002, p. 262.
9. S.T. Das, *Indian Military: It's History and Development*, Sagar Publications, New Delhi, 1969, p. 162, as cited in Pervaiz Iqbal Cheema, *The Armed Forces of Pakistan*, Oxford University Press, Karachi, 2006, p. 51.
10. Hasan Askari Rizvi, *The Military and Politics in Pakistan 1947-86*, Progressive Publishers, Lahore, 1986, p. 33, as cited in Pervaiz Iqbal Cheema, *The Armed Forces of Pakistan*, Oxford University Press, Karachi, 2006, p. 51.
11. Stephen P. Cohen, no. 6, p. 98.
12. Husain Haqqani, *Pakistan: Between Mosque and Military*, Vanguard Books, Lahore, 2005, p. 29.
13. This section is based on Sumita Kumar's article, "Pakistan's Strategic Thinking", *Strategic Analysis,* 35 (3), May 2011, pp. 479-492.
14. Stephen P. Cohen, no. 6, p. 98.
15. See the introductory page of the website of the Pakistan Army which contains the motto, at http://www.pakistanarmy.gov.pk/
16. In the book, Malik mentions that Jihad was not merely military strategy, but the "near equivalent of total or grand strategy", and it was "a continuous and never ending struggle waged on all fronts including political, economic, social, psychological, domestic, moral

and spiritual to attain the object of policy." S.K. Malik, *The Quranic Concept of War*, Himalayan Books, New Delhi, 1979, p. 54.

17. Shuja Nawaz, no. 7.
18. In April 2007, the Pakistani Army announced its plan to create three new army geographical commands to improve the operation of domestic land forces. The Northern Command was likely to be headquartered at Gujranwala or Mangla; the Southern Command at Quetta; and the Central Command at Lahore or Multan. See "Pakistan to Create Three Army Commands", April 2007, at http://www.pakistanidefence.com/news/MonthlyNewsArchive/2007/April2007.htm. Also, see "Pakistan Army Revamp: Northern, Southern, Central Commands to be Setup", April 25, 2007, at http://www.india-defence.com/reports-3081
19. See "COAS visits second leg of Azm-e-Nau III", *Geo Television Network*, April 27, 2010, at http://www.geo.tv/4-27-2010/63915.htm
20. Sher Baz Khan, "Punjab's dominance in army being reduced: ISPR", *Dawn*, September 14, 2007, at http://archives.dawn.com/2007/09/14/top13.htm
21. Defence Wide Budget covers expenditure on the maintenance of paramilitary forces of Pakistan which provide a wide range of services. These forces are: the Coast Guard, the Frontier Corps, the Maritime Security Agency, the National Guard, the Northern Light Infantry, and the Pakistan Rangers.
22. The figures on Pakistan's defence expenditure have been taken from the Pakistan Federal Budget. For details, see http://www.finance.gov.pk/budget/Non-development%202011-2012/Non-development%202011-2012.rar
23. See "U.S. Arms Sales to Pakistan", CRS Report RS22757, and "Pakistan-U.S. Relations", CRS Report RL33498, January 2011, at http://www.fas.org/sgp/crs/row/pakarms.pdf
24. According to Hasan Askari Rizvi, the military's industrial and commercial interests can be categorised into three types. The first comes under the direct administrative control of the army chief. The second type of interests is looked after by the Defence Production Division of the Ministry of Defence. The third type includes four charitable trusts for the welfare of ex-Services personnel, the Fauji Foundation and the Army Welfare Trust of the Army, the Shaheen Foundation of the Air Force and the Bahria Foundation of the Navy. Hasan Askari Rizvi, *Military, State and Society in Pakistan*, McMillan Press Ltd., Hampshire, 2000, pp. 236-238. While these foundations have become a conglomerate of companies with assets of millions of rupees, they have been criticised for being a burden on the economy. For details, see Ayesha Siddiqa-Agha, *Pakistan's Arms Procurement and Buildup, 1979-99: In Search of a Policy*, Palgrave, Hampshire, 2001, p. 84.
25. For a discussion on the reasons for the Army's perpetuation in power, see Sumita Kumar, "The Army in the Power Structure (of Pakistan)" in Ajay Darshan Behera and Mathew Joseph C. (eds.), *Pakistan in a Changing Strategic Context*, Knowledge World, New Delhi in association with Centre for Strategic and Regional Studies, University of Jammu, 2004, pp. 153-158.
26. The dream of *Akhand Bharat* (Undivided India) did excite a fringe group in India during and after partition which was perceived as an imperial conspiracy which was too unnatural to succeed. However, it has died its natural death in India. Interestingly, the ruling elite in Pakistan has not been able to accept Indian acceptance of Pakistan as an independent and sovereign state so far; hence, there is an unreasoned fear of being overwhelmed by a naturally preponderant India.
27. Altaf Gauhar who was information secretary in the Ayub Khan regime and later became chief editor of the daily *Dawn*, wrote in a series of articles in the daily *Nation*, during

September-October 1999, in the immediate aftermath of the Kargil War, that all the wars against India were started by the Pakistan army with the wrong assumption that the 'Hindu' soldiers of India would not be able 'to stand more than a couple of hard blows at the right time and place.' The first article in the series was titled "Four Wars, One Assumption" (*The Nation,* September 5, 1999). Later in 2010, Air Chief Marshal Asghar Khan, who participated in the 1965 war and now founder patron of *Tehreek-i-Istiqlal,* in his interaction with the media in Lahore, reiterated this fact by saying, "I am not favouring India. But it is true that all wars fought between Pakistan and India had been initiated by the respective Pakistani governments." See "Pakistan responsible for wars with India", *Dawn*, January 14, 2010, at http://archives.dawn.com/archives/82394

28. In his interview with the well-known Indian journalist Kuldip Nayar on January 28, 1987, A Q Khan, regarded as the father of the Pakistani bomb, admitted that Pakistan had the ability to produce the nuclear bomb. This was done against the backdrop of 'Operation Brasstacks' (November 1986-March 1987) by India and was meant to act as a deterrent.
29. As this report was being prepared, a US Scholar also came up with a similar reading of Pakistani policy *vis-à-vis* India. See C. Christine Fair, "The Militant Challenge in Pakistan", *Asia Policy*, No. 11, January 2011.

Chapter Seven

'Defenders of the Nation': Evolution and Role of the Sri Lankan Army

M. Mayilvaganan

Introduction: The Security Environment of the Country

Geo-political/Strategic Significance of the Country

The geo-political[1] significance of Sri Lanka in the international arena assumes significance in view of its strategic location between the west and the east along vital sea lines[2] in the Indian Ocean. The presence of natural harbours, such as Trincomalee, has further added to its geo-strategic value. Realising its gifted location in the Indian Ocean, Sri Lanka has always sought to take advantage of the prevailing competition in the region either by playing one against the other or by co-operating with one of the powers. In present times too, it has used the competitive politics of the countries vying for influence in the Indian Ocean to legitimise and seek support for its own 'war against terrorism.'[3]

Geographical Terrain

Sri Lanka as an Island-nation with minimal population is surrounded by passable barriers. In the south, east and west, it is surrounded by the Indian Ocean, and is separated from India in the far northwest by a thin waterway—the Palk Strait.

Threat Perceptions: Key Domestic and External Challenges

Strategically, Sri Lanka has had two challenges, both pivoting around the question of defending the Island-nation. First, from internal separatist groups—Liberation Tigers of Tamil Eelam (LTTE)—which intended to establish a separate Tamil nation on the basis of linguistic and ethnic identity. Second, from India, a regional power with a substantial Tamil population in its southern Tamil Nadu state who share ethnic linkages with the Sri Lanka's restive Tamil minority.[4] Ironically, for the majority Sinhalese and from the Sri Lankan Army's viewpoint, the probability of India as a potential threat to the Sri Lanka's sovereignty and independence has not abated even in the post-LTTE scenario. In short, Sri Lanka has two geopolitical imperatives: to secure its unity and territorial integrity against separatist movements; and to maintain its sovereignty, distinctive identity and culture.[5]

Evolution of the Sri Lankan Army

With the gaining of independence in 1948, began the formation of a native Sri Lankan Army (SLA), then known as the Royal Ceylon Army. The Army Act No. 17 of 1949, passed by the Parliament on April 11, 1949 and later enacted officially through Gazette Extraordinary No. 10028 on October 10, 1949, marked the creation of the national army.[6] The name Royal Ceylon Army was changed into Sri Lankan Army in 1972, when Sri Lanka became an independent republic.[7] Brigadier James Sinclair, Earl of Caithness, was the first commander as well as the general officer commanding of the Ceylon Army at the time of independence. Later, Major General Anton Muttukumaru took command of the Army by becoming the first Sri Lankan commander of the SLA.

Under the 1947 bi-lateral Anglo-Ceylonese Defence Agreement, the British were supposed to oversee the national army. Moreover, the Defence Agreement of 1947 provided the safeguard for the island nation by assurance of support from the British in the event of any attack by a foreign power.[8]

The strength of the SLA at the time of creation was relatively small and consisted of a regular and a volunteer force—the successor of the disbanded CDF (Ceylon Defence Force).[9] Owing to a lack of any major external threat, the growth of the SLA was dawdling till 1970s. For much of the 1950s and 60s, the Army was mainly engaged with the task of building itself through training and recruiting new personnel. In addition, it focused on raising an artillery regiment, an infantry battalion, an engineer's squadron, a medical unit, and a service corps. Meanwhile, the primary duties of the Army promptly moved towards internal security with the increase in human trafficking from South India since 1952. The first internal security operation code named *Operation Monty* was initiated in 1952 in support of Royal Ceylon Navy coastal patrols and police operations, with the aim of countering the influx of illegal South Indian immigrants carried out by smugglers on its north-western coast.[10] Furthermore, the Army was also involved in restoring peace under provincial emergency regulations to help out police during the 1953 *hartal*, the 1956 Gal Oya Valley riots, the 1958 riots, and the 1961 Colombo Port strike.[11]

Later, with *Janatha Vimukthi Peramuna* (People's Liberation Front or the JVP)[12] leading the Marxist revolt, particularly the coordinated attack on 74 police stations on April 5 1971, the SLA undertook its first major counter insurgency operation to thwart the former's attempt to overthrow the government.[13] Prior to it, the Sri Lankan military had literally never fought a war. They had such limited tasks as guarding the presidential palace and maintaining the internal law and order. In fact, according to a report, dated May 9, 1971, published by the *Washington Post*, the SLA all these years had been firing at dummies. However, within a month of the Army's operation, the insurgency suffered a serious setback with most of the JVP insurgents either imprisoned or killed.[14]

After successfully defeating the JVP insurgency in 1971, the SLA was confronted with the challenge of countering highly motivated Tamil rebel groups in the north and the east in the 1980s. Soon the Army had to simultaneously launch a counter-insurgency operation against the revived JVP insurgency in 1987 as well.[15] The operation against the LTTE gradually shaped the SLA's role and its emergence as a strong force. The war with the LTTE was finally won with the dislodging of the Tiger leadership in May 2009. It was an impressive victory for the SLA, boosting its morale as well as profile.

Structure/Formation of the National Army

The SLA is the largest of the three armed services and consists of a regular force,[16] a regular reserve,[17] a volunteer force and a volunteer reserve. Lt. Gen. Jagath Jayasuriya is at present the Commander of the SLA[18] who took over from Lt. Gen. Sarath Fonseka, under whose command the SLA scored a triumphant victory in the recently concluded *Eelam War IV*. He provides operational direction to the defence forces through the National Defence Council (NDC)[19] under the Ministry of Defence. He is assisted by the Chief of Staff of the Army. The Commandant of the Volunteer Force is head of the Army Volunteer Force and is responsible for the administration and recruitment of reserve personnel.

The formations of the SLA grew from time to time keeping in view the changing/rising security requirements of the country. In the initial phase, there were no formations and all units were directly functioning under Army Headquarters. Temporary field headquarters were formed when needed, as was the case during the 1958 communal riots. Similarly, the first field formation was raised in 1963 to prevent illicit immigration from South India.

The Army is currently structured into 13 divisions and several independent brigades. Each division is in command for a particular region and is commanded by a General Officer Commanding of the rank of a Major General. However, almost all the divisions are put in command for the security in the conflict affected north and east. The region assigned to a particular division is further divided into areas, which are assigned to brigades. Each brigade is commanded by an officer of the rank of Brigadier. Generally, number of Infantry Battalions, support arms—Artillery, Engineers and Signals—and support services—Service Corps, Engineering Services, Ordnance Corps, Electrical and Mechanical Engineers—were placed under its command. Apart from this, Armour, Artillery, Engineers and Signals Units are grouped under Brigade Headquarters of their own arm.

In addition, the individual regiments, such as, the Sri Lanka Light Infantry and the Sinhala Regiment operate separately. The infantry battalion—the basic unit of organisation in field operations—has five companies of four platoons each. It is assisted by various regiments[20] and a variety of logistics units such as an armoured regiment, five reconnaissance regiments, three mechanized infantry regiments, five field artillery regiments, three commando regiments, three Special Forces regiments, six field engineering regiments, five signals battalion, and a medical corps.[21] The commando regiment was established in 1986. The Special Force Regiment (SF) is an elite unit of the Army, specialising in hard-hitting encounters and their motto is "*determined, dared, and done.*"[22] Notably, the SF Regiment, which is trained in deep penetration capabilities, has the distinction of taking part in almost all major offensives conducted by the Army since 1986, particularly in the final battle with the Tigers.

At the headquarters level, the Army is divided into a number of branches. The General Staff (GS) branch coordinates operations and training whereas the Adjutant General's (AGs) branch is responsible for personal administration, welfare, medical services and rehabilitation. The Military Secretary is responsible for handling all matters pertaining to officers, such as promotion, posting and discipline.[23] The Quarter Master General's branch is responsible for movement, supply of essential items, construction and maintenance. The Master General of Ordnance's branch deals with procurement and maintenance of vehicles and special equipments. Besides, the headquarters of each field formations has its own staff. For instance, a divisional headquarter is divided into a GS and AG; each headed by a Colonel and is responsible for operations & training and administration & logistics respectively. Similarly, a Major is responsible for operations and administration at the level of a brigade.

Ethnic Composition

At the time of SLA's formation, Tamils and Burghers accounted for 50 per cent of its officer corps.[24] However, gradually the government succeeded in recasting the armed forces in its own way with recruitment at all levels increasingly dominated by the Sinhalese. The proportion of minorities—Tamils—dropped down to less than 5 per cent when 1983 riots took place.[25] Besides, the ethnic conflict tended to discourage male Tamil youths from pursuing a career in the military. At present, almost all enlisted personnel in the armed services are Sinhalese except for some Muslims. In fact, more Muslim youths began to be recruited since 2005. The country's first exclusively Muslim infantry battalion was formed to provide protection to those living in the eastern province.[26] Few Muslim officers are working in the intelligence units too.[27]

Recruitment/Selection Procedure

The selection criterion for the Army has remained essentially same since the British times. Males and females not less than 18 years of age are preferred in the service.[28] Minimum qualifications of three passes at the General Certificate of Education (GCE) Advance Level (A/L) Examination and a minimum of 25 marks for the fourth subject with a minimum aggregate of 180 marks are required. Also, they are required to pass in English Language and an ordinary pass in Mathematics in not more than two sittings. And those having an ordinary pass may apply on condition that they will appear for the next GCE Ordinary Level (O/L) examination and obtain a credit pass in English.[29] Interviews for recruitment are conducted in second stage. In some cases mobile recruitments were held in selected areas. For instance, interviews were conducted at the Ampara Combat Training College to recruit Muslim youths to the Sri Lanka's first all Muslim regiment.[30]

Budgeting

The Sri Lankan government, which had engaged in a long drawn battle with the LTTE, allocated Rs.177.1 billion ($1.66 billion) for its defence forces in its 2008 budget. Quoting the appropriation bill published by the finance ministry, the *Lanka Business Online* (LBO) website reported that the defence ministry will get Rs.18.7 billion as capital expenditure and Rs.158.4 billion as recurrent expenditure in 2009.[31] Despite the final defeat of the Tamil rebels in mid-May 2009, Sri Lanka has raised its defence expenditure by another 20 per cent and subsequently Sri Lankan Parliament on October 8, 2009 approved an additional Rs. 33 billion ($287 million) to pay for hardware and beef up security in former conflict zones. According to the Sri Lankan Government and military, they are in need of another Rs. 20 billion to recruit more soldiers and pay for fuel, medical supplies and compensation for those who were injured or died in combat.[32] In line, Sri Lanka increased the defence spending to Rs. 230 billion ($2.1 billion) in 2012 from Rs. 215 billion (about $1.92 billion) in 2011.[33]

Training

The new recruits undergo extensive training programmes. A number of training schools/academies were established to prepare the new recruits for providing additional training to serving officers and other ranks. Generally, most of the basic training is provided at the Army Training Centre (ATC)[34] in Diyatalawa in the Badulla District. The ATC was later renamed as the Sri Lanka Military Academy (SLMA) and since then it has been totally utilised for training of Officer Cadets. At any one time, five to six hundred Officer Cadets are trained at this institution. At any one time, five to six hundred Officer Cadets are reportedly trained at this institution. During a period of two years, the trainees are trained in leadership, tactics, weapons training, law, military accounting systems and academic studies. Also an intensive course in English Language is conducted during the first six months of training to enhance the English knowledge of the Officer Cadets.[35]

Apart from this, there are number of training centres established for both general and specialised trainings. They are: Army Training School (ATS), Infantry Training Centre (ITC), Combat Training School (CTS),[36] Army Physical Education Centre (APEC), Volunteer Force Training School (VFTS), Marksman Sniper Training School (MSTS), Non-Commissioned Officer Training School (NCOTS), Language Training School (LTS), Institute of Peacekeeping Support Operations Training Sri Lanka (IPSOT-SL), Regimental Training Centres. Apart from this, there is Armoured Corps Training Centre, School of Artillery, School of Military Engineering, School of Mechanical Engineers, School of Signals, Commando Regiment Training School, Engineer Services School, Sri Lanka Army Service Corps School, Sri Lanka Army Military School of Nursing, Sri Lanka Army Ordnance School, Sri Lanka Electrical and Mechanical Engineers School, Sri Lanka Corps of Military Police School, Sri Lanka Army General Service Corps and Ranaviru IT Training Institute.[37]

Among them, the Infantry Training School in Minneriya, the Combat Training School in Ampara, and the Army Training School in Maduru Oya are assigned for commissioned officers and rank. Non Commissioned Officers (NCOs) receive training at the Non Commissioned Officers Training School at Kala Oya. Junior field officers of the Army and their counterparts in the Navy and Air Force are given advanced training and education at the Defence

Services Command and Staff College (DSCSC) at Batalanda, which was established in 1997 as the Army Command and Staff College. Specialised and additional training is given by specialist training schools,[38] regimental training centres, and individual field units.

In 1981, the Sri Lankan Government also formed the General Sir John Kotelawala Defence University (KDU)[39] at Rathmalana near Colombo, devoted completely to defence studies. Annually, about 50 cadets from all three services are admitted to the University's three-year programme of academic work and basic training. The successful cadets with exceptional performance can pursue post-graduate studies in reputed universities/ institutions in accordance with the requirements of the Services to which they belong.

For the advanced training facilities, the Army to an extent depends on military training provided by foreign countries. In particular, the United Kingdom (UK) played a major role in the early years following independence and continues to be an important source of military expertise to the Sri Lankan military. India,[40] Israel, Pakistan, Australia, Malaysia,[41] and the United States (US) are other resource for the Sri Lankan military's advance training. However, it seems that the Sri Lankan Army is presently offering special courses based on lessons drawn from the *Eelam War IV*[42] to the other countries, and Pakistan is reportedly availing of it.

The cadets graduating from the academy/school are commissioned as officers in the regular and volunteer forces. The course for officer cadets runs for 90 weeks and includes training in tactics and administration which helps prepare the cadets to take up the position of platoon commanders. The course covers military and academic subjects. It also trains the cadets physically and helps to further leadership qualities. In short, for the commission course, the cadets undergo a 56 week training programme. Afterwards, there is 10 years of service for regular army officers and five years of service for volunteer officers.

Training is conducted in Sinhala and English. The main purpose of the training is to introduce cadets to the profession of arms and guide them to develop their knowledge and skills and to foster a spirit of comradeship amongst them to develop jointness and a sense of national unity amongst the corps of three services. The SLA is certainly now better equipped, with weaponry and training geared towards meeting any eventuality.

Strength of the National Army

In 2008, the Sri Lankan military stood at 150,000 regular, including 2,960 women plus 10,000 personnel in reserve. The Army has 117,900 personnel[43] with 1,100 reserve, who are organised into 26 regiments at present. Though the actual strength of the Sri Lankan Army today is 'bit of a puzzle', it is reportedly over 200,000. Attempts to suppress the internal strife in 1970s and later efforts to dislodge the LTTE had necessitated the rapid expansion of the Army. Citing a *Wikileak* document, the Norwegian newspaper *Aftenposten* reported that SLA plans to increase the size of the armed forces by a total of 210,000 soldiers over the five years up to 2015, to a final strength of 410,000.[44]

Table 1: Trends of SLA's Expansion

Year	*1970*	*1992*	*1996*	*2002*	*2008*	*2009*
Army	7000[45]	80,000[46]	100,000[47]	118,000[48]	150,000[49]	200,000[50]

Logistics—Sources and Nature of Weaponry

The SLA began to expand the range of its weaponry only after the 1971 uprising and in particular after the LTTE's insurgency. Previously, its weaponry mainly comprised of British Lee Enfield rifles, Sten Submachine guns, Vickers machine guns, Bren machine guns, 6-inch coastal guns, and Bren Gun Carrier, 40 mm anti-aircraft guns, 3.7 inch heavy anti-aircraft guns and 4.2-inch heavy mortars. Initially, the Sri Lanka Government under Sirimavo Bandaranaike went in for new sources of weaponry to counter the Marxist insurgency from the Soviet Union, Yugoslavia, and China.

Later, to meet the threat posed by the LTTE, the Army purchased modern military hardware including 5 inch calibre heavy machine guns, rocket propelled grenade launchers, night vision devices, 106 mm Recoilless rifles, 60 mm and 81 mm Mortars,[51] 40 mm grenade launchers and some sniper rifles. Also, refurbished Armoured Personnel Carriers (APC)[52] were added to the 'A' vehicle fleet of the 1st Reece Regiment of Sri Lankan Armoured Corps and the capability of the Sri Lankan Artillery was enhanced with the induction of Ordnance QF 25 pounders. In 1985, the South African made Buffel was introduced to counter the land mines. Subsequently, the Army developed its own Unicorn in 1987 and the new Unibuffel,[53] both assembled by the Sri Lanka Electrical & Mechanical Engineers Regiment using Indian TATA engine.

In recent years, particularly in the light of the LTTE's air strikes in March 2007 and thereafter with the decisive war against the Tigers in the final stages of *Eelam War IV*, Sri Lanka yet again had to modernise its military hardware. As the US and European regulations disallowed selling of weaponry to nations that are suffering from internal conflicts, Sri Lanka became increasingly reliant on China and Pakistan for weapons procurement. Besides, Sri Lanka continues to receive modern weapons from Israel, Ukraine, India, Britain and other former suppliers. Also, a number of new weapons were reported to have been clandestinely acquired from Czech Republic[54] and Ukraine during the final northern offensive.

List of weaponry that SLA owns include:

- Main battle tanks—T-55AM2
- Infantry fighting vehicles—BMP-2
- Artillery—A 152 mm towed howitzer
- Hand guns—Beretta M9 Pistol; Glock 17, Enfield revolver
- Assault Rifles[55] such as Type 56, AK-47, Type 81, Heckler & Koch G3, M16, M4 Carbine, FN FAL, SAR-80, Type 95
- Sub-Machine guns like H&K MP5, 9 mm Uzi and Sterling submachine guns[56]
- Sniper Rifles—Dragunov, Heckler & Koch PSG1
- Machine guns[57]—PK, Type 56 LMG, HK21 Belt-fed light machine gun, FN minimi general purpose machine gun, FN MAG general purpose machine gun
- Grenade launchers—HK 69 Breech-loading grenade launcher, M203 Grenade launcher; Rocket launchers—RPO-A Shmel man-portable rocket launcher, Type 69 RPG Rocket launchers
- Anti-tank missiles—Baktar-Shikan Anti-tank guided missiles
- Armoured vehicles—Main battle tanks—T-55[58] and T-55AM2, Type 69, Type 59
- Infantry fighting vehicles—BMP-3, BMP-2, BMP-1
- Armoured personnel carriers—TYPE 89 (YW534), TYPE 85 (YW531H) Amphibious armoured personnel carriers (Tracked), Shorland S55, TYPE 63 (YW531), BTR-80 (wheeled), TYPE 92 WZ551 (wheeled), BTR-152 (wheeled), HUSSAR (wheeled)
- Mine-protected APC—Buffel,[59] Unibuffel,[60] Unicorn[61]
- Hotspur—Armoured version of the Land Rover Defender
- Reconnaissance vehicles
- Alvis Saladin Armoured cars, Alvis Saracen Armoured cars and Daimler Ferret Armoured cars
- Engineering Support Vehicles
- VT-55 Armoured recovery vehicle
- MT-55A—Armoured vehicle-launched bridge

Limitations of the National Army

Although the SLA is a strong institution, it remains somewhat beset with financial constraints, shortage of equipments, and inadequate representation of minorities, particularly the Tamils. Also, the SLA has high levels of desertion. Reports suggest that about 36,000 army deserters were at large during the operations against the LTTE in the *Eelam War IV*[62] and a total of 65,000 in the past two decades. Nonetheless, former Army Commander General Fonseka, under President Mahinda Rajapaksa's watch, injected a new spirit into the Army by changing its culture, procedures, and rewarding individuals for battle-gutsiness against Tigers. In short, the erstwhile ceremonial army is a battle-hardened force now.

Civil-Military Relations

The development of civilian-military relations in Sri Lanka began with the rise of insurrections, both Marxist JVP and the Tamil insurgency in the 1970s and the 80s. Gradually, the need for a robust civil-military relationship was felt. The size and ethnic composition of the military institution, their political ideology, their level of cohesion and unity as well as their desire to protect national (read Sinhala) interests, contributed for this enhanced relationship. Besides, the popular sovereignty and the legitimacy of civilian rule cemented by the Sinhalisation of policies since 1956 and class linkages between politicians and the security forces played a part in averting coups in Sri Lanka.[63]

Similarly, the SLA acquired constitutional standing in the legislative process by virtue of the requirement under the Public Security Ordinance passed by the State Council in 1947. With its subsequent amendments, it was deemed to be a law enacted by the parliament both under the 1972 and the 1978 Constitution. These amendments also empowered the SLA through the executive president for indefinite preventive detention with no provision for a substantial judicial review of detention, along with upholding of law and order.

Today, with the dislodging of the Tamil Tigers, the SLA is even empowered to carry out civilian functions in the north and the east along with security responsibilities.[64] In an effort to equip the Army officers with civil affairs, the civil affairs officers of the Sri Lankan armed forces even underwent training course on civil-military relations conducted by the US Centre for Civil-Military Relations (CCMR) at Colombo.[65]

Bilateral and Multilateral Defence/Security Co-operation, both Regional & Extra-Regional

Since 1970s, Sri Lanka has entered into a number of bilateral and multilateral defence cooperation agreements with regional and other powers, such as, India, Israel, the UK, the US, Pakistan, China, Ukraine, Indonesia. Bilateral defence cooperation in the field of military training, exchange of military intelligence and information, maritime surveillance to prevent illegal activities, official visits and bilateral meetings at different levels, participation in training programmes, joint military exercises, etc., were significant features of cooperation with the regional powers. Besides, on the security affairs, Sri Lanka has ongoing cooperation with many countries in training and supply of equipment to the Sri Lankan defence forces.

Since the JVP uprising in 1971, the Sri Lankan Army has been actively and passively supported by India. For instance, Indian Army dispatched infantry troops and logistics to help quell the insurgency in 1971. But, Indian support for the Sri Lankan security forces is basically in the arena of training of personnel, intelligence sharing, and supply of life-saving equipments, such as, flak jackets. In recent years, Pakistan has also emerged as a key arms supplier to Sri Lanka. It has already put forward the draft proposal for a (bilateral) Defence Cooperation Agreement.[66] Apart from training Sri Lankan Army personnel and officers, Pakistan also provides modern lethal weapons for the SLA whereas India at times had refused to supply advanced weapons. For instance, in early 2000, during the critical battle of Elephant Pass, Pakistan provided multi barrel rocket launchers when India refused.[67]

The *Eelam War IV*—final assault on LTTE—further provided an opportunity for the SLA to strengthen its cooperation with other countries, especially in countering regional and global terrorist networks and sharing of vital defence-related information. In fact, the defence cooperation and support from India, Pakistan and China came at a crucial juncture for the SLA, when it was engaged in a series of landmark battles against a three-decade long Tamil insurgency led by the LTTE.

In short, unmindful of India's stated opposition to Sri Lanka turning to Pakistan and China for military hardware to bolster its offensive against the LTTE, Sri Lanka has in recent years inked several significant defence agreements with these countries.[68]

National Army in People's Perception

The SLA's image among the Sri Lankans varies from the majority Sinhalese to the ethnic minorities. For the Sinhalese, the SLA is seen as a defender or a redeemer, which liberated the motherland from the clutches of the Tamil insurgents. The image of the SLA among the majority Sinhala population peaked with the killing of the LTTE Chief Vellupillai Prabakaran and the extermination of the Tigers' top leadership. Conversely, for the majority of the Tamils, the SLA is a tormenter. But, understandably for the Sri Lankan Muslims, the SLA is just a redeemer—a rescuer from the tyranny of the LTTE. They have no lucid 'love' nor 'hate' for the SLA. They have been clandestinely supportive of the SLA given their antagonism towards the LTTE and to protect their political interests. The ambiguous stance of the Sri Lankan Muslims has been largely due to their sandwiched status in the Sri Lankan society—among the Sinhalese in the south and the Tamils in the north and the east.

Future Prospects

The SLA's reputation and importance within the Sri Lankan polity and in nation-building assumes more significance with the military victory against the LTTE in May 2009. Also, the victory against the Tamil Tigers has made it an unusually influential institution in the political decision-making apparatus, certainly much more than any of the other services. In fact, SLA counter-terrorism policy has been termed as the most effective one in the 21st century and is recommended for other countries to study today.[69] The former Army Commander Gen. Fonseka and his aides were at one point of time hugely popular among the Sinhalese population and in the Colombo power circle. As result of his popularity, Gen. Fonseka declared his candidacy in the January 26, 2010 presidential elections. In fact, he had emerged as a unanimous opposition candidate against President Rajapaksa owing to his popularity among the Sinhalese.[70] This became evident as Gen. Fonseka was frequently giving statements to the media during the war, not just on battleground progress but also on political matters.[71]

It is noteworthy that the SLA has since been in the limelight by way of engaging the political actors in the national development and post-war reconstruction process. Besides, the SLA is likely to increase its strength probably by another 100,000 in next few years to prevent the potential resurgence of the Tamil Tigers or any other such group.[72] Establishing an ethnic Tamil regiment within the Army is one of the possibilities that the SLA could be focusing on.[73] Apart from this, the SLA may be focusing its attention on strengthening its capability in terms of resource and technology. Yet, the SLA's progress and reputation depends on the competence of the Sri Lankan Government and its effort to 'win the hearts and minds of the ethnic minority.'

NOTES

1. Geopolitics may be roughly defined here as the influence of geography upon politics, and how distance, terrain and climate affect the affairs of states and people.
2. The Sri Lankan Prime Minister D.S. Senanayake described the geo-location of Sri Lanka in the Indian Ocean as "the strategic highway."
3. It is in the context of its ethnic problem that Sri Lanka's simultaneous cooperation and antagonism with powers like India must be understood. Sri Lanka played the same card to sustain the allegedly 'genocidal war' against its Tamil minorities.
4. Invasions from southern India in the historical past on Sinhala kingdoms and support from south India for Lankan Tamil rebels in the recent past is partially a cause for perceived threat perceptions from India.
5. India's strong influence or 'Indian-ness' is quite evident in Sri Lanka. Nevertheless, Sri Lanka has always tried to assert its distinct identity from 'Indian-ness'. See P. Sahadevan, "India and Sri Lanka: A Changing Relationship", *Dialogue*, 5 (3), January-March 2004, at http://www.asthabharati.org/Dia_Jan.04/India%20sahadevan.htm
6. See "Sri Lankan Army: Establishment", at http://www.army.lk/estab.php.
7. In May 1972, when Ceylon was proclaimed a republic and its name was changed from the Dominion of Ceylon to the Republic of Sri Lanka, all army units were also renamed accordingly.
8. Besides, through the defence agreement, British got the advisory role in building the SLA. The British Army Training Team (BATT)—an advisory group—carried out training for ex-members of the Ceylon Defence Force (CDF) within the Ceylon Army apart from regular training given to SLA officers at the British Army Staff College, Camberley, and Royal Military Academy, Sandhurst.
9. CDF was formed in 1910 by reforming the Ceylon Volunteer Force (CVF) which existed as the military reserve during the British rule under the command of the British Army. In fact, during World War II, Ceylon Garrison Artillery of CDF was deployed outside Ceylon as part of the British force to support the Allied and Commonwealth forces in the Indian Ocean, particularly, in defence of Seychelles and the Cocos Islands. It later developed into a regular force. See Oscar Abeyaratna, *The History of the Ceylon Light Infantry*, Ceylon Daily News, Colombo, 1945. Also, see Anton Muttukumaru, *The Military History of Ceylon*, Navrang, New Delhi, 1987.
10. Later in 1963, the operation was renamed as Task Force Anti-Illicit Immigration (TaFII) that continued until it was disbanded in 1981.
11. During the 1950s and 1960s, the Army was called upon to carry out essential services whenever industrial workers went on strike organised by the left wing parties and trade unions for various reasons, the most notable being the 1961 Colombo Port strike during which ships threatened to bypass the Colombo Port and the country almost starved. See Sergei de Silva-Ranasinghe, "An evolving army and its role through time", *Sunday Times,* October 16, 2005, at http://www.sundaytimes.lk/051016/plus/4.html
12. The JVP was founded in 1965 with the aim of providing a leading force for a socialist revolution in Sri Lanka.
13. The Sri Lankan Government under Srimavo Bandaranaike had called on India to provide basic security to the capital as the Sri Lankan Army had no combat experience since World War II and no training in counter insurgency warfare. Indian troops guarded Bandaranaike International Airport and the Indian Air Force helicopters assisted the counter offensive. See A.C. Alles, *The J.V.P., 1969-1989*, A.C. Alles, Colombo, 1990.
14. An estimated 10,000 people were killed. However, they were successful in seizing and holding major areas in southern and central provinces of Sri Lanka before they were

defeated by the security forces. Their attempt to seize power created a major crisis for the Sri Lankan Government and forced a fundamental reassessment of the nation's security needs. See Jagath P. Senaratne, *Political Violence in Sri Lanka, 1977-1990: Riots, Insurrections, Counter-insurgencies, Foreign Intervention*, VU University Press, Amsterdam, 1997.

15. The JVP rebelled again in 1987 after its attempt to operate as a legal political party failed. The Army had to fight hard this time as the second round of insurgency was both longer—lasting about two years—and more devastating than the first. The SLA's intelligence penetrated the JVP and gradually paved the way for defeating it using brutal tactics. Some estimates suggest that it resulted in over 60,000 deaths and disappearances. Because of its profound societal penetration during this period, the JVP earned the nickname "the alternative government" and by mid-1989 many observers expected the organisation's victory over the state. See Mick Moore, *Thoroughly Modern Revolutionaries: The JVP in Sri Lanka*, Cambridge University Press, Cambridge, 1993.
16. The regular force consists of officers and soldiers who are appointed or enlisted for the purpose of rendering continuous service under this Act during the period of their engagement.
17. The Regular Reserve consists of officers and soldiers who by the order of the president are transferred from the Regular Force in accordance with the terms of their enlistment.
18. Lt. Gen. Jagath Jayasuriya, VSV USP ndu psc, is the 19th Commander of the Sri Lankan Army. He assumed office on July 15, 2009 and was the Commander, Security Forces Wanni since August 2007 till he assumed the office of the Commander of the Army. He was actively engaged in the overall military planning and operations in the Wanni in the final war against the LTTE. For details, see http://www.army.lk/commander.php.
19. NDC is charged with formulating and executing the defence policy, and procurements for the armed forces.
20. List of current Sri Lanka Army regiments and corps are: Sri Lanka Armoured Corps (SLAC); Sri Lanka Artillery (SLA); Sri Lanka Engineers (SLE); Sri Lanka Signals Corps (SLSC); Sri Lanka Light Infantry (SLLI); Sri Lanka Sinhala Regiment (SLSR); Gemunu Watch (GW); Gajaba Regiment (GR); Vijayabahu Infantry Regiment (VIR); Commando Regiment (CR); Special Forces Regiment (SF); Mechanized Infantry Regiment; Military Intelligence Corps; Engineer Services Regiment; Sri Lanka Army Service Corps; Sri Lanka Army Medical Corps; Sri Lanka Army Ordnance Corps; Sri Lanka Electrical and Mechanical Engineers; Sri Lanka Corps of Military Police; Sri Lanka Army General Service Corps; Sri Lanka Army Women's Corps; Sri Lanka Rifle Corps; Sri Lanka Army Pioneer Corps; and Sri Lanka National Guard.
21. IISS, *The Military Balance 2007*.
22. The Special Forces (SF) renamed in 1988 was started as the Combat Trekker Team (CTT) in 1985 with two officers and 38 other ranks and it was renamed in 1986 as the Rapid Deployment Force (RDF). See Dhakeshi Yatawara, "True sons of Mother Lanka", *Sunday Observer*, August 15, 2010, at http://www.sundayobserver.lk/2010/08/15/spe10.asp
23. Each branch is headed by an officer of the rank of Major General who is directly responsible to the Commander of the Army for the smooth functioning of the Branch. Under each branch, there are several Directorates, each headed by a Brigadier.
24. The Burghers are a community of mixed European descent.
25. The retirement of the British-educated cadre of Tamil and Burgher officers gradually depleted the ranks of minority members.
26. The Sri Lankan Army recruits Muslims for its exclusively Muslim battalion. The new regiment, according to the Lankan government, will comprise some 800 personnel.

Champika Liyanaarachchi, "Muslim Regiment to the Sri Lanka Army", *Daily Mirror*, March 29, 2006.

27. Ibid.
28. However, during the 1971 insurrection, government recruited new soldiers, which specifically excluded recruitment of anyone under the age of 35 in view of the perception that much of the youth population was supportive of the JVP–led insurgency. See *Responses to Information Requests*, July 24, 2007, at http://www2.irb-cisr.gc.ca/en/research/rir/?action=record.viewrec&gotorec=451400.
29. See "Sri Lanka Army Career: Join Us", at http://www.army.lk/careers.php
30. "Lanka to create first Muslim battalion", *Lanka Newspapers*, March 28, 2006, at http://www.lankanewspapers.com/news/2006/3/6213.html
31. The government's allocation for the defence ministry in 2008 was Rs.166.44 billion. The reported hike in the defence budget was justified in view of the SLA's advancement towards the LTTE's 'administrative capital' Kilinochchi. See "Sri Lanka proposes $1.66 bn defence budget for 2009", *Thaindian News*, October 2, 2008, at http://www.thaindian.com/newsportal/uncategorized/sri-lanka-proposes-166-bn-defence-budget-for-2009_100102762.html.
32. Papers presented to parliament showed that, "It is important to acquire vehicles and hire heavy equipment for troop transport and to construct new camps." See "Military Outlay", *Lanka Business Online*, October 9, 2009, at http://www.lbo.lk/fullstory.php?nid=2048117281. Also, see "Sri Lanka to maintain defence budget—Gotabhaya", *Siber News*, August 20, 2009, at http://www.sibernews.com/200908203575.html
33. "Sri Lanka passes highest ever defense budget despite war ending in 2009", *Xinhua News*, December 19, 2011, at http://news.xinhuanet.com/english/world/2011-12/19/c_131315537.htm
34. The Army Training Centre (ATC) was earlier known as the Army Recruit Training Depot (ARTD) which was formed in Diyatalawa on February 6, 1950 for training recruits. See "Sri Lanka Army: Training", at http://www.army.lk/training.php
35. Ibid.
36. The Konduwattuwan Combat Training College in Ampara was the venue where the Eastern Command of the Sri Lankan Army earlier gave training to some 500 Muslim youths as home guards in 1990.
37. The new Ranaviru IT Training Institute was established by the Army IT Unit at Kandy, Anuradhapura and Panagoda. These IT Institutes will reportedly provide IT facilities to War Hero families. See "Third New Ranaviru IT Institute Opened as Army Enters New Technical Vistas", September 14, 2010, at http://www.army.lk/detailed.php?NewsId=2634
38. Special Forces Training School was established on February 15, 1992. It conducts basic and specialised training for all Special Forces personnel. It also conducts special courses to train instructors from other battalions in the Army and has also helped to train Navy Special Boat Squadron personnel and Sri Lanka Air Force Regiment Special Force.
39. The KDU was initially established as "General Sir John Kotelawala Defence Academy" by the Parliamentary Act No. 68 of 1981 and was subsequently elevated to University status by the amendment Act No. 27 of 1988, thereby empowering it to award Bachelors' and Post-graduate degrees in Defence Studies. Indeed, the idea of a defence university was first mooted in Sri Lankan Armed Forces' recommendations of 1979 to the Government of Sri Lanka on the need to enable young officers to gain higher academic qualifications. For details, see the official website of KDU, at http://www.kda.lk/
40. India provides maximum slots to the Sri Lankan military, numbering around 700

annually, out of its quota of 1500 vacancies for the training of military personnel from foreign countries.

41. Malaysian Armed Force Staff College offers training course for the foreign armed forces.
42. In an exclusive interview to *The Asian Age*, the Sri Lankan Defence Secretary Gotabhaya Rajapaksa had stated that his country's military victory over the LTTE offers lessons for the international community. See "Any country facing terrorism should follow Lankan model", September 16, 2010, at http://www.army.lk/detailed.php?NewsId=2624
43. IISS, *The Military Balance 2008*.
44. "Sri Lanka: Army's Five-Year Strategy for Expansion", *Aftenposten*, October 12, 2011, at http://www.aftenposten.no/spesial/wikileaksdokumenter/01062009-SRI-LANKA-ARMYS-FIVE-YEAR-STRATEGY-FOR-EXPANSION-5118506.html
45. Cited in Angela S. Burger, "Changing Civil-Military Relations in Sri Lanka", *Asian Survey*, 32 (8), August 1992, p. 10.
46. Ibid. In 1990, the figure was 40,000; The *India Today* reported on July 15, 1991 that it was 60,000; and a Sri Lankan Army General reported in April 1992, in an interview in New Delhi, a 20,000 increase in the past year to the figure of 80,000.
47. "Sri Lankan Army Seeks to Expand Strength", Asia Pacific, *Jane's Defence Weekly*, June 12, 1996, at http://www.janes.com/articles/Janes-Defence-Weekly-96/SRI-LANKAN-ARMY-SEEKS-TO-EXPAND-STRENGTH.html
48. "Sri Lanka—Armed Forces", *Encyclopaedia of the Nations*, at http://www.nations encyclopedia.com/Asia-and-Oceania/Sri-Lanka-ARMED-FORCES.html.
49. "Army now 150,000 strong recruits more, readies for big battles on the Vanni front", *The Island*, November 2, 2008, at http://www.island.lk/2008/02/11/news2.html
50. "Army to play development role in Sri Lanka: Samarasinghe", *The Hindu*, September 19, 2009, at http://beta.thehindu.com/news/international/article22348.ece.
51. "Sri Lanka orders emergency military supplies from Pakistan", *IRNA*, New Delhi, April 3, 2008, at http://www.globalsecurity.org/military/library/news/2008/04/mil-080403-irna01.htm
52. These APCs enabled the Armoured Corps to have their own assault troops to provide close combat protection to their Alvis Saladin and Ferret Scout Cars which were vulnerable to anti-tank weapons.
53. Anton Nonis, "The Evolution of the Indigenous Armoured Vehicle: From Unicorn to Unibuffel", *Sunday Observer*, April 25, 2004, at http://www.sundayobserver.lk/2004/04/25/fea22.html.
54. According to *Jane's Defence Weekly*, Sri Lanka had received more than 40 T-55A2/AM2 MBTs, eight MT-55A bridgelayers, 16 VT-55 armoured recovery vehicles, three mobile workshop vehicles and 12 TATRA T815 tanks transporters other than 10,000 122mm rockets for 16 multi-barrelled rocket launchers from the Czech government in early 2010. See "Sri Lankan Army inspects Czech main battle tanks", *Jane's Defence Weekly*, July 19, 2000.
55. Chris Smith, "In the Shadow of a Cease-fire: The Impacts of Small Arms Availability and Misuse in Sri Lanka", *Small Arms Survey*, Occasional Paper No. 11, October 2003.
56. The main suppliers of these are Pakistan and China. See P.K. Balachandran, "Naval Surveillance is the Millstone around LTTE's Neck", *The Hindustan Times*, October 14, 2003.
57. 13.6 million Pounds worth of equipment (armoured vehicles, machine gun components and semi-automatic pistols) from Britain, 10,000 rockets worth 1.1 million pounds from Slovakia, and 1.75 million pounds worth of guns and ammunition from Bulgaria. See *SIPRI Yearbook* 2009; The *Military Balance*, 2007.

58. Reportedly, Sri Lanka has asked Pakistan to service its T-55 main battle tanks at the height of the conflict. See Robert Karniol, "Sri Lanka looks to Pakistan as conflict looms", *Jane's Defence Weekly*, June 14, 2006, p. 32.
59. The African Buffels were first imported to Sri Lanka in 1985. They were deployed in the Northern and Eastern regions. By 1989, 29 of these machines were being used on the country's battlefields.
60. Unibuffel are bullet-proofed and is protected against land mine explosions. It has an efficient communications system established between the driver and the troop compartment. The vehicle is designed to carry a contingent of 12 persons including the driver and the gunner. The vehicle is powered by a TATA engine which could easily cater to rough terrain. Earlier, SLA had depended extensively on South African imported APVs till it developed Unibuffel. The imported APV, popularly known as 'Buffel', was costly at over Rs.11 million. The locally made vehicle 'Unibuffel', however, costs only three million rupees, saving seven million rupees on each machine for the SLA. It has been named 'Unibuffel' to differentiate it from the South African version. Nonis, n. 53.
61. Ibid. An army model called the Unicorn was created during 1987. A distinct feature of the Unicorn was that the driver-passenger compartment was undivided. According to soldiers in the battlefield, this feature made communication among the two sections easier than that in a Buffel where the driver was separated from the passengers. The manufacturing of Unicorns was carried out up to 2000. By that time, the Army had made a range of Unicorns with the final one being classified as Unicorn Mark VI. Each was an improvement over the previous one. A total of 93 Unicorns were produced, with Unicorn VI being the most advanced version.
62. Camelia Nathaniel, "Army arrests deserters", *Ceylon Today*, May 08, 2012, at http://www.ceylontoday.lk/16-5824-news-detail-army-arrests-deserters.html
63. There were at least two attempted and two implemented *coup d'etats* in Sri Lanka. Besides, the officer corps at the higher level is considerably politicised, divided between the two mainline parties—UNP and SLFP. Understandably, there are JVP sympathisers too. For *coup d'etats* in Sri Lanka, see "Ceylon: Delayed Revolt", *Time*, March 03, 1961, at http://www.time.com/time/magazine/article/0,9171,897670,00.html?promoid=googlep. Also, see "The Kataragama factor and the 1962 coup", *The Sunday Times*, August 13, 2000, at http://sundaytimes.lk/000813/news3.html
64. Nanda Wickremasinghe, "Sri Lankan military takes over urban development", May 13, 2010, at http://www.wsws.org/articles/2010/may2010/sril-m13.shtml
65. About 20 Military Officers including 9 Army Officers attended the lectures conducted by a panel of US lecturers including US Army personnel on various aspects of Civil-Military Relations. See "US Civil Military Relations Centre Trains SL Defence Forces", September 20, 2010, at http://www.army.lk/detailed.php?NewsId=2641
66. P. Karunakharan, "Pakistan seeks to expedite defence pact with Sri Lanka", *Thaindian News*, August 1, 2008, at http://www.thaindian.com/newsportal/uncategorized/pakistan-seeks-to-expedite-defence-pact-with-sri-lanka_10078599.html.
67. Ashwani Talwar, "Pak multi-barrel rocket launchers sent to Lanka", *Indian Express*, June 5, 2000, at http://www.expressindia.com/ie/daily/20000605/ifr05025.html.
68. As India provided only "defensive weapons", SLA went to China and Pakistan for their weapons requirements like Buffel. Reportedly, Sri Lanka had signed a classified $37.6 million deal with China's Poly Technologies in April 2007 to supply its defence forces with ammunition and ordnance for the army and navy in addition to varied small arms. Sri Lanka cited "security compulsions" as its drive for seeking military equipments from China, Pakistan and other suppliers. See Rahul Bedi, "Sri Lanka turns to Pakistan, China

for military needs", June 02, 2007, at http://www.indianmuslims.info/news/2007/jun/02/sri_lanka_turns_pakistan_china_military_needs.html.

69. "Sri Lanka army to share anti-terror expertise with others", *NDTV News*, January 06, 2011, at http://www.ndtv.com/article/world/sri-lanka-army-to-share-anti-terror-expertise-with-others-77535
70. He was imprisoned after a failed presidential bid in 2010 on the ground of "committing military offences" while in service. For details, see "Sri Lanka election loser Sarath Fonseka arrested", *BBC News*, February 08, 2010, at http://news.bbc.co.uk/2/hi/8504882.stm
71. For instance, he would respond to international criticism of the government's war tactics and alleged human rights abuses, which generally should have been the responsibility of the foreign minister, president, or a civilian authority.
72. Sri Lankan military had stated that it wants to boost up its manpower by more than 100,000 troops to be deployed in areas that were previously under rebel control. The troop build up, which would increase the number of Sri Lankan forces from 200,000 to 300,000, was announced by the then Army Chief Gen. Fonseka amidst fears in Colombo that the Tamil Tigers living abroad may try to resurrect the group under a new leadership. See "Lankan Army Strength to be Raised by 100,000", *The Outlook*, Colombo, May 26, 2009, at http://news.outlookindia.com/item.aspx?660433. Also, see "Military Outlay", *Lanka Business Online*, October 09, 2009, at http://www.lbo.lk/fullstory.php?nid=2048117281.
73. The Minister for National Integration & Reconciliation Vinyagamoorthi Muralitharan *alias* Karuna Amman made known the SLA plan citing his conversation with the army chief. See "'Tamil unit' for Sri Lanka's army", *BBC News,* June 29, 2009, at http://news.bbc.co.uk/2/hi/south_asia/8124836.stm

Index